DOGFIGHT

DOGFIGHT

How Apple and Google Went to War and Started a Revolution

FRED VOGELSTEIN

Sarah Crichton Books

Farrar, Straus and Giroux

New York

Sarah Crichton Books
Farrar, Straus and Giroux
18 West 18th Street, New York 10011

Library of Congress Cataloging-in-Publication Data
Vogelstein, Fred.
    Dogfight : how Apple and Google went to war and started a
revolution / Fred Vogelstein. — First edition.
        pages   cm
    Includes bibliographical references and index.
    ISBN 978-0-374-10920-2 (hardback) — ISBN 978-0-374-71100-9
(ebook)
    1. Computer industry.   2. Apple Computer, Inc.   3. Google (Firm).
4. Competition.   I. Title.

HD9696.2.A2 V64 2013
338.4'7004—dc23

                                                    2013021855

Designed by Jonathan D. Lippincott

Farrar, Straus and Giroux books may be purchased for educational, business, or
promotional use. For information on bulk purchases, please contact the Macmillan
Corporate and Premium Sales Department at 1-800-221-7945, extension 5442,
or write to specialmarkets@macmillan.com.

www.fsgbooks.com
www.twitter.com/fsgbooks • www.facebook.com/fsgbooks

1   3   5   7   9   10   8   6   4   2

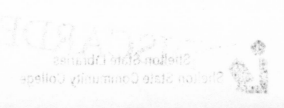

For Evelyn, Sam, and Beatrice

Contents

DOGFIGHT

Introduction

When Steve Jobs stood before the world at the beginning of 2007 and said he was going to reinvent the cell phone, the expectations were modest—at best. Jobs had upended the music business with the iPod and iTunes. But taking on the cell phone industry? That seemed unlikely. The wireless carriers, who controlled the market, had been foiling cell phone innovators for years. And the iPhone, while cool looking, seemed no match for their iron grip on the industry. It was more expensive than most phones out there. And it was arguably less capable. It ran on a slower cell/data network. And it required users to type on a virtual, not a physical, keyboard. To some critics, that meant the iPhone was dead on arrival.

If anything, Jobs undersold the iPhone that day. It truly was a breakthrough. The iPhone wasn't really a phone, but the first mainstream pocket computer that made calls. With its touchscreen, it did so many things that other phones could never do that consumers overlooked its shortcomings. Consumers got used to the virtual keyboard, and Apple continued to make it better and better. It cut the price to equal that of other phones. It quickly upgraded the slower cell/data radios to make its technology competitive. It developed displays with unheard-of resolutions. It bought a chip design company to make sure the iPhone was always the fastest device out there. It rolled out a completely new version of the iPhone software every year. And it designed iconic television ads—as it had done for the iPod—that made consumers feel special about owning one.

The subsequent frenzy of demand gave Apple and Jobs the leverage to turn the tables on the wireless carriers and start telling *them* what to do. More important, it ignited a technology revolution that today touches almost every corner of civilization. The iPhone has become one of the most popular cell phones of all time, selling more than 135 million units in 2012 alone. It has become the platform for a new and hugely profitable software industry—phone apps—that has generated more than $10 billion in total revenues since starting five years ago, in 2008. And the iPhone has become the source of an entire rethink of how humans interact with machines—with their fingers instead of buttons or a mouse. The iPhone and its progeny—the iPod Touch and the iPad—haven't just changed the way the world thinks about cell phones, they have changed the way the world thinks about computers for the first time in a generation, arguably since the advent of the Macintosh in 1984.

Since 2010, when Jobs followed the iPhone with the iPad, the questioning has grown frenzied. Who said our computer had to sit under our desk or on our lap? Can't it just be a screen that fits in our pocket or purse, or something we leave lying around the house? Indeed, if you compare iPad sales to sales of desktops and laptops, Apple is now the largest PC maker in the world. It now sells more iPads per quarter than Dell or HP sells laptops and desktops. Apple's total sales of iPhones, iPads, and iPod Touches now exceed 200 million devices a year. That's about the same number of TVs sold by all manufacturers every year and about four times the number of cars sold worldwide. All of this has turned Apple, the corporation, into a colossus larger than even Jobs's enormous ambitions. Once on the precipice of bankruptcy, in 1997, Apple today is one of the most valuable and profitable companies anywhere.

And yet Apple behaves like a corporation under siege—because despite all this success, it is. From the moment in late

2007 that Google unveiled Android—and its own plan to dominate the world of mobile phones and other mobile devices—Google hasn't just *tried* to compete with the iPhone, it has *succeeded* in competing with the iPhone. Android took hold in 2010, and it has exploded in popularity since. To Apple's astonishment, there are now more smartphones and tablets running Android software than there are iPhones, iPads, and iPod Touches running Apple's software, known as iOS. In 2012 there was even debate about whether the iPhone was the most popular smartphone anymore. During the third quarter of 2012, some surveys said, Samsung sold more Android-powered Galaxys than Apple sold iPhones.

Apple ended the "who has the most popular smartphone" discussion at the end of 2012, when it unveiled the iPhone 5. But more and more wonder whether this is even relevant anymore. The differences between the two platforms are narrowing by the day. Sure, they are different structurally. Apple makes every inch of the iPhone—the hardware and the software (though the devices are assembled in China). Google just makes the software for Android phones. It allows phone manufacturers such as Samsung to make the hardware. But both platforms now have an equivalent number of pluses and minuses: Apple's platform is a little easier to use, but it only offers three products—the iPhone, the iPad, and the iPod Touch. Google's platform offers many more phone choices, and often has the latest phone features ahead of Apple, but it lacks the polish of Apple's interface. Still, both platforms are now equally available among large carriers worldwide, and, with the exception of Apple stores, they are available for purchase in the same places.

Seeing Apple's market dominance challenged so swiftly and broadly was uniquely painful for Jobs and remains that way for the company's other executives. Jobs thought, and Apple executives still think, that Google and the Android community cheated to create their success. They think that Google executives stole Apple's software to build Android, and that Android's largest phone maker, Samsung, copied Apple's designs to build its supersuccessful

Galaxy phones. They feel betrayed. Apple and Google weren't just business partners when the iPhone was unveiled in early 2007. They were spiritual allies—the yin and yang of the technology revolution. This was one of the closest alliances in American business. Apple made great devices. Google made great software. Google's founders considered Jobs to be a mentor. Google's then CEO, Eric Schmidt, sat on Apple's board of directors. They had a common enemy: Microsoft. Together they planned for a long and prosperous marriage.

Then, as can happen in a marriage, the relationship frayed. Secrets were kept. Promises were broken. And the two went to war. When Jobs died in October 2011, there was hope that the dogfight would feel less like personal betrayal and quiet down—that Apple's new CEO, Tim Cook, would take the emotion out of the battle and find a way to settle it. But if anything, Apple has gotten *more* aggressive and nasty toward Google since then. It still has dozens of patent lawsuits in at least seven countries pending against the Android community—mostly against Samsung and Motorola (owned by Google). In the summer of 2012, it took the unheard-of step of having its fight with Samsung, Google's top distributor of Android phones, tried in front of a jury in San Jose. It won a $1 billion judgment, though that is being appealed. In September 2012 Apple stopped selling the iPhone preloaded with Google Maps. It replaced the app with one of its own, despite wide consumer complaints that the app was inferior. Apple is believed to be working on a video service to compete with YouTube, which Google owns.

Apple has even begun replacing some Google search technology in the iPhone with search technology from its old enemy, Microsoft. Now when you use Siri, the iPhone's voice recognition feature, Apple's newest software no longer uses Google search. Instead, she queries Microsoft's Bing search engine, which has been clawing at Google for a decade over search market share. To get Siri to use Google's search, you have to specifically ask her to "search Google" before each request. Google is still the default search engine inside the iPhone's web browser. But for those with long memories, the idea that Apple would dump any Google technology for Microsoft's—when Microsoft was the bitter enemy of both for so long—is an astonishing development.

Google's public posture in its fight with Apple has consistently been "Who, us? We're just a bunch of geeks out to change the world." But in its quiet, nerdy way Google has fought back ferociously. It defied Apple's demands that it remove software from Android phones or face patent lawsuits. It employed tactics to make Jobs look like an unhinged tyrant. And it bought the cell phone maker Motorola for $12.5 billion in 2012, its largest acquisition by far. It said the only purpose of the purchase was to buy Motorola's patents. It said it would be easier to fight a litigious opponent like Apple if it owned the company that invented the modern cell phone and all the patents associated with that. That's true, but the claim hid another equally powerful reason: the acquisition means that Google will always be able to make phones to compete with Apple no matter how successful Apple is with its lawsuits against other phone and tablet manufacturers. The purchase also gives Google leverage in case new challengers emerge.

Last, Google now finds itself doing something most thought it would never do: it is making its own consumer electronics from scratch to compete with Apple devices in the living room. Google has all the pieces not only to hook users on cell phones running its Android software, but to reach them wherever they go, inside or outside their homes.

• • •

Usually, the story of two companies and their powerful leaders going at it makes a great magazine piece and little more. Company X attacks company Y. Company Y fights back. One wins. One loses. But this is a much bigger tale than that. It's hard to imagine a more revolutionary object than the object the two companies started fighting over: the smartphone. The smartphone has fundamentally changed the way humans get and process information, and that is changing the world in ways that are almost too large to imagine. Ponder the individual impacts of the book, the newspaper, the telephone, the radio, the tape recorder, the camera, the video camera, the compass, the television, the VCR and the DVD, the personal computer, the cell phone, the video game, and the iPod. The smartphone is all those things in one device that fits in your pocket. It is radically changing the way we learn in school, the way doctors treat patients, the way we travel and explore. Entertainment and all media are accessed in entirely new ways. That sounds like something Jobs might have said at one of his famous product launches. But it is not an exaggeration.

What this means is that Apple versus Google isn't just a run-of-the-mill spat between two rich companies. It is the defining business battle of a generation. It is an inflection point, such as the moment when the PC was invented, when the Internet browser took hold, when Google reinvented web search, and when Facebook created the social network. In this massive reexamination of how technology, media, and communications intersect, two of the most powerful companies in the world to dominate that new landscape are in open warfare.

Yes, invariably this reminds you of previous fights among entrepreneurs in Silicon Valley, such as Apple versus Microsoft in the 1980s or Microsoft versus Netscape in the 1990s. But the stakes are infinitely higher now. In the 1980s personal computing was a nascent market, and both Apple and Microsoft were new companies. In the 1990s people saw the potential of the Internet, especially in a device that fit in your pocket. But wireless bandwidth was still too slow and expensive. Today, 1.8 billion cell phones are sold worldwide every year, and in five to ten years most of them are going to be smartphones. No one knows how big the tablet market is going to be yet, but the tablet is already becoming an important new technology for people to read books, newspapers, and magazines, not to mention watch TV or play video games. In other words, the stakes of this battle are infinitely higher than any earlier struggles.

It's not just that there is a lot more money to be made and lost in the Apple/Google fight than in previous Silicon Valley battles. It's that the fight feels—to the players, at least—like a winner-take-all situation. Why? Because they're not just fighting over which side has the hottest devices, they're battling for control of the online stores and communities these devices connect to—the so-called cloud. A lot of what we buy via Apple's iTunes store—apps, music, movies, TV shows, books, etc.—doesn't work easily on Android devices or at all, and vice versa. And both companies know that the more money each of us spends on apps and other media from one store, the less likely we are to switch to the other. They know we will ask, "Why rebuy all that content just to buy an Android phone instead of an iPhone?" Many companies have free apps that work on both platforms, but even having to redownload them, and re-set them up, is enough to keep many users from switching. In Silicon Valley parlance, it's a platform war. Whether your example is Microsoft with Windows and Office, eBay with auctions, Apple with the iPod, Amazon with books, Google with search, or Facebook with social media, history suggests that the winner in fights like this gets more than 75 percent of the market share, while the loser struggles to stay in that business.

This is a big deal. In the coming years most of what we consider information—news, entertainment, communications—will get funneled through either Apple's or Google's platform. Doubt me? It's already happening. We now spend as much time connected to the Internet as we do watching television, and more and more of our access to the Internet comes through smartphones and tablets. Think about how much time you spend staring at your phone or tablet now—not just responding to email, reading the news, tweeting, facebooking, watching a video, playing games, or surfing the web. Include the seconds you spend in elevators, standing in line, at stoplights, in the restroom too. Now ask yourself this question: Who controls what you see on your television? Your cable company. Who controls what you see on your smartphone? Ultimately, it is Apple and Google.

I remember when, as a contributing editor for *Wired*, I first started thinking about the mobile revolution. At that time the top-selling phones worldwide came from Nokia, RIM (which makes the BlackBerry), Sony Ericsson, and Motorola. Then the iPhone was announced. It quickly seemed inevitable that Apple and Google would end up fighting. Few agreed with me. An editor friend of mine said the idea seemed preposterous. How could Apple and Google compete when they were in entirely different businesses? he asked. Technically he was right. Apple makes money selling the devices it creates. Google makes money selling online advertising. What he and many missed is that those are now only means to a much bigger end. Both companies see themselves as becoming new kinds of content distribution engines—twenty-first-century TV networks, if you will. They won't make content as the TV networks do today; but their control of huge global audiences, and their enormous balance sheets, will enable them to have a big impact on what gets made and who sees it.

This may seem counterintuitive. It's hard to imagine the geeks at Apple or Google producing *Mad Men*. But makers of movies and TV shows essentially care about only two things: How much is their project going to cost? And how many people are going to see it? No two companies have more reach than Apple and Google. Fewer still have more money. Together they controlled $200 billion in cash alone by mid-2013. That's not only enough to buy and/or finance an unlimited amount of content for their audience; it's actually enough to buy most of Hollywood. The market capitalizations of News Corp., Time Warner, Viacom, and CBS total that much combined. Although most people don't think of Apple and Google as entertainment giants, Apple through iTunes controls roughly 25 percent of all music purchased and 6 to 10 percent of the $18 billion home video market. Meanwhile, Google is investing millions of dollars in original programming for YouTube, which is already a video destination for tens of millions of consumers around the world.

This isn't to suggest that there won't be enormous room for

new and old companies to build substantial businesses of their own in this new world. In early 2013 Netflix boasted 30 million subscribers, as many as HBO. Two years ago it looked to be a company that might not make it. Studios jacked up the price of their content to unaffordable levels. Movie and TV-show selection fell and customers started to leave. So Netflix—a technology company based in Los Gatos, not a Hollywood studio—started financing its own programming. Its first stab at this, the series *House of Cards*, with Kevin Spacey, has been an enormous hit. Amazon and Microsoft are getting production facilities up and running too. Meanwhile, Facebook, with more than 1 billion members—half the Internet—has become a favorite stop for Hollywood agents looking to use this giant global audience as another way to finance and distribute their clients' work.

But despite the power of Facebook, Amazon, Netflix, and Microsoft, at the moment they all still have to largely go through two companies—Apple and Google—to get to the increasingly massive audiences using smartphones and tablets for their news, entertainment, and communications. What this means is that the Apple/Google fight is not just a story about the future of Silicon Valley. It is about the future of media and communications in New York and Hollywood as well. Hundreds of billions of dollars in revenue are at stake, and for at least the next two years, and probably the next five, these companies, their allies, and their hangers-on will be going at it full bore.

• • •

In many ways what is happening now is what media, communications, and software moguls have been predicting for a generation: The fruits of Silicon Valley's labor and those of New York and Hollywood are converging. This is as close to tragic irony in business as one ever gets. For two decades—the 1980s and 1990s—a procession of celebrated media executives marshaled the best technology they could assemble to position themselves for the new world they saw coming. They spent hundreds of billions of dollars buying one another to bulk up. But their timing was so off, their innovations were so bad, and their mergers were so disastrous—such as AOL's purchase of Time Warner in 2001—that by 2005 convergence had become a discredited idea, and few dared to mention the word.

Where did all these very smart and very wealthy people go wrong? They had the wrong devices in mind. The media and communications tycoons all predicted that the convergence would happen on the personal computer—that their equipment supplying television programming, such as set-top boxes, would ultimately control our personal computers too. The software tycoons—largely Microsoft and Bill Gates—predicted that it would be personal computers that would take over our television sets. Instead, the touchscreen smartphone and touchscreen tablet are driving all the changes—two devices that hadn't been invented until recently. The problem with the television is that it is a lousy device to do any kind of work on. The problem with the PC is that it is a lousy device to consume entertainment on. The smartphones and tablets, because they are portable and so easy to use, are turning out to be the perfect blend of both. You'd never pull out a laptop to play a game or watch a movie when you're standing in line or sitting in the back of a cab. But we do that with our smartphones and tablets all the time. We accept the trade-off of screen size for portability because, unlike with previous portable devices, there are no other compromises we need to make. Their screens, while small, are actually sharper than those of most televisions. Their batteries last all day. They turn on immediately. They are connected to wireless networks that are fast enough to stream movies. And they are powerful enough to effectively run the same applications as every other machine we have.

· · ·

By the end of this book you'll have a good idea who *I* think is winning the Apple/Google fight. But you'll also develop enough respect for what each side has had to go through just to stay in the game that you might feel bad rooting for either side. One of the things that I didn't expect when I took on this project was how hard it is to conceive and build the products that Steve Jobs liked to casually pull out of his pocket onstage. Whether you are an Apple engineer, a Google engineer, or *any* engineer, building products that change the world isn't just work. It's a quest. It leaves its participants not only tired the way all jobs sometimes do but mentally and physically exhausted—even traumatized—at the end. Part of Jobs's appeal as a leader and a celebrity was that he successfully hid all this from public view. He made innovation look easy. Now he is gone. And, as you'll see in the following pages, there are many engineers at both companies who want the rest of the world to know what changing the world *really* has been like. Before there could be the smartphones and tablets we all now buy and take for granted, there was yelling, screaming, backstabbing, dejection, panic, and fear over what it would take to get those projects off the ground and into consumers' hands. They want you to understand what the iPhone and Android projects were like at the beginning—and so that is where this book will start.

1

The Moon Mission

The fifty-five miles from Campbell to San Francisco is one of the nicest commutes anywhere. The journey mostly zips along the Junipero Serra Freeway, a grand and remarkably empty highway that abuts the east side of the Santa Cruz Mountains. Known as 280 to locals, it is one of the best places in Silicon Valley to spot a start-up tycoon speed-testing his Ferrari and one of the worst places for cell phone reception. For Andy Grignon in his Porsche Carrera, therefore, it was the perfect place for him to be alone with his thoughts early on January 8, 2007.

This wasn't Grignon's typical route to work. He was a senior engineer at Apple in Cupertino, the town just west of Campbell. His morning drive typically covered seven miles and took exactly fifteen minutes. But today was different. He was going to watch his boss, Steve Jobs, make history at the Macworld trade show in San Francisco. Apple fans had for years begged Jobs to put a cell phone inside their iPods so they could stop carrying two devices in their pockets. Jobs was about to fulfill that wish. Grignon and some colleagues would spend the night at a nearby hotel, and at 10:00 a.m. the following day they—along with the rest of the world—would watch Jobs unveil the first iPhone.

Getting invited to one of Jobs's famous product announcements was supposed to be a great honor. It anointed you as a player. Only a few dozen Apple employees, including top executives, got an invite. The rest of the spots were reserved for Apple's board of directors, CEOs of partners—such as Eric Schmidt of Google and Stan Sigman at AT&T—and journalists from around the world. Grignon got an invite because he was the senior engineer for all the radios in the iPhone. This is a big job. Cell phones do innumerable useful things for us today, but at their most basic they are fancy two-way radios. Grignon was in charge of the equipment that allowed the phone to be a phone. If the phone didn't make calls, connect with Bluetooth headsets, or connect to Wi-Fi setups, Grignon had to answer for it. As one of the iPhone's earliest engineers, he'd dedicated two and a half years of his life—often seven days a week—to the project. Few deserved to be there more than he did.

But as Grignon drove north, he didn't feel excited. He felt terrified. Most onstage product demonstrations in Silicon Valley are canned. The thinking goes, why let bad Internet or cell phone connections ruin an otherwise good presentation? Jobs's presentations were live, however. It was one of the things that made his shows so captivating. But for those in the background, such as Grignon, few parts of the job caused more stress. Grignon couldn't remember the last time a Jobs show of this magnitude had gone sideways. Part of what made Steve Jobs such a legend was that noticeable product-demo glitches almost never happened. But Grignon found it hard to recall the last time Jobs was so unprepared going into a show.

Grignon had been part of the iPhone launch-preparation team at Apple and later at the presentation site in San Francisco's Moscone Center. But he had rarely seen Jobs make it all the way through his ninety-minute show without a glitch. Jobs had been rehearsing for five days, yet even on the last day of rehearsals the iPhone was still randomly dropping calls, losing the Internet connection, freezing, or just shutting down.

"At first it was just really cool to be at rehearsals at all—kind of like a cred badge. 'Fuck yeah, I get to hang out with Steve,'" Grignon said. Like everything else that surrounded Jobs, the preparations were as secret as a U.S. missile attack on Afghanistan. Those who were truly in felt as if they were at the center of the universe. From Thursday through the end of the following week, Apple completely took over Moscone. Backstage it built an eight-by-eight-foot electronics lab to house and test the iPhones. Next to that it built a greenroom with a sofa for Jobs. Then it posted more than a dozen security guards twenty-four hours a day in front of those rooms and at doors throughout the building. No one got in or out without having his or her ID electronically checked and compared with a master list that Jobs had personally approved. More security checkpoints needed to be cleared once visitors got inside. The auditorium where Jobs was rehearsing was off-limits to all but a small group of executives. Jobs was so obsessed with leaks that he tried to have all the contractors Apple had hired for the announcement—from people manning booths and doing demos to those responsible for lighting and sound—sleep in the building the night before his presentation. Aides talked him out of it.

"It quickly got really uncomfortable," Grignon said. "Very rarely did I see him become completely unglued. It happened. But mostly he just looked at you and very directly said in a very loud and stern voice, 'You are fucking up my company,' or, 'If we fail, it will be because of you.' He was just very intense. And you would always feel an inch tall [when he was done chewing you out]." Grignon said that you would always ask yourself two questions during one of these lectures: "'Is it my shit that broke this time?' and 'Is it the nth time it broke or the first time?'—because that actually mattered. The nth time would frustrate him, but by then he might have figured out a way around it. But if it was the first time, it added a whole new level of instability to the program." Grignon, like everyone else at rehearsals, knew that if those glitches showed up during the real presentation, Jobs would not be blaming himself for the problems, he would come after people like Grignon. "It felt like we'd gone through the demo a hundred times and that each time something went wrong," Grignon said. "It wasn't a good feeling."

• • •

The iPhone didn't work right for a good reason; it wasn't close to being finished. Jobs was showing off a prototype. He just didn't want the public to know that. But the list of things that still needed to be done before the iPhone could be sold was enormous. A production line had yet to be set up. Only about a hundred iPhones even existed, all of them of varying degrees of quality. Some had noticeable gaps between the screen and the plastic edge, others had scuff marks on the screen. Thus no one in the public was allowed to touch an iPhone after Jobs unveiled it, despite a day of press briefings and a whole exhibit set up for them in the convention center. The worry was that even the best prototypes wouldn't stand close scrutiny, Grignon said. They'd look fine at a distance and for Jobs's demo, but if you held one in your hand, "You would laugh and say, 'Wow, this thing really looks unfinished.'"

The phone's software was in even worse shape. A big chunk of the previous four months had been consumed figuring out why the iPhone's processor and its cell radio wouldn't reliably communicate. This huge problem was akin to a car with an engine that occasionally doesn't respond to the accelerator, or wheels that occasionally don't respond to the brake pedal. "It almost brought the iPhone program to a halt," Grignon said. "We had never seen a problem this complicated." This was ordinarily not a problem for phone makers, but Apple's obsession with secrecy had kept Samsung, the manufacturer of the phone's processor, and Infineon, the maker of the phone's cell radio, from working together until Apple, in desperation, flew teams of engineers from each company to Cupertino to help fix the problem.

Jobs rarely backed himself into corners like this. He was well-known as a master taskmaster, seeming to always know just how hard he could push his staff so that they delivered the impossible. But he always had a backup, a Plan B, that he could go to if his timetable was off. Six months prior he'd shown off Apple's upcoming operating system, Leopard. But that was after letting the date for the final unveiling slip.

But Jobs had no choice but to show off the iPhone. He had given this opening keynote at every Macworld since he'd returned as Apple's CEO in 1997, and because he gave public presentations only once or twice a year, he had conditioned Apple fans to expect big things from them. He'd introduced iTunes here, the iMac that looked like a fancy desk lamp, the Safari web browser, the Mac mini, and the iPod shuffle.

It wasn't just his own company that Jobs had to worry about disappointing this time. AT&T was expecting Jobs to unveil the iPhone at Macworld too. In exchange for being the exclusive carrier of the iPhone in the United States, AT&T had given Jobs total control of the design, manufacture, and marketing of the iPhone. It had never done anything like this before. If Jobs didn't launch on time, AT&T could back out of its deal. It's not hard to explain that a product called the iPhone that couldn't make calls would sell poorly. Days before, Jobs had flown to Las Vegas to give AT&T's top mobile executives a limited demo of the iPhone. But they were expecting a full show at Macworld.

Lastly, the iPhone was truly the only cool new thing Apple was working on. The iPhone had been such an all-encompassing project at Apple that this time there *was* no backup plan. "It was Apple TV or the iPhone," Grignon said. "And if he had gone to Macworld with just Apple TV [an experimental product back then], the world would have said, 'What the hell was that?' "

. . .

The iPhone's problems were manifest. It could play a section of a song or a video, but it couldn't play an entire clip without crashing. It worked fine if you sent an email and then surfed the web. If you did those things in reverse, however, it did not. Hours of trial and error had helped the iPhone team develop what engineers called "the golden path," a specific set of tasks, performed in a specific way and in a specific order, that made the phone look as if it worked.

But even when Jobs stayed on the golden path, it required all manner of last-minute work-arounds to make the iPhone functional. On announcement day the software that ran Grignon's radios still had bugs. So too did the software that managed the iPhone's memory. And no one knew whether the extra electronics Jobs had required to be added to the demo units would make these problems worse.

Jobs had required the demo phones he would use onstage to have their screens mirrored on the big screen behind him. To show a gadget on a big screen, most companies just point a video camera connected to a projector at the gadget. That was unacceptable to Jobs. The audience would see his finger on the iPhone screen, which would mar the look of his presentation. Instead, he had Apple engineers spend weeks fitting extra circuit boards attached to video cables onto the backs of the iPhones he would have onstage. The video cables then connected to the projector showing the iPhone image on the screen. When Jobs touched the iPhone's calendar app icon, for example, his finger wouldn't appear, but the image on the big screen would respond. The effect was magical. People in the audience felt as if they were holding an iPhone in their own hands. But making the setup work flawlessly given the iPhone's other major problems seemed hard to justify at the time. "It was all just so monkey-patched together with some of the ugliest hacks you could imagine," Grignon said.

The software in the iPhone's Wi-Fi radio was so unstable that Grignon and his team ultimately soldered antenna wires to the demo phones and ran them offstage along the wires to the projection setup. The iPhone would still connect wirelessly to the network, but the signal wouldn't have to travel as far. Even then, Grignon and his team needed to make sure no one in the audience could get on the frequency they were using. "Even if the base station's ID was hidden [and therefore not showing up when laptops scanned for Wi-Fi signals], you had five thousand nerds in the audience. They would have figured out how to hack into the signal." The solution, Grignon said, was simply to tweak the AirPort software to think it was operating in Japan instead of the United States. Japanese Wi-Fi uses some frequencies that are not permitted in the U.S.

There was even less they could do to make sure the phone

call Jobs planned to make from the stage went through. All Grignon and his team could do was make sure the signal was good and pray. They had AT&T bring in a portable cell tower so they knew reception would be strong. Then, with Jobs's support, they preprogrammed the phone's display to always show five bars of signal strength regardless of the true signal. The chances of the radio's crashing during the few minutes that Jobs would use it to make a call were small, but the chances of its crashing at some point during the ninety-minute presentation were high. "If the radio crashed and restarted, as we suspected it might, we didn't want people in the audience to see that. So we just hard-coded it to always show five bars," Grignon said.

None of these kluges fixed the iPhone's biggest problem: it often ran out of memory and had to be restarted if asked to do more than a handful of tasks at a time. Jobs had a number of demo units onstage with him to manage this problem. If memory ran low on one, he'd switch to another while the first was restarted. But given how many demos Jobs planned, Grignon worried that there were far too many potential points of failure. If disaster didn't strike during one of the dozen demos, it was sure to happen during Jobs's grand finale, when Jobs planned to show all the iPhone's top features operating at the same time on the same phone. He'd play some music, take a call, put it on hold and take another call, find and email a photo to the second caller, look up something on the Internet for the first caller, and then return to his music. "Me and my guys were all so nervous about this. We only had 120 megabytes of memory in those phones, and because they weren't finished, all these apps were still big and bloated," Grignon said.

The idea that one of the biggest moments of his career might implode made Grignon's stomach hurt. At forty, Grignon looks like the kind of guy you'd want to drink with—and he is. When he moved from Campbell to Half Moon Bay in 2010, he quickly became friendly with the sommelier at the Ritz-Carlton Hotel. He even had a wine fridge in his office. But behind that gregarious exterior is a fierce intellect and an ultracompetitive streak.

Once when trying to get to the bottom of a slew of software bugs in an iPhone subcontractor's equipment, he turned the AC on high in the conference room he used to make the subcontractors uncomfortably cold. When that didn't get them moving fast enough, he tried a more aggressive approach: he accused them of holding out on him and threw his laptop against the wall.

By 2007 he'd spent virtually his entire fifteen-year career at Apple or companies affiliated with it. While at the University of Iowa in 1993, he and his friend Jeremy Wyld—now cofounder with Grignon of Quake Labs—reprogrammed the Newton MessagePad to wirelessly connect to the Internet. That was quite a feat back then, and it helped them both get jobs at Apple right out of school. Wyld actually worked on the Newton team, and Grignon worked in Apple's famous R & D lab—the Advanced Technology Group—on video conferencing technology. Even though the Newton did not succeed as a product, many still think of it as the first mainstream handheld computer. But by 2000 Grignon had found his way to Pixo, a company spun out of Apple that was building operating systems for cell phones and other small devices. When Pixo's software found its way into the first iPod in 2002, Grignon found himself back at Apple again.

By then, thanks to his work at Pixo, he'd become well known for two other areas of expertise besides building video conferencing technology: computer radio transmitters (what we now call wireless) and the workings of software inside small handheld devices such as cell phones. Grignon works in an entirely different world from that inhabited by most software engineers in the Valley. Most rarely have to think about whether their code takes up too much space on a hard drive or overloads a chip's abilities. Hardware on desktop and laptop computers is both powerful, modifiable, and cheap. Memory, hard drives, even processors, can be upgraded inexpensively, and computers are either connected to electric outlets or giant batteries. In Grignon's world of embedded software, the hardware is fixed. Code that is too big won't run. Meanwhile, a tiny battery—which might power a laptop for a couple of minutes—needs enough juice to last all day. When Jobs decided to build the iPhone at the end of 2004, Grignon had a perfect set of skills to become one of the early engineers on the project.

Now, in 2007, he was emotionally exhausted. He'd gained fifty pounds. He'd stressed his marriage. It had been a grueling two years. Apple had never built a phone before, and the iPhone team quickly discovered the process didn't resemble building computers or iPods at all. "It was very dramatic," Grignon said. "It had been drilled into everyone's head that this was the next big thing to come out of Apple. So you put all these supersmart people with huge egos into very tight, confined quarters, with that kind of pressure, and crazy stuff starts to happen."

• • •

The iPhone didn't start out as Apple's "next big thing." Jobs had to be talked into building a phone. It had been a topic of conversation among his inner circle almost from the moment Apple launched the iPod in 2001. The conceptual reasoning was obvious: Why would consumers carry two or three devices for email, phone calls, and music when they could carry one?

But every time Jobs and his executives examined the idea in detail, it seemed like a suicide mission. Phone chips and bandwidth were too slow for anyone to want to surf the Internet and download music or video over a cell phone connection. Email was a fine function to add to a phone. But Apple couldn't leverage all the work it had put into building a music player such as the iPod to do that. Research in Motion's BlackBerry was fast locking up that market, anyway. Apple even considerd buying Motorola in 2003, but executives quickly concluded it would be too big an acquisition for the company then.

Worst of all, if Apple wanted to make and sell a phone in the United States, it would be at the beck and call of the U.S. wireless carriers. Back then, phone manufacturers such as Motorola were the serfs of high tech in the United States. They depended on carriers' marketing dollars to get consumers into stores, and then they depended on carriers to make the phones affordable by subsidizing their purchase price. That made manufacturers powerless to resist carriers' meddling in how each phone should be built. Manufacturers occasionally pushed back against this dominance and were always met with the same response from the carriers: "You can build the phone your way, but we might not subsidize it, market it, or allow it on our network." Manufacturers always caved in the face of this threat.

Jobs was personally offended by this way of doing business and wanted no part of it. "We're not the greatest at selling to the Fortune 500, and there are five hundred of them—five hundred CIOs [chief information officers] that are orifices you have to go through to get" that business. "In the cell phone business there are five. We don't even like dealing with five hundred companies. We'd rather run an ad for millions and let everyone make up their own mind. You can imagine what we thought about dealing with five," he said during an onstage interview at the All Things D conference in May 2003. Translation: I am not about to spend hundreds of millions of dollars to have a bunch of suits tell me how to build and sell my phone.

That sounded tough and principled. But by the end of 2003, as the iPod became Apple's most important product since the Macintosh, it was also starting to look misguided. Cell phone makers were putting music-listening applications in their phones. And companies such as Amazon, Walmart, and Yahoo! were beginning to sell downloadable music. Executives such as iPod boss Tony Fadell worried that if consumers suddenly gave up their iPods for music phones, Apple's business—only five years removed from its flirt with bankruptcy—would be crushed. "We didn't really have a hit on our hands [with the iPod] until late 2003, early 2004, so we were saying maybe we don't have the market domination—the retail channels—to expand the iPod's business properly," Fadell said.

It's hard to imagine a time when the iPod wasn't an iconic product, selling more than 50 million units a year; but back then Apple had sold only 1.3 million devices in two years and was still having trouble getting retailers such as Best Buy to carry it. "So we were thinking, 'How do we get above the noise? How do we make sure that we are at least competitive so that anyone who is carrying a cell phone can get iTunes music?' Because if we lost iTunes, we would have lost the whole formula," Fadell said.

Publicly, Jobs continued his harangue against the carriers. At the D conference in 2004, Stewart Alsop, Jr., the venture capitalist and former journalist, actually begged Jobs to make a smartphone that would improve on the popular Treo. "Is there any way you can get over your feelings about the carriers?" Alsop asked, offering to connect Jobs with Verizon CEO Ivan Seidenberg, who was also in the audience. Not a chance, Jobs said. "We've visited with the handset manufacturers and even talked to the Treo guys. They tell us horror stories." But privately, Jobs was thinking hard about the content of Alsop's pitch.

• • •

Jobs's first answer to the growing competition wasn't the iPhone, but something much more modest—a music phone called the Rokr, to be built in partnership with Motorola and Cingular, the big wireless carrier that would, via two mergers, become AT&T. The deal, agreed to in early 2004, seemed like the best of all worlds for Apple. It would license its iTunes software to Motorola to be put on Motorola's supersuccessful Razr cell phone, and Motorola would handle the rest. Apple would get a license fee for letting Motorola use the software, and Jobs wouldn't have to deal with the wireless carriers. iTunes would help Motorola sell more phones, get Cingular more wireless customers, and enable Apple to compete with the music phones it feared. "We thought that if consumers chose to get a music phone instead of an iPod, at least they would be using iTunes," Fadell said.

Instead, the Rokr was an embarrassment. When Jobs unveiled it nearly eighteen months later in September 2005, it was not capable of over-the-air music downloads, the device's main selling point. It was big and chunky—nothing like the sleek Razr that Motorola had made famous. And its music capacity was artificially limited to a hundred songs.

The tension between the partners, especially Apple and Motorola, was obvious quickly after Jobs was done demoing the device onstage at Moscone Center in San Francisco. Jobs had released the first iPod nano at the same time, and when a reporter asked Motorola CEO Ed Zander a few weeks later if he felt upstaged by the other products Jobs had unveiled, his answer was succinct: "Screw the nano." *Wired* magazine soon put a story of the fiasco on its cover under the headline YOU CALL *THIS* THE PHONE OF THE FUTURE?

Jobs successfully pinned the Rokr screwup on Motorola, but the fiasco was mostly Apple's fault. Yes, Motorola had produced an ugly phone, and it continued to produce phones that didn't sell well for the next four years until Zander resigned. But the Rokr project's real problem was that Jobs's reason for the deal evaporated almost as soon as it was signed, Fadell said. The deal was designed as a defensive maneuver, a hedge against companies' trying to build music phones without having to deal with the carriers themselves. But with each passing month in 2004 it became clearer that the last thing Apple needed to do with iTunes and the iPod was to play defense. It didn't need the Rokr to help it more broadly distribute iTunes. It just needed to hang on as iPod sales took off like a rocket ship. In the summer 2003 Apple was selling only about three hundred thousand iPods a quarter. At the beginning of 2004 it was selling only eight hundred thousand a quarter. But by summer 2004 sales exploded. It sold 2 million during the quarter that ended September 30, 2004, and another 4.5 million in the final quarter of the year. By the time ugly Rokr prototypes showed up in the fall of 2004, many Apple executives saw clearly that they were on the wrong path, and by year-end Jobs had all but abandoned the project. He was still driving the iTunes team to deliver the software that would go in the Rokr, but he was listening more carefully to executives who thought the Rokr project had been folly from the start.

It wasn't just the iPod's success in 2004 that diluted Apple's enthusiasm for the Rokr. By the end of the year, building its own phone no longer seemed like such a bad idea. By then it looked like most homes and cell phones would soon have Wi-Fi, which would provide high, reliable bandwidth over the home-owner's DSL or cable connection. And outside-the-home cell phone bandwidth looked like it would soon be fast enough to stream video and run a fully functioning Internet browser. Phone processor chips were finally fast enough to run cool-looking phone software. Most important, doing business with the carriers was starting to seem less onerous. By the fall of 2004, Sprint was beginning to sell its wireless bandwidth wholesale. That meant that by buying and reselling Sprint bandwidth, Apple could become its own wireless carrier—an MVNO, short for "mobile virtual network operator." Now Apple could build a phone and barely have to deal with the carriers at all. Disney, on whose board Jobs sat, was already in discussions with Sprint about just such a deal to provide its own wireless service. Jobs was asking a lot of questions about whether Apple should pursue one as well.

. . .

Cingular executives involved in the Rokr project such as Jim Ryan watched Jobs's interest in an MVNO with Sprint grow, and it terrified them. They worried that if Apple became a wireless carrier, it would cut prices to win customers and crush profits in the industry as other carriers cut prices to compete. So while they had access to Jobs and his team, they gently lobbied him to cut a deal with them instead. If Jobs would agree to an exclusive deal with Cingular, they said, they would be willing to throw out the rule book on carrier–manufacturer relations and give Jobs the control he needed to build a revolutionary device.

Ryan, who has never talked publicly about those days until now, said the experience taxed every ounce of his negotiating skills. He'd been assembling complex carrier deals for nearly a decade and was known in the industry as one of the early thinkers about the future of wireless. He'd grown Cingular's wireless data business from almost nothing to $4 billion in revenue in three years. But Apple and Jobs had little experience negotiating with carriers, making it much harder for Ryan to predict how they would respond to his various offers. "Jobs hated the idea of a deal with us at first. *Hated* it," Ryan said. "He was thinking that he didn't want a carrier like us anywhere near his brand. What he hadn't thought through was the reality of just how damn hard it is to deliver mobile service." Throughout 2004, during the dozens of hours he and his team spent in meetings with Apple executives in Cupertino, Ryan kept reminding Jobs and other Apple executives that if Apple became a carrier itself, it would get stuck with all the hassles of running an inherently unpredictable asset—a cell phone network. A deal with Cingular would insulate Apple from all that. "Funny as it sounds, that was one of our big selling points to them," Ryan said. "Every time the phone drops a call, you blame the carrier. Every time something good happens, you thank Apple."

Cingular wasn't just playing defense. Executives such as Ryan thought partnering with the inventor of the iPod would transform the way customers thought about their own company. Apple's explosive success with the iPod in 2004 and 2005—it sold 8.2 million iPods in 2004 and another 32 million in 2005—had taken Jobs's status as a business and cultural icon to unparalleled heights. The likely torrent of new customers who would come to Cingular if it were the carrier for a phone as revolutionary as the iPod had been made them salivate.

Another Cingular executive who worked on the deal but who would not be named put it this way to me when I was working on a story for *Wired* in 2008: "Jobs was cool. He was hip. There were studies done in colleges that asked, 'What is the one thing you can't live without?' For twenty years it was beer. Now it was the iPod. Things like that made us say this guy has got something. That probably gave us that much more energy to make sure this deal happened."

While Cingular was lobbying Jobs from the outside, a handful of Apple executives, such as Mike Bell and Steve Sakoman, were pushing Jobs to sign off on building a phone from the inside. "We were spending all this time putting iPod features in Motorola phones. That just seemed ass-backwards to me," said Bell, who now is cohead of Intel's mobile-device effort. He told Jobs that the cell phone itself was on the verge of becoming the most important consumer electronics device of all time, that no one was good at making them, and that, therefore, "if we [Apple] just took the iPod-user experience and some of the other stuff we were working on, we could own the market."

Bell was a perfect executive to be making this pitch. He'd been at Apple fifteen years and had helped build some of the products, such as the iMac, that enabled Apple to avoid bankruptcy in 1997. Most important, because he ran not only a chunk of the Mac software division but the software group responsible for Apple's AirPort Wi-Fi devices, he knew more about the wireless industry than most other senior executives inside Apple. He doesn't claim credit for being the father of the iPhone. He ultimately didn't run or even work on the project. Fadell ran it, before Scott Forstall took it over. But even today most say Bell was an important catalyst.

"So I argued with Steve for a couple of months and finally sent him an email on November seventh, 2004," Bell said. "I said, 'Steve, I know you don't want to do a phone, but here's why we should do it: [Design director Jony Ive] has some really cool designs for future iPods that no one has seen. We ought to take one of those, put some Apple software around it, and make a phone out of it ourselves instead of putting our stuff on other people's phones.' He calls me back about an hour later and we talk for two hours, and he finally says, 'Okay, I think we should go do it.' So Steve and I and Jony [Ive] and Sakoman had lunch three or four days later and kicked off the iPhone project."

It wasn't just Bell's persistence and Ive's designs that helped convince Jobs. Sakoman came to lunch having already done some early engineering work about what it might take to build a phone. He'd been at Palm until 2003, where, among other things, he helped build the software that went inside Treo smartphones. And as vice president of software technology at Apple, he had become the executive most familiar with the software inside the iPod. If Apple was going to make a smartphone, the iPod was a logical place to start. That's what consumers were expecting Apple to do. So by the time Sakoman arrived for lunch, he and his team had already figured out a way to put a Wi-Fi chip inside an iPod and get it to connect to the Internet.

They'd even begun working on new software for the music player—a version of Linux—so that it could handle the increased demands of being a phone and an Internet browser. Linux, the open-source software made famous by Linus Torvalds in the 1990s, had not supplanted Microsoft Windows as many geeks predicted it would. But by then it had become the software of choice for less powerful and sophisticated electronics. Sakoman briefed Jobs on his team's progress and later that afternoon told his team, "You better start figuring this out because this [phone project] is going ahead."

Bell says one reason why he remembers the meeting is that he'd never seen anyone eat the way Jobs did that day. "You know how you remember certain things because of their bizarreness? So we're meeting outside at the Apple cafeteria, and when Steve walks out, on his tray is a glass bowl full of avocado halves. Not one or two, but, like, fifteen covered in salad dressing. So I remember sitting there with Jony and Sakoman and watching Steve mow through a mound of avocados. I guess, having read Walter Isaacson's biography [of Jobs], it was one of those food phases he was in to cure his cancer, but at the time I had no idea what was up."

• • •

The final deal between Apple and AT&T, which acquired Cingular in 2006, took more than a year to hammer out. But it would prove easy compared to what Apple went through just to build the device. Many executives and engineers, riding high from their success with the iPod, assumed it would be just like building a small Macintosh. Instead, Apple designed and built not one iPhone but three entirely different devices in those two years. One executive on the project thinks Apple made six fully working prototypes just of the device it ultimately sold—each with its own set of hardware, software, and design tweaks. Many on the team were so burned-out, they left the company shortly after the first phone hit store shelves. "It was like the first moon mission," said Fadell, who was one of the key executives on the project, and who left Apple to start his own company, Nest, in 2010. "I'm used to a certain level of unknowns in a project, but there were so many new things here that it was just staggering."

Jobs wanted the iPhone to run a modified version of OS X, the software that comes with every Mac. But no one had ever put a gigantic program like OS X on a phone chip before. The software would have to be a tenth the size, and even then there wasn't a phone chip being made in 2005 that could run it fast enough and with a long enough battery life. The chips that run Apple laptops were never considered because they generated too much heat and would suck a phone battery dry in minutes. Millions of lines of code would have to be stripped out or rewritten, and until 2006 engineers would have to simulate chip speed and battery drain because actual chips weren't available until then. "Initially we just worked on Gumstix boards [cheap circuit boards hobbyists buy]," said Nitin Ganatra, one of the early software engineers. "We started with the Mac address book—a list of names—and to see if we could make it scroll [on a screen] at between thirty to sixty frames a second. We just wanted to figure out if there was any way to make this [OS X on a phone chip] work—whether we were even in the right ballpark. We wanted to know if we could push bits fast enough to get that iPhone look and feel. If we couldn't get it to work on a Gumstix board, we knew we might have a problem."

No one had ever put a capacitive multitouch screen in a mainstream consumer product before either. Capacitive touch technology—which creates "a touch" when a finger or other conductive item completes a circuit on the device—had been around since the 1960s. Elevator buttons in office buildings and screens on ATMs often used it. And research into multitouch technologies had been around since the 1980s. Trackpads on laptops were probably the most sophisticated use of this technology because they could recognize the difference between one- and two-finger inputs. But it was also well known that to build the multitouch screen Apple put on the iPhone and produce it in volume was a challenge few had the money or guts to take on. The next steps—to embed the technology invisibly in a piece of glass, to make it smart enough to display a virtual keyboard with autocorrect, and to make it sophisticated enough to reliably manipulate content such as photos or web pages on that screen—made it hugely expensive even to produce a working prototype. Few production lines even had experience manufacturing multitouch screens. There were touchscreens in consumer electronics, but over the years these had typically been *pressure-sensitive* touchscreen devices on which users pushed on-screen buttons with a finger or a stylus. The PalmPilot and its successors such as the Palm Treo were popular implementations of this technology. Even if multitouch iPhone screens had been *easy* to make, it wasn't at all clear to Apple's executive team that the features they enabled, such as onscreen keyboards and "tap to zoom," were enhancements that consumers wanted.

As early as 2003 a handful of Apple engineers, who had done cutting-edge academic work with touch interfaces, had figured out how to put multitouch technology in a tablet. But the project was mothballed. "The story was that Steve wanted a device that he could use to read email while on the toilet. That was the extent of the product spec," said Josh Strickon, one of the earliest engineers on that project. "But you couldn't build a device with enough battery life to take out of the house, and you couldn't get a chip with enough graphics capability to make it useful. We spent a lot of time trying to figure out just what to do." Before joining Apple in 2003, Strickon had been a student at MIT for a decade, getting his B.A., master's, and Ph.D. in engineering. He was a huge proponent of touchscreen technology, having built a multitouch device for his master's thesis. But he said given the lack of consensus at Apple about what to do with the prototypes he and his fellow engineers developed, he left the company in 2004 thinking it wasn't going to do anything with multitouch.

Tim Bucher, one of Apple's top executives at the time and the company's biggest multitouch proponent, said part of the problem was that the prototypes they were building used software, OS X, that was designed to be used with a mouse, not a finger. "We were using ten- or twelve-inch screens with Mac mini–like guts . . . and then you would launch these demos that would do the different multitouch gestures. One demo was a keyboard application that would rise from the bottom—very much what ended up shipping in the iPhone two years later. But it wasn't very pretty. It was very much wires, chewing gum, and bailing wire. It left too much to the imagination." Bucher, who has never before talked publicly about his work at Apple, had hoped to keep pushing the effort forward, but he lost a political battle with other top executives and left Apple in early 2005.

Few even thought about making touchscreen technology the centerpiece of a new kind of phone until Jobs started pushing the idea in mid-2005. "He said, 'Tony, come over here. Here's something we're working on. What do you think? Do you think we could make a phone out of this?'" Fadell said. "So we sat there and played with the demo (he was showing me) for a while. It was huge. It filled the room. There was a projector mounted on the ceiling and it would project the Mac screen onto this surface that was maybe three or four feet square. Then you could touch the Mac screen and move things around and draw on it. I knew about it [the touchscreen prototype], but I didn't know about it in detail because it was a Mac thing [Fadell ran the iPod division]. So we all sat down and had a serious discussion about it—about what could be done."

Fadell had serious doubts about whether such an enormous prototype could be shrunk so much. But he also knew better than to answer no to Steve Jobs. He was one of Apple's superstars, and he didn't get there by being timid about thorny technological problems. He'd joined Apple in 2001 as a consultant to help build the first iPod. By 2005, with iPod sales exploding, he had become, at thirty-six, arguably the single most important line executive at the company.

"I understood how it could be done," Fadell said. "But it's one thing to think that, and another to take a room full of special, one-off gear and make a million phone-sized versions of that in a cost-effective, reliable manner." The to-do list was exhausting just to think about. "You had to go to LCD vendors [companies that make the screens that go in computer monitors and TVs] who knew how to embed technology like this in glass; you had to find time on their line; and then you had to come up with compensation and calibrating algorithms to keep the pixel electronics [in the LCD] from generating all kinds of noise in the touch-screen [sitting on top of it.] It was a whole project just to make the touchscreen device. We tried two or three ways of actually making the touchscreen until we could make one in enough volume that would work."

Shrinking OS X and building a multitouch screen, while innovative and difficult, were at least within the skills Apple had already mastered as a corporation. No one was better equipped to rethink OS X's design. Apple knew LCD manufacturers because it put an LCD in every laptop and iPod. The peculiarities of mobile phone physics, on the other hand, were an entirely new field, and it took those working on the iPhone into 2006 to realize how little they knew.

To ensure the iPhone's tiny antenna could do its job effectively, Apple spent millions buying and assembling special robot-equipped testing rooms. To make sure the iPhone didn't generate too much radiation, Apple built models of human heads—complete with goo to simulate brain density—and measured the effects. To predict the iPhone's performance on a network, Apple engineers bought nearly a dozen server-size radio-frequency simulators for millions of dollars apiece. One senior executive believes Apple spent more than $150 million building the first iPhone.

. . .

The first iPhone prototype was not ambitious. Jobs hoped that he would be able to develop a touchscreen iPhone running OS X. But in 2005 he had no idea how long that would take. So Apple's first iPhone looked very much like the joke slide Jobs had put up when introducing the real iPhone—an iPod with an old fashioned rotary dial on it. The prototype was an iPod with a phone radio that used the iPod click wheel as a dialer. It grew out of the work Steve Sakoman had used to pitch Jobs on a phone project in the first place. "It was an easy way to get to market, but it was not cool like the devices we have today," Grignon said. He worked for Sakoman at the time and is one of the names on the click wheel dialer patent.

The second iPhone prototype in early 2006 was much closer to what Jobs would ultimately unveil. It incorporated a touchscreen and OS X, but it was made entirely of brushed aluminum. Jobs and Ive were exceedingly proud of it. But since neither of them were experts in the physics of radio waves, they hadn't realized they'd created a beautiful brick. Radio waves don't travel through metal well. "I and Ruben Caballero [Apple's antenna expert] had to go up to the boardroom and explain to Steve and Ive that you cannot put radio waves through metal," said Phil Kearney, one of Bell's deputies, who left in 2008. "And it was not an easy explanation. Most of the designers are artists. The last science class they took was in eighth grade. But they have a lot of power at Apple. So they ask, 'Why can't we just make a little seam for the radio waves to escape through?' And you have to explain to them why you just can't."

Jon Rubinstein, Apple's top hardware executive then and known to many as the Podfather for driving the creation and development in the iPod, said there were even long discussions about how big the phone would be. "I was actually pushing to do two sizes—to have a regular iPhone and an iPhone mini like we had with the iPod. I thought one could be a smartphone and one could be a dumber phone. But we never got a lot of traction on the small one, and in order to do one of these projects you really need to put all your wood behind one arrow."

It all made the iPhone project so complex that it occasionally threatened to derail the entire corporation. Many of the top engineers in the company were being sucked into the project, forcing slowdowns in the timetables of other projects. Had the iPhone been a dud or not gotten off the ground at all, Apple would have had no other big products ready to announce for a long time. Worse, its top engineers, frustrated by the failure, would have left Apple for other jobs, according to 2012 testimony by Scott Forstall, one of Apple's top executives on the project and Apple's head of iOS software until October 2012. He testified during the *Apple v. Samsung* patent trial.

Even Apple's experience designing screens for iPods didn't help the company design the iPhone screen. After much debate, Jobs decided the iPhone screen needed to be made of hard Plexiglas. He and his executives thought a glass screen would shatter when dropped—until Jobs saw how scratched a plastic prototype had gotten when he carried it around in his pocket with his keys. "Jobs goes, 'Look at this. Look at this. What's with the screen?'" said an executive who witnessed the exchange. "And the guy [a midlevel executive] takes the prototype and says, 'Well, Steve, we have a glass prototype, but it fails the one-meter drop test one hundred out of one hundred times, and blah blah blah . . .' Jobs cuts him off and says, 'I just want to know if you are going to make the fucking thing work.'"

There was a good reason the executive argued with Jobs. This was September 2006. The iPhone would be unveiled in four months. And Jobs wanted to rethink the phone's most prominent component.

Through his friend John Seely Brown, Jobs reached out to Wendell Weeks, the CEO of glassmaker Corning in upstate New York, invited him to Cupertino, and told him he needed the hardest glass ever made for the screen of the iPhone. Weeks told him about a process developed for fighter-jet cockpits in the 1960s. But Weeks said the Defense Department never ended up using the material, known as gorilla glass, so it had never found a market. He said Corning had stopped making it decades ago. Jobs wanted Weeks to start production immediately, convincing Weeks that he could in fact get Jobs the glass he needed in six months. Weeks told Jobs's biographer Walter Isaacson that he remains amazed at what Jobs convinced him to do. Corning took a factory in Harrodsburg, Kentucky, that had been making LCD displays and converted it, getting Jobs the glass he needed on time. "We produced glass that had never been made. We put our best scientists and engineers on it and we just made it work," Weeks said.

"I still remember *PC Magazine* doing a screen durability test once the phone came out in July 2007," said Bob Borchers, Apple's then head of iPhone marketing. "They put it in a bag of coins and shook it up. They put keys in the bag and shook it up. They dropped it a few times on a carpet. And then they went out on the street and dropped it on the concrete three times. It survived all of that. We all laughed, looked at each other, and said, 'Right, we knew that.'"

. . .

On top of all that, Jobs's obsession with secrecy meant that despite being exhausted from working eighty hours a week, the few hundred engineers and designers working on the project couldn't talk about the project to anyone else. If Apple found out you'd told a friend in a bar, or even your spouse, you could be fired. Before a manager could ask you to join the project, you had to sign a nondisclosure agreement in his office. Then, after he told you what the project was, you had to sign another document confirming that you had indeed signed the NDA and would tell no one. "We put a sign on over the front door of the iPhone building that said FIGHT CLUB because the first rule of fight club is you don't talk about fight club," Forstall would explain in his court testimony. "Steve didn't want to hire anyone from outside of Apple to work on the software, but he said I could hire anyone in the company I wanted," Forstall said. "So I'd bring recruits into my office. Sit them down and tell them, 'You are a superstar at Apple. Whatever you are doing now, you'll do fine. But I have another project that I want you to consider. I can't tell you what it is. All I can say is that you will have to give up untold nights and weekends and that you will work harder than you have ever worked in your life."

"My favorite part," said one of the early iPhone engineers, "was what all the vendors said the day after the unveiling." Big companies such as Marvell Electronics, which made the Wi-Fi radio chip, and CSR, which provided the Bluetooth radio chip, hadn't been told they were going to be in a new phone. They thought they were going to be in a new iPod. "We actually had fake schematics and fake industrial designs," the engineer said. Grignon said that Apple even went as far as to impersonate employees of another company when they traveled, especially to Cingular (and, later, AT&T) in Texas. "The whole thing was you didn't want the receptionist or whoever happens to be walking by to see all [pre-printed Apple] badges lying out."

On the other hand, Jobs wanted a handful of the top engineers on the iPhone project to use iPhone prototypes as their permanent phones. "It wasn't 'Carry an iPhone—and a Treo,'" Grignon said. "It was 'Carry an iPhone and live on it,' because that's how we found bugs. If you can't make a phone call because of a bug, you are going to be extra-motivated to start yelling to get that fixed. But it made for some awkward times where, if you were, say, in a club or an airport, you could spot an iPhone user a mile away because they were the person hunched over with their arms around their phone doing something mysterious. Snorting a line of coke—or using an iPhone?"

One of the most obvious manifestations of Jobs's obsession with secrecy was the growth of lockdown areas all over campus—places that those not working on the iPhone could no longer go. "Each building is split in half, and there is this corridor that runs through the middle of them with common areas, and after one weekend they just put doors around the common areas so that if you were not on the project, and you were used to using that space, it was now off-limits," Grignon said. "Steve loved this stuff. He loved to set up division. But it was a big 'fuck you' to the people who couldn't get in. Everyone knows who the rock stars are in a company, and when you start to see them all slowly get plucked out of your area and put in a big room behind glass doors that you don't have access to, it feels bad."

Even people within the iPhone project itself couldn't talk to one another. Engineers designing the iPhone's electronics weren't allowed to see the software it would run. When they needed software to test the electronics, they were given proxy code, not the real thing. If you were working on the software, you used a simulator to test hardware performance.

And no one outside Jobs's inner circle was allowed into chief designer Jony Ive's wing on the first floor of Building 2. The security surrounding Ive's prototypes was so tight that employees believed the badge reader called security if you tried to badge in and weren't authorized. "It was weird, because it wasn't like you could avoid going by it. It was right off the lobby, behind a big metal door. Every now and then you'd see the door open and you'd try to look in and see, but you never tried to do more than that," said an engineer whose first job out of college was working on the iPhone. Forstall said during his testimony that some labs required you to "badge in" four times.

The four months leading up to announcement day were particularly rough, Grignon said. Screaming matches broke out routinely in the hallways. Engineers, frazzled from all-night coding sessions, quit, only to rejoin days later after catching up on their sleep. Forstall's chief of staff, Kim Vorath, slammed the door to her office so hard that the handle bent and locked her in; it took colleagues more than an hour and some well-placed whacks with an aluminum bat to free her. "We were all standing there watching it," Grignon said. "Part of it was funny. But it was also one of those moments where you step back and realize how fucked-up it all is."

. . .

To Grignon's amazement and to that of many others in the audience, Jobs's iPhone demo on January 9, 2007, was flawless. He started the show saying, "This is a day I have been waiting for two and a half years." Then he regaled the audience with a myriad of tales about why consumers hated their cell phones. Then he solved all their problems—definitively. Virtually everyone in the audience had been expecting Jobs to announce a phone, yet they were still in awe.

He used the iPhone to play some music and watch a movie clip to show off the phone's beautiful screen. He made a phone call to show off the phone's reinvented address book and voice mail. He sent an email and a text, showing how easy it was to type on the phone's touchscreen keyboard. He scrolled through a bunch of photos, showing how simple pinches and spreads of two fingers could make the pictures bigger or smaller. He navigated Amazon's and *The New York Times'* websites to show that the iPhone's Internet browser was as good as the one on his computer. He found a Starbucks with Google Maps—and called the number from the stage—to show how it was impossible to get lost with an iPhone.

By the end, Grignon wasn't just happy, he was drunk. He'd brought a flask of Scotch to calm his nerves. "And so there we were in the fifth row or something—engineers, managers, all of us—doing shots of Scotch after every segment of the demo. There were about five or six of us, and after each piece of the demo, the person who was responsible for that portion did a shot. When the finale came—and it worked along with everything before it, we all just drained the flask. It was the best demo any of us had ever seen. And the rest of the day turned out to be just a shit show for the entire iPhone team. We just spent the entire rest of the day drinking in the city. It was just a mess, but it was great."

2

The iPhone Is Good.
Android Will Be Better.

For all its fame and notoriety, Silicon Valley, as a place, isn't much of a tourist attraction. There is no sign or Walk of Fame as in Hollywood. There isn't an address, such as Wall Street, where the New York Stock Exchange has been for 150 years. It is just a slew of office parks sprawling thirty miles southeast from the San Francisco Airport to San Jose.

But a visual encapsulation of the Valley's brilliant, driven, and zany gestalt *does* exist. You just have to know someone at Google to go see it. Located thirty-five miles southeast of San Francisco next to Highway 101 in Mountain View, Google's sprawling campus resembles few other corporate facilities in the world. The company started in a Stanford University dorm room in 1998 and has in fifteen years grown into one of the most important and powerful companies in the world. Google now controls more than sixty-five buildings in Mountain View and employs a third of its roughly fifty-five thousand workers there. Size hasn't made Google slow or stuffy. Visual signs of its unconventional approach to problem solving remain everywhere. Googlers on red, green, and blue bicycles and motorized scooters zip from building to building. A fifteen-foot-high replica of a T. rex named Stan presides over the main outdoor lunch patio. A few feet away is a replica of Space-ShipOne, Burt Rutan's first manned private spaceship in 2004. Many lobbies have pianos and vibrating massage chairs; and many restrooms have heated Japanese toilet seats—an odd experience on a hot day when the person before you has forgotten to turn the heater off. Google uses so many solar panels for power that it ranks as one of the largest corporate solar installations in the world. Meanwhile, an entire fleet of Wi-Fi-enabled commuter buses run to and from San Francisco, Berkeley/Oakland, and San Jose. They not only encourage employees to conserve gas by not driving, but they allow Google to tap into a bigger population of potential employees. Food and drink everywhere on campus are free.

It feels like a college campus, and that's exactly how it's supposed to feel. The source of Google's success has been the quality of the engineers it hires out of top colleges. Rather than make them feel as if they've just joined the marines—as other corporations might—Google wants to keep them feeling that they've never left school so that they stay creatively wide-eyed. The campus has a swimming pool, gyms, a convenience store, a day-care center, a place to get haircuts, and drop-off dry cleaning. Almost every building has a laundry room. One summer back in 2004 a bunch of summer interns tried to live at Google rather than search for housing. They slept on couches and ran their whole lives out of the Googleplex until they were told they were violating the fire code.

"We made an explicit decision to keep the buildings crowded," Google executive chairman and former CEO Eric Schmidt told me back then. "There's kind of a certain amount of noise that kind of gets everybody to work and gets them excited. It's really based on how computer-science graduate schools work. If you go to a graduate school, like go to the Stanford Computer Science building, you'll see two, three, or even four in an office. That model is one which is very familiar to our programmers and for us because we were all in those offices too, and we know it's a very productive environment."

Over the years these perks and oddities have been so widely imitated by other corporations that it is now impossible to explain Silicon Valley *without* mentioning them. Google's company bus fleet is arguably driving an entire reconfiguration of work-life patterns in the Bay Area. Most big Silicon Valley companies now offer such buses. The one downside of working in Silicon Valley after college used to be living in suburban Mountain View, Palo Alto, or Sunnyvale. City life in San Francisco wasn't worth the more than two hours of driving it required to live there. Google's buses, which all have Wi-Fi, make those commutes not only tolerable but some of the most productive hours of the day. So many high-tech workers now live in San Francisco that some of the newest technology companies have followed them. A decade ago companies such as Zynga and Twitter would have automatically located in Silicon Valley. When they started more than six years ago, they located in San Francisco. Benchmark Capital, a top venture capital firm, just opened its first office in their neighborhood too.

All this has made Google a rigorous yet chaotic place to work. Especially back in 2005 there were often dozens of engineering projects going at the same time. Many of them had conflicting ambitions. And some were so secret that only a handful of top executives knew about them. The most secret and ambitious of these was Google's own smartphone effort—the Android project. Tucked in a first-floor corner of Google's Building 44, surrounded by Google ad reps, its four dozen engineers thought that they too were on track to deliver a revolutionary device that would change the mobile phone industry forever. By January 2007, they'd all worked sixty-to-eighty-hour weeks for fifteen months—some for more than two years—writing and testing code, negotiating software licenses, and flying all over the world to find the right parts, suppliers, and manufacturers. They had been working with prototypes for six months and had planned a launch by the end of the year . . . until Jobs took the stage to unveil the iPhone.

• • •

Chris DeSalvo's reaction to the iPhone was immediate and visceral. "As a consumer I was blown away. I wanted one immediately. But as a Google engineer, I thought, 'We're going to have to start over.'"

For most of Silicon Valley—including most of Google—the iPhone's unveiling was something to celebrate. Jobs had once again done the impossible. Four years before he'd talked an intransigent music industry into letting him put their catalog on iTunes for ninety-nine cents a song. Now he had convinced a wireless carrier to let him build a revolutionary smartphone. But for the Google Android team, the iPhone was a kick in the stomach. "What we had suddenly looked just so . . . nineties," DeSalvo said. "It's just one of those things that are obvious when you see it."

DeSalvo wasn't prone to panic. Like many veteran engineers in the Valley, laconic would be a good description of his personality. He's an expert sailor who had just returned from taking his family on a three-week excursion in Indonesia. He'd been writing software for two decades, first for video-game developers, then for Apple, and by 2000 for a start-up called Danger. There were few software-development issues he hadn't encountered. After joining Google and the Android team in Mountain View at the end of 2005 and spending a year writing thousands of lines of code out of a utility closet (he likes writing code in silence), he'd moved to Chapel Hill, North Carolina, the week before to help the team integrate a recent acquisition. But as he watched Jobs's presentation from a run-down office above a T-shirt shop there, he knew his boss, Andy Rubin, would be thinking the same thing he was. He and Rubin had worked together for most of the previous seven years, when DeSalvo had been an engineer at Danger, Rubin's first start-up. Rubin was one of the most competitive people DeSalvo knew. Rubin was not about to release a product that suddenly looked so dated.

Six hundred miles away in Las Vegas, on his way to a meeting with one of the myriad handset makers and carriers that descend on the city for the Consumer Electronics Show, Rubin reacted exactly as DeSalvo predicted. He was so astonished by what Jobs was unveiling that, on his way to a meeting, he had his driver pull over so that he could finish watching the webcast. "Holy crap," he said to one of his colleagues in the car. "I guess we're not going to ship *that* phone."

What the Android team had been working on, a phone code-named Sooner, sported software that was arguably *more* revolutionary than what had just been revealed in the iPhone. In addition to having a full Internet browser, and running all of Google's great web applications, such as search, Maps, and YouTube, the software was designed not just to run on Sooner, but on any smartphone, tablet, or other portable device not yet conceived. It would never need to be tethered to a laptop or desktop. It would allow multiple applications to run at the same time, and it would easily connect to an online store of other applications that Google would seed and encourage. By contrast, the iPhone needed to connect to iTunes regularly, it wouldn't run more than one application at a time, and in the beginning it had no plans to allow anything resembling an application store.

However, the Sooner phone was ugly. It looked like a BlackBerry, with a traditional keyboard and a small screen that wasn't touch-enabled. Rubin and his team, along with partners HTC and T-Mobile, believed consumers would care more about the great software it contained than its looks. This was conventional wisdom back then. Revolutionary phone designs rarely succeeded. The Nokia N-Gage, which in 2003 tried to combine a gaming system with a phone and email device, often gets mentioned here. RIM had become one of the dominant smartphone makers on the planet by making BlackBerry's unadorned functionality one of its main selling points: you got a phone, an incredible keyboard, secure email, all in one indestructible package.

The iPhone, in contrast, was not only cool looking, but it used those cool looks to create entirely new ways to interact with a phone—ways that Android engineers either hadn't thought possible or had considered too risky. By using a virtual keyboard and replacing most real buttons with software-generated buttons on a big touchscreen, every application could now have its own unique set of controls. Play, Pause, and Stop buttons only appeared if you were listening to music or watching video. When you went to type a web address into the browser, the keyboard appeared, but it disappeared when you hit Enter. Without the physical keyboard taking up half the phone, the iPhone had a screen twice the size of virtually every other phone on the market. It all worked the same way whether the user held the phone in portrait or landscape mode. Apple had installed an accelerometer to use gravity to tell the phone how to orient the screen.

A lot was wrong with the first iPhone too. Rubin and the Android team—along with many others—did not think users would take to typing on a screen without the tactile feedback of a physical keyboard. That is why the first Android phone—the T-Mobile G1 from HTC, nearly two years later—had a slide-out keyboard. But what was also undeniable to the Android team was that they had underestimated Jobs. At the very least, Jobs had come up with a new way of interacting with a device—with a finger instead of a stylus or dedicated buttons—and likely a lot more. "We knew that Apple was going to announce a phone. Everyone knew that. We just didn't think it would be that good," said Ethan Beard, one of Android's early business development executives.

Within weeks the Android team had completely reconfigured its objectives. A phone with a touchscreen, code-named Dream, that had been in the early stages of development, became the focus. Its launch was pushed out a year until fall 2008. Engineers started drilling into it all the things the iPhone *didn't* do to differentiate their phone when launch day *did* occur. Erick Tseng, then Android's project manager, remembers suddenly feeling the nervous excitement of a pending public performance. Tseng had joined Google the year before out of Stanford business school after Eric Schmidt, himself, sold him on the promise of Android. "I never got the feeling that we should scrap what we were doing—that the iPhone meant game over. But a bar had been set, and whatever we decided to launch, we wanted to make sure that it cleared the bar."

• • •

In many ways the Android project is the perfect reflection of Google's zany and chaotic culture. At most companies, outlandish ideas are discouraged in favor of ideas that are doable. At Google, especially back then, the reverse was true. The easiest way to get on cofounder and now CEO Larry Page's bad side was not to think big enough and to clutter a pitch with how much money an idea could make. Back in 2006 Page famously gave Sheryl Sandberg praise for making a mistake that cost Google several million dollars. That was when Sandberg was a Google vice president in charge of its automated ad system, not the chief operating officer of Facebook. "God, I feel really bad about this," Sandberg told Page, according to *Fortune* magazine. But instead of hammering her for the error, Page said, "I'm so glad you made this mistake because I want to run a company where we are moving too quickly and doing too much, not being too cautious and doing too little. If we don't have any of these mistakes, we're just not taking enough risk."

The cell phone industry in 2005 was a perfect example of a hairy Google-size problem. The software industry for mobile phones was one of the most dysfunctional in all technology. There wasn't enough wireless bandwidth for users to surf the Internet on a phone without frustration. Phones weren't powerful enough to run anything but rudimentary software. But the biggest problem, as Jobs had learned, was that the industry was ruled by an oligopoly: Few companies besides the carriers and the phone makers were writing software for phones, and what existed was terrible. Wireless bandwidth would improve and phone chips would get more powerful; but back then it looked as if the carriers and phone makers would control it all. "We had done a deal with Vodafone [the big European carrier] to try to get Google search on their phones," said one top Google executive who would not give his name. "But the search they offered us was that we could put some results on, but that they would control most of them, and that our results would be at the bottom of every query. They didn't have a good mobile browser. Ringtones [that they were selling] sometimes got prioritized in search results. All the carriers were doing this. They thought they could provide all the services inside a walled garden [as AOL had in the 1990s], and that this control was the best way to make money."

The reason few developers built software for mobile phones was because anytime they tried, they lost money. There was no standardization in the industry. Virtually every phone ran its own software and set of applications, meaning software written for a Samsung phone often wouldn't run on a Motorola phone, which wouldn't run on a Nokia. Software platforms were incompatible even within companies. For example, there were a handful of different versions of Symbian. Put simply, the mobile industry screamed "money pit" to any enterprising developer. Most stayed away. The most lucrative business was not writing apps for phones. It was owning a testing company that would make sure your apps worked on all the phones in the market. Larry Page has never been shy talking about how frustrating those days were for him and Google. "We had a closet full of over 100 phones [that we were developing software for], and we were building our software pretty much one device at a time," he said in his 2012 report to shareholders. In various remarks over the years he has described the experience as both "awful" and "incredibly painful."

But Page and the rest of Google's executives knew that someone would figure out the mobile business eventually, and they were particularly concerned that that company would be Microsoft. Back then, Microsoft was still the richest and most powerful technology company in the world, and it was finally getting traction with its Windows CE mobile phones and software. Windows CE smartphones were still a niche market, but if consumers took to the platform en masse as they did later with the iPhone, Google's entire business could be in jeopardy.

This wasn't an exaggeration. Back then, Microsoft and Google were in the midst of a nasty battle of their own for dominance in search, and for top dog in the tech world. After two decades of being the first-choice workplace of top engineering talent, Microsoft was now losing many of those battles to Google. Chairman

Bill Gates and CEO Steve Ballmer had made it clear they took Google's challenge personally. Gates seemed particularly affected by it. Once or twice he made fun of the way Page and his Google cofounder Sergey Brin dressed. He said their search engine's popularity was "a fad." Then, in the same breath, he would issue the ultimate compliment, saying that of all his competitors over the years, Google was the most like Microsoft.

Google executives were convinced that if Windows on mobile devices caught on, Microsoft would interfere with users' access to Google search on those devices in favor of its own search engine. The government's successful antitrust trial against Microsoft in the 1990s made it difficult for the company to use its monopoly on desktops and laptops to bully competitors. It could not, for example, make Microsoft's the default search engine in Windows without giving users a choice between its search engine and those from Google, Yahoo, and others. However, on smartphones, few rules governed how fiercely Microsoft could compete. It didn't have a monopoly there. Google worried that if Microsoft made it hard enough to use Google search on its mobile devices and easy enough to use Microsoft search, many users would just switch search engines. This was the way Microsoft killed Netscape with Internet Explorer in the 1990s. If users stopped using Google's search engine and began using a competitor's such as Microsoft's, Google's business would quickly run aground. Google made all its money back then from the search ads that appeared next to its search results. "It's hard to relate to that [fear of Microsoft] now, but at the time we were very concerned that Microsoft's mobile strategy would be successful," Schmidt said in 2012 during testimony in the *Oracle v. Google* copyright trial.

All these fears and frustrations were top of the mind for Page when he agreed to meet with Rubin in early 2005 in the first-floor conference room of Google's Building 43. Back then, Page's office was on the second floor overlooking Google's main courtyard. He and Brin shared it and continued that setup until Page became CEO in 2011. The space looked more like the dorm room of two engineering students than anything you would expect to see in a major corporation. You had to work to see their two desks and computers because the room was so jammed with their latest electronic-gadget passions—cameras typically for Page, along with Brin's radio-controlled planes and cars and his roller-hockey gear. When Brin and Page were not there, the office was often filled with other programmers, who felt free to take it over. Rubin had reached out to Page because Rubin had started Android the year before and had enough software written to show potential customers such as carriers. He thought some kind of sign from Google—such as an email from Page saying that Android was doing interesting work—would help Rubin raise more money to keep going and give his sales pitch more zing.

• • •

Few people can just email Larry Page directly and successfully ask for a meeting, but back then Rubin was one of them. Three years earlier, when Google was still scrabbling for users, attention, and revenue, Rubin had made Google the default search engine on the T-Mobile Sidekick, the device Rubin designed and built when he ran Danger. Page remembered the gesture not just because Google had desperately needed search traffic at the time, but also because he thought the Sidekick was one of best-engineered mobile devices he'd ever seen.

The Sidekick was odd looking—shaped like a bar of soap with a screen in the middle. To operate it, one flipped up the screen, rotating it 180 degrees, and typed on the keyboard underneath. Its nonstandard looks and a nonexistent marketing budget kept it from being a hit product. But it had a cult following among two groups: savvy high school and college students and Silicon Valley engineers. Students liked that it was the first mobile device to have instant-messaging software built in. Engineers such as Page loved that it was the first mobile device to allow users to surf the Internet the same way as on their office computers. BlackBerry had mobile email down to a science, and everyone at Google had a BlackBerry. But the Internet browsers on it and other mobile devices were terrible. To deal with smaller bandwidth back then, browsers were designed to show only the bare bones of a web page's content—typically just text. But that also made the browsing experience all but useless for businesses. One of the things that wouldn't work in these crippled browsers were Google search ads. You couldn't click on them. Soon Page and Brin were walking around with Sidekicks themselves, enthralling their friends and colleagues with a mobile device that nearly replaced their laptops.

According to *Wired*, when Page arrived for the meeting, late as usual, Rubin jumped to the whiteboard to begin his pitch: phones with computer capabilities, not laptops or desktops, were the future of technology. It was a huge market, Rubin said. More than 700 million cell phones were sold worldwide every year, compared to 200 million computers, and that gap was widening. But the phone business was stuck in the dark ages. Android would fix that problem by convincing carriers and phone makers that they didn't need to spend money on their own proprietary software. Frustrated consumers would flock to phones that worked better. Software developers would rush to write software for a platform in such demand. A self-reinforcing software ecosystem would be born.

Page listened gamely. He looked at the prototype Rubin had brought with him. But Page had pretty much decided what he was going to do before the meeting even started: What if Google just bought Android? he asked. He later told Steven Levy, the author of *In the Plex*, "We had that vision [about what the future of mobile should look like], and Andy came along and we were like 'Yeah we should do it. He's the guy.'" Google bought Android for about $50 million plus incentives, and by July 2005 Rubin and his seven other Android cofounders were sharing their vision of the world with the rest of Google's management team.

• • •

Rubin was surprised and thrilled about Google's decision to buy his company. "At Danger we had a great niche product [the

Sidekick] that everyone loved. But I wanted to get beyond niche and make a mass-market product," he said. And no company was more mass-market than Google. When reflecting on those days, he likes to tell a before-and-after story about a presentation he gave to phone maker Samsung in Seoul:

> I walk into the boardroom with my entire team—me and six people. Then twenty executives walk in and stand on the other side of the table in the boardroom. We're sitting down because I wasn't accustomed to Asian culture and whatnot at the time. Their CEO walks in. Everyone sits only after he sits, like a military tribunal. Then I go into pitch mode. I pitch the whole Android vision to them like they are a venture capitalist. And at the end and I am out of breath, with the whole thing laid out . . . there is silence. Literally silence, like there are crickets in the room. Then I hear whispering in a nonnative language, and one of the lieutenants, having whispered with the CEO, says, "Are you dreaming?" The whole vision that I presented, their response was "You and what army are going to go and create this? You have six people. Are you high?" is basically what they said. They laughed me out of the boardroom. This happened two weeks before Google acquired us. The next day [after the acquisition was announced] a very nervous lieutenant of the CEO calls me up and says, "I demand we meet immediately to discuss your very, very interesting proposal that you gave us [when you were in Seoul]."

Because of Google, Rubin no longer had to worry about running out of money and having potential vendors and customers not return his calls. But after the euphoria of the acquisition wore off, it became clear that even at Google getting Android off the ground was going to be one of the hardest things Rubin had undertaken in his life. Just navigating Google itself was initially a challenge for Rubin and his team. There was no hard-and-fast org chart, as in other companies. Every employee seemed right out of college. And the Google culture, with its famous "Don't be evil" and "That's not Googley" sanctimony, seemed weird for someone such as Rubin, who had already been in the workplace twenty years. He couldn't even drive his car to work because it was too fancy for the Google parking lot. Google was by then filled with millionaires who had gotten rich on the 2004 IPO. But in an effort to preserve Google's brand as a revolutionary company with a revolutionary product—the anti-Microsoft—all cars fancier than a 3 Series BMW were banned. During this period Brin and Page—now worth more than $5 billion apiece—famously drove Priuses to work. That meant Rubin's Ferrari was not allowed.

Rubin also had to adjust to no longer being the boss. He ran Google's Android division, but even by the end of 2005 that was only about a dozen people in a corporation with fifty-seven hundred. But Google clearly didn't treat Android like any of its many other small acquisitions. In those the founders rarely stayed, quickly discovering that actually working at Google was frustrating. Google often bought companies just to test out a new technology and/or hire talented engineers, but without a clear game plan. Page didn't want Rubin to become frustrated like that, and he specifically tasked executives such as Alan Eustace—who helped Page negotiate the purchase of Android—to make sure Rubin felt that he had the access to the people and resources he needed. Google immediately opened its wallet to the tune of $10 million to help Rubin buy necessary software licenses. Schmidt personally helped negotiate some of them. To ensure the secrecy of their project, the Android team was allowed to keep its software code separate from the rest of Google, and inaccessible to anyone without Rubin's permission. Page gave Rubin the rare privilege of being able to hire his own staff, instead of going through Google's famously rigorous and lengthy hiring process.

But all this attention didn't spare Rubin from having to navigate Google's wacky politics. For starters, it wasn't clear to him for a while who Google's ultimate boss was. Eric Schmidt was the CEO and played a critical role in helping Google deal with its hypergrowth back then. He was also the public face of the company, which he did well and which Page and Brin had much less interest in doing. He had been a CEO before—at Novell—and an executive at Sun Microsystems for fourteen years before that. But Schmidt, who joined Google in 2001, was not a founder as were Page and Brin, which made his true role slightly murkier.

Officially, the three ran Google as a triumvirate, but Google employees debated about how much power Schmidt actually had—whether Brin and Page called the shots, with Schmidt filling a largely ceremonial role, providing "adult supervision" in Silicon Valley parlance. Schmidt didn't help with this confusion by describing his job the way a chief operating officer would, not a CEO. In an interview with me in 2004 he said,

> My primary responsibility is making the trains run on time, so I try to make sure that the meetings happen, that all of the functions of a properly running company are in place and people are paying attention. Larry and Sergey have driven the top-level strategy and much of the technology strategy. I contribute by organizing the strategy process, but it's really their strategy and their technology strategy. And if there is a disagreement among the three of us . . . we'll have a significant conversation, and somebody will eventually say yes. A few months later somebody, one of the three, will say, 'Well, maybe the other guy was actually right.' So there's a very healthy respect now between the three of us and it's a wonderful thing. We're best friends and we're very good colleagues.

Rubin also noted to colleagues that it seemed to him as if Page and Schmidt didn't completely agree on what Android should become. Schmidt wanted Android to be software only, and for a while he wondered if it should just be low-level software, without fancy graphics or animations. This was Rubin's original vision: give phone makers and carriers code that runs all phones and applications the same way, but allows them to decide things such as what the opening screen would look like, and what kinds of graphic flourishes each phone would have. Page, however, was more interested in having Google build a phone. "I remember talking to Andy about this," one Android executive told me. "He said he always made sure never to demonstrate an Android feature to Page without a prototype of the actual hardware it would run on."

Then there were legal issues. Most of Android was open-source software, meaning no one owned it, and the code could be modified by anyone in any way. But not all of it was open source, and Google negotiated licenses for those portions for tens of millions of dollars. Rubin hoped a big chunk of licensed code would come from Sun Microsystems, makers of Java. Sun had spent ten years building Java as an alternative to Microsoft's Windows. It typically gave the software away for free, on the condition the user didn't modify it in a major way. Rubin used it for the operating system on the Sidekick, and it was, back then, a widely used language by engineers coming out of top universities. But Android wanted to modify Java more than Sun would allow. No amount of money seemed able to move Sun from this view. Payments as high as $35 million were discussed. This created two problems for Rubin: Without the Java code, Rubin had to spend months of extra time creating a work-around. Second, it infuriated Sun, which believed Google had copied portions of Java to build the work-around. It ultimately became the focus of a messy lawsuit that went to trial in 2012. Google was not held liable, but Sun, now owned by Oracle, is appealing that decision.

Finally, Rubin had the enormous task of just doing what he'd promised to do: build a mobile phone operating system that carriers and manufacturers would want to use and that software developers in addition to Google would want to write programs for. There certainly was precedent for it. It's what Bill Gates did to transform the PC industry and become the world's richest man. Most of us now just assume that any PC we buy will run Microsoft Windows or Apple OS X, and that it will have an Intel processor running on a certain kind of circuit board that connects to every printer, mouse, keyboard, monitor, and almost every other electronic device. But in the 1980s, the PC industry was just like the mobile industry in 2005. Not until Gates came along and used MS-DOS and Windows to create a platform for developers to write to did the PC application business take off. "I remember at the time telling Andy, 'This is going to be really hard, really, really difficult. I don't want you to get discouraged, but I think the chances are low on this,'" said Alan Eustace, Google's head of engineering and Rubin's boss at the time. "And then he and I would laugh about that because he was a true believer. It wasn't that I was a skeptic. I supported the project all the time. It's just that we both knew it was going to be hard."

Some of the issues in building Android were similar to the ones Apple faced. Few people had put an operating system as sophisticated as Android on a phone chip. Meanwhile, all the testing had to be done on simulators because the actual chips and displays Rubin wanted to put on the Dream phone weren't going to be manufactured for another year. But Google was in an even worse position than Apple to take on these challenges. At Apple the iPhone had nearly brought the company to its knees, but at least Apple was used to building things that consumers wanted to buy. Google had no such experience. Google made money selling advertising. Everything else it built—web software—it gave away for free. It had no fancy industrial-design division comparable to Apple's. Indeed, the idea of a finished product of any sort was anathema to Googlers. To them the beauty of building web software was that it was *never* finished. When a feature was mostly done, Google would release it, then refine it over time based on consumer usage with updates to their servers.

Google also viewed marketing with the kind of contempt only an engineer could muster. If a product was good, word of mouth on the web would get people to use it. If it was not good, people would not use it. The idea that Google might be selling more than just a cool phone, but amorphous feelings of satisfaction and self-confidence—the way Jobs sold Apple's devices—seemed silly. This thinking was firmly rooted in Google's DNA as a corporation. In Google's early years executives had hired the famed consultant Sergio Zyman—the former head of marketing for Coca-Cola—to draw up a plan to get the world excited about their new company. After he spent months working on a plan, the founders rejected the whole marketing concept and did not renew Zyman's contract. They believed—correctly—that Google's search engine would sell itself. Google didn't even have a director-of-marketing position until 2001.

• • •

Rubin and the Android team believed they could compensate for these deficits by partnering with wireless carriers and phone makers. That was the whole point of Android, after all: everyone would do what they did best. Google would write software, manufacturers would make phones, and carriers would supply bandwidth and sales and marketing heft. HTC and T-Mobile were committed to the project. They had helped Rubin build the Sidekick when he was at Danger.

Rubin's problem was that T-Mobile wasn't a big enough carrier in the United States to get Android on enough phones, and the two other big US wireless carriers, AT&T and Verizon, were deeply suspicious of anyone from Google interested in a business deal. For all Android's promise and Rubin's ability to sell that promise, by the end of 2006 the rest of Google was starting to scare people, telecom companies in particular. Google had clearly created a new and incredibly profitable form of advertising, and it was recording profits and amassing cash at astonishing rates. In 2003 it had seemed like a friendly, plucky start-up. By the end of 2006 it was a colossus with nearly eleven thousand employees, $3 billion in profits, and more than 60 percent market share in search advertising. Would Google soon replace Microsoft as the big bad monopoly in tech? some started to ask.

Executives at companies such as Verizon had experienced Microsoft's aggressive behavior firsthand in the 1990s as Gates started trying to leverage his desktop monopoly into adjacent industries. Convinced that Windows would soon become the hub for the convergence of our PCs and TVs, Microsoft invested $1 billion in Comcast, $5 billion in AT&T, and another $500 million in smaller cable and telephone companies. Carriers worried that Gates didn't just want to speed the adoption of broadband Internet and install Windows on every cable set-top box. They believed he wanted to make phone companies irrelevant.

Google, if anything, made the telecom industry *more* jumpy than Microsoft. For years Schmidt, Page, and Brin had had a team of engineers doing nothing but experimenting with ways to route around the telecom industry. As Google quickly became the most powerful company on the web, powerful enough to control the search-advertising business and spend $1.65 billion to buy YouTube in 2006, the telecom companies worried that Google might soon announce that it was becoming a carrier itself. By the spring of 2007, when Google announced it was buying online ad firm DoubleClick, these worries had crept into executive suites worldwide as well as into the halls of antitrust regulators in Washington and the European Union. "Google's vision of Android is Microsoft's vision of owning the operating system of every PC," a platform monopoly, former Verizon CEO Ivan Seidenberg told author Ken Auletta. "Guys like me want to make sure that there is a distribution of platforms and devices. Is it in Google's interest to disintermediate us? Yeah."

• • •

When Rubin and the Android team were done dealing with the initial shock of how good the iPhone was, little drama surrounded what needed to be done.

Rubin is at his core a start-up CEO—messianically convinced

that his path is the best one regardless of whether people and circumstance agree with him. He was used to setbacks. The iPhone was good, but what he was doing was going to be different—and better. It would be technically superior to the iPhone and more widely distributed. Rubin believed that all the software engineers at carriers and phone makers added 20 percent to the cost of a phone. With Android, they wouldn't need that infrastructure and would be able to sell their phones for less. And the iPhone would help focus Google's attention on the Android project. When the iPhone was announced, Rubin had about four dozen people. Two years later he'd have more than a hundred.

In retrospect, having the iPhone beat the first Android phones to market was arguably a *good* thing, some at Google have told me. Apple spent tens of millions of dollars educating consumers about how to use these new devices with a touchscreen. By the time Android phones started to arrive two years later, the iPhone had become hugely popular. That meant that those carriers who didn't have the iPhone—which was everyone but AT&T at the time—were looking for an alternative. This wasn't a short-term problem. AT&T's contract with Apple gave them exclusive rights in the United States for four years. "They [the carriers and manufacturers] saw the writing on the wall, and that definitely helped Android. It helped cause people to sit up and take notice and take Android seriously," Eustace said.

For Rubin and the Android team, the more complicated issue to emerge from the iPhone's unveiling was their own company's involvement in the iPhone's project. Google, they learned, was Apple's key partner in the venture. While Google's top executives had been backing Android for two years, they had also tasked another team to work secretly with Apple to get Google's search, Maps, and YouTube software on Jobs's new device. Indeed, Jobs had made the inclusion of Google software one of the iPhone's selling points during his unveiling. He said the iPhone was the "Internet in your pocket for the first time ever" and "You can't think about the Internet without thinking about Google." Google CEO Eric

Schmidt had joined Jobs onstage during the unveiling to reinforce the depth of their partnership. "Steve, my congratulations to you. This product is going to be hot," Schmidt said during three minutes of remarks.

The Android team knew Schmidt was on the Apple board. What they didn't know was how tight the companies had become. While they were developing Android, a handful of engineers in another building a few hundred yards away had almost become an Apple satellite operation, with more knowledge about the iPhone project than all but a few dozen Apple employees. Inside Apple, Jobs strictly controlled and siloed access to the various portions of the iPhone project. At Google, some members of the team developing Maps, search, and YouTube for the iPhone had seen almost everything—the chips Apple was using, the touchscreen, the software. A few had even seen the most recent prototypes and used the phone before the announcement. "Apple particularly wanted the Google Maps product," said one of the engineers. "Steve, I think, personally liked it a lot and wanted to make sure it was integrated into the iPhone. So we knew the iPhone was coming."

Having two product teams seemingly in competition with each other wasn't a new thing at Google. Many of Google's best creations, such as Google News and Gmail, grew out of that philosophy. But the engineers at Android had also come to believe that maybe they were different. Cofounder Larry Page was their patron. They had privileges and perks that few other teams of their size at Google had. And they felt justified in having them. To them, it wasn't just that Rubin had started Android or built the Sidekick, it was that he probably knew more about the mobile phone business than anyone else at Google, maybe all of Silicon Valley.

Then forty-four, he'd been building cutting-edge mobile products in Silicon Valley since the early 1990s. It was his vocation and his avocation. People describe his home as something akin to Tony Stark's basement laboratory in *Iron Man*—a space jammed with robotic arms, the latest computers and electronics, and prototypes of various projects. Like many electronics whizzes in Silicon Valley, he had Tony Stark's respect for authority too.

At Apple in the late 1980s he got in trouble for reprogramming the corporate phone system to make it seem as if CEO John Sculley were leaving his colleagues messages about stock grants, according to John Markoff's 2007 profile in *The New York Times*. At General Magic, an Apple spin-off that wrote some of the first software for handheld computers, he and some colleagues built lofts above their cubicles so they could more efficiently work around the clock. After Microsoft bought his next employer, WebTV, in the mid-1990s, he outfitted a mobile robot with a web camera and microphone and sent it wandering around the company, without mentioning to anyone that it was connected to the Internet. The sights and sounds it recorded were beamed worldwide until Microsoft security, which was not amused, discovered the problem and turned it off. Danger, the company that made the Sidekick, got its name from what the robot in the 1960s TV show *Lost in Space* barked whenever it sensed, well, danger.

This loyalty to Rubin made his team worry about Google's conflict of interest. Why should they even continue working on Android? Apple was now clearly light-years ahead of them, and Google's top management was clearly behind that effort. Trying to compete with both Apple and their own company with a project that then seemed so inferior seemed like a waste of time.

"Frankly, the iPhone created a morale problem," said one of the senior engineers. "Some of the engineers actually said, 'Oh my God, we're doomed. This is Apple. This is the Second Coming. What are we going to do now?'"

Rubin and those on down had the additional frustration of watching Jobs, in their view, wrongly take credit for innovations that were not his or Apple's. Jobs was an amazing innovator who had an unparalleled sense for when to release a product, how to design the hardware *and* the software, and how to make consumers lust after it. No one else comes close to his record of doing this again and again. It was genius. But he didn't invent most of the technology in the iPhone. What made Jobs so successful is that he never wanted to be first at anything. Business and technology history is littered with inventors who never made a dime off their inventions. Jobs understood that a multiyear gap always exists between when something is discovered and when it becomes viable as a consumer product. But when he announced the iPhone, Jobs broke with this practice and declared, for example, that the iPhone had the "first fully usable" Internet browser on a phone.

For Rubin and others on the Android team this was not just a matter of principle. It was personal. He and those on his team at Danger believed that *they* had created the first usable Internet browser on a phone five years earlier, in 2002. Rubin is cryptic but clear when you ask him about this: "Apple is the second adopter of the web standard." DeSalvo is more direct: "Only one in ten engineers have probably even heard of Danger now, yet many of the things associated with the modern smartphone we did first on the Sidekick." The Sidekick, not the iPhone, was the first to have downloadable games. It even worked with cochlear implants. "Obviously we were five years too early. If we had launched in 2005, though, we would have owned the world. I guess I don't think we get enough credit for what we did."

3

Twenty-Four Weeks, Three Days, and Three Hours Until Launch

A handful of Apple engineers had been worried about the Android effort for months; they knew how envious Google was of the iPhone. But Jobs believed in the Apple-Google partnership, and in his relationship with Schmidt and Google's founders Brin and Page. More important, Android seemed like the least of Apple's problems in early 2007. The iPhone was to go on sale in six months, and Apple was obviously going to need every hour to get it ready.

That Jobs's demo had been nearly flawless was an enormous relief. It was remarkable, actually. Apple had taken a barely working iPhone prototype and, with some engineering sleight of hand, made millions want to buy one right away. But what would happen on June 29, when many of those consumers would line up at the Apple stores to buy one? They would expect the iPhones to work as flawlessly as Jobs made them look onstage. But all Apple had now, in January, were a few dozen prototypes that had been personally picked up at an Asian factory by Apple executives and flown back as carry-on luggage. They couldn't withstand ordinary shipping, let alone daily use. "We had to figure out how to build iPhones in mass quantity," Borchers said. Anyone can make one hundred of something. Making a million of them is something else altogether. "How do you build and test antennas, for example? Every unit that came off the production line would need to be tested and characterized because there is great variability in how antennas get built on an assembly line. That affects the radio performance." Apple was so obsessive about leaving nothing to chance that it actually designed and built its own testing setup at Apple headquarters to address these issues. "Then we brought Foxconn [Apple's Asian manufacturing partner] in and said, 'Replicate this five hundred times or whatever it takes to get it done.'"

It wasn't simply a matter of refining and producing parts that worked right. Key features of the iPhone were far from perfected. Its memory and the virtual keyboard, already one of its most controversial features, still didn't work right. Touching the letter *e*— the most frequently used letter in the alphabet—often caused other letters to pop up around the keyboard. Instead of appearing instantly after being "typed," letters would emerge after annoying lags. Microsoft CEO Steve Ballmer had been among the many declaring the iPhone a failed product because it didn't have a physical keyboard. Apple executives were worried too. They weren't comfortable using the keyboard either. "Everyone was concerned about touching on something that doesn't have any physical feedback," one of the executives said. But Jobs was unyielding on the issue. "Steve's rationale was just what he said onstage. 'You put keys on, and now you've got these fixed keys that don't work for every app. Worse, you've lost half your screen real estate.' So everyone understood that this was incredibly important to get right—a make-or-break kind of thing."

Apple needed to reengineer the iPhone's display screen too. While Jobs had decreed it would be glass, not plastic, and had found a source for the material the previous fall, it was not as simple a matter as swapping one screen for the other. While Corning supplied the glass, that was only one of many steps necessary to create a working iPhone touchscreen. The multitouch sensors had to be embedded in the glass, not just attached to it, in order to work correctly. But the process of embedding the sensors in glass was entirely different from embedding them in plastic. Glass is heavier than plastic too, so Apple's engineers needed a stronger adhesive to hold the assembly in place. They had to readjust how all the buttons would work on a phone now made with a stiffer material (glass doesn't bend like plastic). They had to re-balance the device to account for the difference in screen weight. "It was a really, really big deal," said an executive involved in the process. "I think Jeff Williams [Apple's head of manufacturing] found every glass-cutting machine in China to make that happen."

Lastly, Apple had to invent its own call-testing protocols to get the phone accepted on AT&T's network. Manufacturers typically just let the carriers do this, but Apple wanted its own data in case of complaints about the iPhone's call quality. It imagined AT&T using its data to blame call problems on the iPhone when they were largely the network's fault. It wanted a way to refute that, Borchers said. "So we loaded [several] phones and computers into my VW Jetta and just went in loops and looked for call drops," said Shuvo Chatterjee. The phones were programmed to autodial certain num-bers at certain intervals, with the computers to measure the results.

"Now Apple has a whole process, with special vans, but back then we were making it up as we went along in terms of what needed to be tested," Chatterjee said. "Sometimes it would be 'Scott [Forstall who] had a call drop. Go figure out what's going on.' So we'd drive by his house and try to figure out if there was a dead zone. That happened with Steve too. There were a couple of times where we drove around their houses enough that we wor-ried that neighbors would call the police."

. . .

Ultimately it fell to Borchers to coordinate and manage most of these issues. As the iPhone's head of product marketing, he and his team essentially were the iPhone project managers, helping Jobs coordinate and edit the work of the various teams, before developing its entire marketing plan. He and his team were all engineers themselves—Borchers had a bachelor's degree in me-chanical engineering from Stanford and a master's degree from MIT—but their particular specialty was taking complicated engi-neering details and explaining them in laymen's terms. If a feature could not easily be explained, Borchers's job was to ask why it was important to the project in the first place. "We helped decide the DNA of the product, nurtured that DNA through the development process, and then translated that into the message the product goes out with," he said. "So we got very involved with what features were going in and what it was going to look like."

Many customers associated Borchers with the first iPhone as much as they did Jobs because Borchers starred in the widely viewed instructional video. No one had ever seen a device like the iPhone before, and Apple wanted to make sure that new users would not feel flummoxed by a device with only one physical button besides On/Off, Volume Up/Down, and Silent/Ringer. As part of the marketing run-up to launch, Borchers had planned to have Jobs tape a thirty-minute video showing customers in detail how to use the iPhone. But at the last minute Jobs told Borchers to do it instead. "We had built a studio for Steve [on the first floor] in Building One so he could just drop down [from his fourth-floor office], do it, and go back to work. But I think he realized it was just going to be a ton of his time. So instead I spent a month doing takes and rehearsals in makeup and getting shaved twice a day and wearing one of Steve's mock black turtlenecks." Today, Borchers has the shirt displayed in Plexiglas on the wall of his office at Opus Capital, the venture capital firm he joined when he left Apple in 2009. "You can't find any others like them, so that's what the clothespins are for. They pinned them along the back so it fit me because I [at five feet eight] am smaller than Steve [who was six feet two]."

Borchers had ended up at Apple after three years at Nike, and then four years at Nokia, when it was the most dominant phone manufacturer in the world. He'd joined Apple in 2004 to help market the iPod to car companies such as BMW and develop accessories with companies such as his former employer Nike. When Apple decided to build the iPhone at the end of 2004, he was one of the first managers tapped to work on the project. He was well-known among senior executives partially because he'd interviewed for a higher-ranking Apple job in 2002, only to have Jobs decide at the last minute that he wanted an internal candidate. "I remember sitting in a conference room, having Steve walk in, look at my CV, and ask, 'Why are you even remotely qualified for this job?' Ten minutes in, he says, 'Okay, I've heard what I need.' I thought, 'Well, okay. At least I got one brush with Steve.'"

That rejection turned into a blessing. Borchers came in a notch lower on the organizational chart a year later, earned Jobs's confidence over the following year, and became a natural to work on the iPhone because of his Nokia background. "So at the end of 2004 I became one of the first marketing employees for the iPhone."

Borchers's job gave him great insight into all aspects of the iPhone project. But at age forty-seven, it also gave him more responsibility than he'd ever had before in his life. He'd be a key player at every public presentation Apple would make for the iPhone. He'd help write many of Jobs's slides. And he'd have a say in every bit of advertising and PR associated with the device. It also meant that by the end of Macworld 2007, Borchers was more tired than he could ever have imagined.

Borchers had been one of the managers responsible for everything Apple did at Macworld, and when he wasn't spending twelve-plus hours a day at the convention center through the weekend, he was in his car driving the forty miles from San Francisco to his home in Pleasanton. He'd driven all two dozen of the demo iPhones up to the convention center in the trunk of his Acura the previous Thursday—bagged in plastic and sitting in two subdivided boxes one might use for liquor. He'd driven them all back the following Friday night. A car with a member of Apple's security team followed him up and back while he worried what would happen to his Apple career if he got pulled over or got into an accident. There were no other phones, so had his car gone into a ditch or caught fire, there would have been no iPhone to unveil. "I drove them into the basement of Moscone and hand-carried them up to a special locked room we'd built where we had engineers waiting to unpack them and retest them for what felt like the sixty-fifth time that day."

In between these two incredibly tense drives, Borchers had been the conductor of how every iPhone looked and was displayed at Macworld. He'd been responsible for scheduling rehearsals, making sure the right people and equipment were always in place, and for making sure security was sufficient so that any pictures of the phone didn't leak out. He was so busy he didn't even get a chance to watch the keynote live. While Jobs was speaking, Borchers was installing iPhones in spinning Plexiglas display cases on the show floor, and making sure the demonstrators Apple had hired for the event had devices to demo.

Only the morning after returning home to Pleasanton did Borchers realize what a long six days it had been. He'd spent the night before the Tuesday keynote at a San Francisco hotel up the street from Moscone, but he'd forgotten to check out, and he'd left all his luggage in his room.

• • •

Getting the iPhone ready for sale wasn't the only distraction Apple engineers had to contend with in early 2007. To get the iPhone built, Jobs had pitted two of his star executives against each other—Scott Forstall and Tony Fadell—to see who could come up with the best product. The fallout from that two-year fight was now rippling through the corporation. It had been an ugly war, full of accusations of sabotage and backstabbing, pitting friends against friends. It had left many people on both sides feeling that Apple no longer resembled the company they had joined. Instead of being the counterculture underdog, they worried it had been transformed into a soulless profit machine, a big company with IBM-style corporate politics. There is no virtue in being a struggling company, as Apple was for so many years, and the dwindling resources of a company nearing bankruptcy—as Apple was when Jobs returned in 1997—created its own brand of snake-pit politics. But most at Apple in 2007 hadn't been there then. Apple may have been founded in 1976, but to most of its employees it was going through the growing pains of a ten-year-old company, not a thirty-year-old company. From 2002 to 2007 the number of employees at Apple had doubled to twenty thousand. While some believe tensions with Forstall prompted Fadell to resign three years later, Fadell compellingly rejects this. He says he and his wife, who ran HR, left to be with their young children, despite Jobs's efforts to make them stay. They left millions of dollars in stocks behind. Either way, the iPhone took Apple's business to new heights. In addition to becoming a cultural icon, the iPhone alone generates more revenue for Apple than the entire Microsoft Corporation does. Apple became the most valuable company in the world because of their work.

But Forstall had been so aggressive in his effort to beat Fadell that it scared people. Many wondered whether there was anything he wouldn't do to get ahead. CEO Tim Cook would eventually push Forstall out of Apple in 2012. But back in 2007 it looked as if he were going to be there forever, and when he was put in charge of all iPhone software in 2007, a huge exodus of talent followed. Those who stayed got to watch Forstall's naked ambition on full display. Even his fans admit that before he left, he had become a cliché of a difficult boss—someone who takes credit for underlings' good work, but is swift to blame them for his own screwups. When Jobs was alive, Forstall drove colleagues mad with his sanctimonious "Steve wouldn't like that" critique, and he made no secret of his seeing himself as the eventual Apple CEO. In 2011, *Bloomberg Businessweek* reported that chief designer Jony Ive and head of technology Bob Mansfield were so suspicious of Forstall they refused to meet with him unless CEO Tim Cook was present too. I've heard that was true for iTunes boss Eddy Cue as well.

It wasn't shocking to see Jobs play two executives off against each other; he was well-known for his Machiavellian side. But what was surprising was that Jobs let the fight go on so long and affect so many people at Apple.

"It was incredibly destructive," one executive said. "I think Steve would have been great during ancient Roman times, where you could watch people get thrown to the lions and be eaten. He played them [Fadell and Forstall] off each other. Tony was the golden boy for a while, then Forstall, then back to Tony, then back to Forstall. It became a circus. Remember 'Spy vs. Spy' [a 1960s comic strip that pitted a white spy (the United States) against a black one (the Soviet Union)] in *Mad* magazine? It was like that— comical—if it hadn't wasted so much time." Another executive, remarkably, made the same comparison. "The first time I saw [the movie] *Gladiator* [in 2007], I told my husband, 'This feels familiar,'" she said. (Forstall would not be interviewed for this project. Fadell is not shy about his feelings, though. After Apple pushed Forstall out, Fadell told the BBC, "Scott got what he deserved.")

In retrospect, many at Apple believe that it ultimately wasn't a fair fight. Fadell's expertise was hardware; Forstall's was software. That gave Forstall a built-in advantage because many believed that Jobs was much more interested in the software and industrial design of Apple products than the innards. But while the fight was going on, it wasn't at all clear how it was going to turn out.

Grignon knows firsthand how nasty the fight between Forstall and Fadell was. He wound up in the middle and ended up feeling pulled in opposite directions like a piece of warm taffy. Even before work on the iPhone started, Grignon discovered simmering tension between the two executives. In 2004 Forstall tried to block Grignon from taking a job in Fadell's division. Grignon had worked for Forstall for three years building products called Dashboard and iChat. He thought they were decent work friends. They would go rock climbing together on the weekends. But when Fadell offered him a better opportunity inside Apple, Forstall went out of his way to block it. He told Grignon that he supported his decision to move. Then Forstall went behind Grignon's back to Jobs himself to stop it. "And he made enough noise to Steve that Steve actually intervened on my transfer to Tony's org. He sat Forstall [and some other executives] in a room and basically beat them all down saying, 'Okay, you can have Andy and nobody else.

Nobody else gets to transfer from software [under Forstall] to iPod [under Fadell].' That's when the animosity between them really started."

The fight was like a religious war. When work on the iPhone began, Forstall constructed an elaborate secret organization to work on the project. It was so secret that it wasn't clear for a while if Fadell even knew about it. From his office on the second floor of IL 2 on Apple's campus, Forstall started pulling in some of the best engineers from around the company, creating lockdown areas all over the building as he went. "If you were working weekends, you'd see the construction crews come in all the time putting up walls, security doors . . . everything . . . so that by Monday there was a new lockdown area. I've never seen walls put up that fast. Looking back, it's almost comical to think about," said Shuvo Chatterjee. "As they reconfigured, some of us were moving almost once every two months. For a while, I just kept everything permanently in boxes because I knew if I unpacked, I'd have to pack up and move again right away."

"It became a maze," Nitin Ganatra said. "You'd open this door and the previous door would close behind you. It was Sarah Wincester-y in some ways."

Officially the iPhone was being run by Fadell. Fadell ran the iPod division, and it seemed natural to build the iPhone by starting with an iPod and just improving it. Forstall had a different and vastly more risky idea: figure out a way to shrink the software that ran on Macs and make it run on a phone. "We had all assumed the iPhone would run a version of the software we had designed for P1 [a version of the iPod OS designed for the first prototype]," said one of Fadell's iPhone engineers. "But totally in parallel, Forstall and his team were working on a version of OS X to run the phone. We didn't know."

Jobs wanted to run OS X on the iPhone. He just didn't think it could be done. When Forstall's team actually did it, Forstall won control of the iPhone project. "There is no hardware-software guy at Apple," said another iPhone engineer. "This has been a point of contention for a lot of people in the history of Apple. Hardware guys think they know software. And software guys think they know hardware. But Steve wouldn't have it [be drawn into that debate among his executives]. So when Scott said, 'Hey, Steve, there is this kick-ass software team in Tony's org, and I want it,' Steve is like, 'Well, of course. You're the software guy. They're doing software, they should be on your team.' By the time the iPhone went on sale in mid-2007, Forstall controlled many of its software engineers. And when Apple launched the iPod Touch a few months later, Forstall controlled that too.

. . .

Fadell has gone on to start Nest, a company that makes the first good-looking, powerful, and easy-to-use home thermostat. Not surprisingly, it has all the design and software flourishes of an Apple product. It is one of the most talked about new ventures in Silicon Valley. But allies and enemies alike still talk about his fight with Forstall as if it were yesterday.

Fadell was truly Apple's first golden boy of Jobs's second stint at the company. At thirty-two he'd come to work at Apple only knowing that he was to work on some secret project he was told he was suited for. Four years later, as the line executive in charge of iPod, he was one of the most powerful people at Apple. By the fall of 2006, iPods represented 40 percent of Apple's $19 billion in revenue. And its market share, at more than 70 percent, seemed unassailable. Apple was selling more Macs too, but those sales represented less than 10 percent of all personal computers. The iPod's success, meanwhile, had turned Jobs into a business icon once again.

Fadell had been exactly what Apple needed in 2001. He was young, brash, and smart, having been part of cutting-edge portable-hardware engineering in the Valley for fifteen years. He once told a reporter that he would have ended up in jail had he not discovered computers. He occasionally showed up for work with bleached hair. He was not good at holding his tongue when faced with sub-standard work or ideas. His first job out of college was at General Magic, a company Bill Atkinson and Andy Hertzfeld spun out of Apple in the early 1990s in the hope of developing some of the first software ever written exclusively for mobile devices. The project failed and Fadell found himself at Philips, the giant Dutch con-glomerate, where he quickly became the company's youngest executive. He ran the company's new mobile-computing group, where he developed some early PDAs (the Velo and Nino), which sold decently. They also introduced him to the power of digital music on portable devices.

Fadell was getting ready to start his own company when Ap-ple's head of hardware, Jon Rubinstein, called, trying to recruit Fadell for a job that, astonishingly, he was not allowed to disclose. According to Steven Levy's book *The Perfect Thing*, Fadell took the call on a ski slope in Colorado in January and expressed inter-est on the spot. He had idolized Apple since he was twelve, ac-cording to Levy. That was when he'd spent the summer of '81 caddying to save up enough money to buy an Apple II. Weeks after Rubinstein's call, Fadell joined Apple, only discovering then that he was being hired as a consultant to help build the first iPod.

Grignon and others have said that Fadell's rise never sat well with Forstall. Up until Fadell joined Apple, Jobs's inner circle was composed of people he'd worked closely with at least from the beginning of his return in 1997, and in some cases from his days running NeXT, the computer company he'd founded after get-ting fired from Apple in 1985. Forstall had worked longer with Jobs than almost any other executive. He'd joined NeXT when he'd graduated from Stanford in 1992. Yet he wasn't part of Jobs's inner circle for a long time, and Fadell was. And Fadell, who was the same age as Forstall, was rising much faster in the corpora-tion than Forstall. Fadell ran the iPod division, which generated 40 percent of Apple's revenue. Forstall was in charge of the application software that came with a Mac—things such as Address Book, Mail, Safari, and Photo Booth.

But then Forstall and Jobs bonded. It was in 2003–4, and colleagues believe it was because Forstall developed a severe stomach ailment around the time that Jobs was first diagnosed with pancreatic cancer. Jobs, who at first tried to treat his own cancer with diet, developed a regimen for Forstall that appeared to cure him. After that, said Grignon, Forstall began coming to more and more of Jobs's Monday senior-staff meetings. Ordinarily Forstall would not even have known about the iPhone project; he wasn't senior enough. "So as soon as he found out through those inner-circle discussions that Jobs wanted to build a phone, that's when he started to wedge himself in," Grignon said.

Forstall couldn't have been more different from Fadell. Forstall was smooth, engaging, and had Jobs's flair for the dramatic gesture, having acted in high school plays in addition to studying computer science. Even then, say classmates, it was clear how ambitious and determined he was. As *Bloomberg Businessweek* put it in 2011, "In many ways, Forstall is a mini-Steve. He's a hard-driving manager who obsesses over every detail. He has Jobs's knack for translating technical, feature-set jargon into plain English. He's known to have a taste for the Mercedes-Benz SL55 AMG, in silver, the same car Jobs drove, and even has a signature on-stage costume: black shoes, jeans, and a black zippered sweater."

For two years Forstall and Fadell fought about everything, often forcing Jobs to mediate disagreements over the smallest matters. Nitin Ganatra, who worked for Forstall, recalls one moment in 2006 when Jobs had to decide which group's boot loader would run on the iPhone. It sounds like engineering minutia, and it is. The boot loader is the first piece of software that runs on a computer. It tells the processor to look for and start the disk that has the machine's software on it. "We were like, 'Why does Steve have to come in and make a decision about something this small? Can't Scott and Tony figure it out on their own?'"

Another engineer, who reported to Fadell, expresses his frustration with the fight more bluntly: "For two years I worked Thanksgiving, Christmas, and New Year's—insane hours—and it was hard to have to deal with this other political bullshit too."

. . .

Despite the feuding and relentless deadline pressure, the iPhone—remarkably—stayed on schedule for its June 29 launch. When it finally went on sale, the last Friday of the month, the event was covered by the global news media as if Elvis Presley or John Lennon had risen from the dead. News crews camped out at Apple stores across the country to witness the pandemonium as eager customers waited on line for hours. During one live shot on FOX News in front of the New York City Apple store at Fifty-Ninth Street and Fifth Avenue, someone eager for attention stepped in front of the camera and grabbed reporter Laura Ingle's microphone out of her hand while she was in midsentence. It almost seemed planned—though it was in not—because she was in the middle of interviewing *Newsweek*'s Steven Levy, who was one of the four journalists in the world to have gotten a review model ahead of the general public. Before the man grabbed the microphone, Ingle had given her audience a buildup, saying, in a hushed voice, "I don't want to create a mob scene, but he's got one . . . We're going to need some security around here probably, but show us what you've got."

Levy wrote about it months later in a *Newsweek* column: "Shaken but undaunted, we restarted. It got even scarier. People pressed in close, fingers stretching toward the device, Michelangelo style. Afterward, a production assistant warned me that I should have a bodyguard with me until the sale began at 6 p.m. I made it through the day without extra muscle, but I still marvel at the phenomenon. For two weeks a gizmo took its place among Iraq and Paris Hilton as a dominant news event."

Apple sold 270,000 iPhones in the first two days they were available. In the next six months Apple sold another 3.4 million iPhones, driving many to conclude that it had changed the cell phone industry forever.

Looking back, the iPhone launch feels like an even more remarkable accomplishment than it did at the time. For all the iPhone's revolutionary design and features, a lot was wrong with it too. At $499 for the base model, it was too expensive. Virtually every other smartphone sold for closer to half that price. Consumers got the freedom to switch cell carriers or cancel their cell service anytime they wanted in return for paying so much more for the iPhone. Other, cheaper phones required customers to keep service up and running with one carrier for two years. But was that added flexibility worth $250 or more? Most thought it was not.

The iPhone ran on the slower 2G cell network when most high-end phones were running on the newer and much faster 3G network. The iPhone had taken so long to build that the chips enabling 3G reception weren't useable when the phone was designed. Most other phones had GPS. The iPhone did not. Most phones had removable batteries and expandable memories. The iPhone had neither. The iPhone didn't run video made with Adobe's Flash technology, which at the time seemed to be every video but those on YouTube. YouTube used Flash to stream videos to desktop and laptop computers but a different technology that used less bandwidth to stream to mobile devices. Most companies didn't have the money or the technological prowess of Google to do likewise then.

Seemingly obvious features such as the ability to search your address book or to copy and paste text or to use the camera to record video were missing from the first iPhone too. Critics pointed out these flaws as if Apple had not thought of them. The problem was much more straightforward: Apple just hadn't had time to put them all in. "There were moments where we said, 'Well, this is really embarrassing,'" said Grignon. "But then we'd have to say, 'Okay. It's going to be embarrassing. But we have to ship. Even though it is a stupid, small, easy thing to fix, we have to prioritize and fix only the things that are the worst."

There was no app store, or plans to launch one. The iTunes app store, which Apple didn't unveil until 2008, has been as important to the iPhone's success as the device itself. It generates $4.5 billion in revenue a year for mobile-software developers and another $1.9 billion a year for Apple. It has been one of the engines driving Silicon Valley's boom. But Jobs, like the rest of Apple, was so focused on getting the device ready for sale that he didn't see the potential at first. "I remember asking Steve what he wanted to accomplish with the iPhone," Bob Borchers said. "He said he wanted to build a phone people could fall in love with. It wasn't 'Let's revolutionize XYZ.' It was 'Let's think about how to build something cool. If they fall in love with it, then we can figure out what they want to do with it.' When we launched the iPhone, we called it a revolutionary phone, the best iPod ever created, and an Internet communications device. But we had no idea what an Internet communications device even was."

Jobs understood why consumers would see the iPhone as a Macintosh for your pocket. It ran OS X after all. But he also hated the idea that consumers would see the iPhone this way. Computers are things that run software from developers all over the world—outside Apple. He didn't want the iPhone to become that at all. After the unveiling, when software developers began clamoring for permission to make programs for the iPhone, Jobs said no publicly and emphatically. "You don't want your phone to be like a PC," he told John Markoff of *The New York Times* right after the announcement. "The last thing you want is to have loaded three apps on your phone and then you go to make a call and it doesn't work anymore. These are more like iPods than they are like computers."

But the iPhone had so many other cool new features that consumers overlooked its flaws. It wasn't just that the iPhone had a new kind of touchscreen, or ran the most sophisticated software ever put in a phone, or had an Internet browser that wasn't crippled, or had voice mail that could be listened to in any order, or ran Google Maps and YouTube, or was a music and movie player and a camera. It's that it appeared to do all those things well and beautifully at the same time. Strangers would accost you in places and ask if they could touch it—as if you had just bought the most beautiful sports car in the world. Its touchscreen worked so well that devices long taken for granted as integral parts of the computing experience—the mouse, the trackpad, and the stylus—suddenly seemed like kluges. They seemed like bad substitutes for what we should have been able to do all along—point and click with our digits instead of a mechanical substitute. All of this captivated not just consumers but investors. A year after Jobs had unveiled the iPhone, Apple's stock price had doubled.

Apple helped create and then took full advantage of all the hype. On launch day it sent top executives to various stores in big cities to witness it all and help whip up the crowds. Head of Global Marketing Phil Schiller went to Chicago. Jony Ive and his design crew went to San Francisco.

Steve Jobs's store was, naturally, the one in downtown Palo Alto at the corner of University Avenue and Kipling Street. It was a mile and a half from his house and he often showed up there unannounced when he was in town. The appropriate high-tech luminaries had already gathered when he arrived. Apple cofounder Steve Wozniak and early Apple employees Bill Atkinson and Andy Hertzfeld were already standing on line. But it also seemed as if Jobs had some internal flames to fan of his own, said one of the engineers who was there along with Grignon and many others who had worked on the project, including Fadell and Forstall. "So there's this reunion of the original Mac guys, and it's really cool. And then Steve goes up to Tony [Fadell] and proceeds to go over in a corner of the store and talk to him for an hour and ignore Forstall just to fuck with him."

"Up until that day, for the previous six months, everything had been Tony's fault. Any hardware problems or ship delays or manufacturing problems—all Tony's fault. Scott could do no wrong. But that was the day the press reviews came out, and the iPhone's email [software] wasn't working for people, but everyone loved the hardware. So now Scott was the bad boy, and Tony was the golden boy. And it was funny, because Steve did it in a way in which his back was to Forstall so that Tony got to look at Scott while it was all happening. I'm not joking. The look on Scott's face was incredible. It was like his daddy told him he didn't love him anymore."

4

I Thought We Were Friends

Back at Google, the Android team's initial worries about the commitment to the project were proving unfounded. Rubin got permission to hire dozens more engineers in 2007 and, if anything, found senior management paying *too* much attention to him. During presentations with Schmidt, Brin, and Page, they leaned on him hard for not getting Android up and running fast enough. They threw out ideas at a frenetic pace and were unyielding when they didn't like what they saw. Notes from one meeting in July 2007 included Schmidt's declaring that there weren't enough people at Google writing software for Android and that that needed to change "ASAP." It also included admonitions from Page, who said that Android needed to get faster and easier to use, and from Brin, who was concerned that the software needed to better accommodate power users who might store more than ten thousand contacts.

Page was particularly specific. All screens needed to load in less than two hundred milliseconds, he said, and the Android needed to be user-friendly enough so that anyone could navigate the phone with one hand while driving. In another meeting Schmidt, unhappy with the operation or design of the slide-out keyboard planned for the Dream phone, said to one of the Android product managers, "First impressions really matter here. Don't fuck it up."

But at the same time, Google showed zero sign of backing

away from its relationship with Apple and the iPhone. Rubin and the Android team may have felt competitive with Jobs and Apple from the moment the iPhone was announced, but Google's ruling triumvirate didn't feel that way at all. After the iPhone was available for sale June 29, Brin and Page were never without one, and in Android meetings they often critically compared those features planned for the Android with the iPhone's features. DeSalvo said he remembers a number of meetings in which "one of them would ask, 'Why are we even doing this project? I have a phone. It's got Google services. It does Gmail. It does Calendar. Why do I need this Android thing?' It used to really piss me off."

Brin and Page won't discuss the thinking behind their remarks, but Schmidt will. He says Google was absolutely two-faced about the iPhone and Android back then, and for good reasons: Google desperately needed to get Google search and its other applications on mobile phones. It had been trying and failing for years. And the iPhone and the Android, while promising, were new enough that choosing one over the other seemed foolish.

In 2007 Google and Apple didn't even seem to be in the same business. Google made money from search ads. Apple made it on selling devices. "It was not obvious to us in 2006, 2007, and 2008 that it would be a two-horse race between Apple and Google," Schmidt said. "These are network platforms, and it is traditional that you end up with a couple [of dominant companies] as opposed to ten [companies]. But it was not obvious back then who would be the winners. Symbian was still quite strong from Nokia [then the largest phone maker in the world]. Windows Mobile had some level of traction. And, of course, BlackBerry was quite strong [with a lock on almost every corporation in the world]."

So, while Brin, Page, and Schmidt were pushing the Android team hard, they were also beefing up the Google iPhone team. Most notably, they put Vic Gundotra, a newly hired but well-known executive from Microsoft, in charge of running it. Gundotra, who was thirty-seven, had spent his entire career working for Bill Gates and Steve Ballmer, becoming their point person for the company's relationship with all external Windows software developers—tens of thousands of geeks worldwide. Gundotra was well-known for his technical acumen, his near-Steve-Jobs-quality presentations, and his willingness to take risks and be controversial. Microsoft's incredible growth and dominance during the 1990s was in no small part the result of his tireless evangelism, convincing legions of programmers worldwide to write software for Windows when few thought it would succeed. It was such a coup for Google to hire Gundotra that even when Microsoft said it would enforce his one-year noncompete agreement—a rare step—Google hired him anyway. Google just paid him not to work for a year, until the end of June 2007.

Gundotra's 2007 start date at Google has been compared to a "tornado whipping through a Midwestern town." He put executives on the spot in management meetings, asking questions about their businesses' profitability. When outlandish ideas were proposed, he asked whether their promoters had drawn up business plans. These are normal questions at most companies. At Google, which prided itself on making a product popular before making it profitable, they could get you fired.

But Gundotra thrived, and he quickly made Google's success in mobile not just a business imperative but a cause. He went to conferences and talked about how he carried and used more than a dozen phones; why Google was going to be on every mobile platform; and how, as he liked to put it, "we've seen this movie before. The exact same dynamic that happened on the PC will happen on mobile phones." The difference this time, he said, was that Google and Apple were on the right side and Microsoft was on the wrong side of that evolution. He'd been thinking about the future of mobile since 2005 when his young daughter suggested he use his phone to find answers to questions instead of saying, "I don't know." He'd ended up at Google because he couldn't convince Microsoft to listen to his ideas.

What made Gundotra such a disruptive force at Google was that he quickly realized Google's future in mobile depended almost exclusively on the iPhone. He was supposed to figure out a way to get Google's applications on *all* mobile platforms. But he quickly realized that that was a waste of time—that the iPhone was such a revolutionary device that it would soon catapult it and all other Apple devices to the top of the heap. Not only would the iPhone rocket Apple past other mobile phone makers such as Nokia and RIM, makers of the BlackBerry, it would signal the end of Microsoft's dominance—with Windows and Office—of desktop computing too. "You could see it. It was a game changer. No one had done anything like it," he said.

For Gundotra, the list of things that made the iPhone revolutionary was endless: The iPhone was beautiful. Apple was free to control it without dreaded carrier intervention. It was the first device powerful enough to run Google's applications the same way they ran on a desktop. And it had a full Internet browser that allowed Google's search ads to appear and work normally. This was great for Google because it would help its applications and search ads become even more ubiquitous. It was also great for Google because, as Gundotra had predicted, it was terrible for Microsoft. Microsoft's power stemmed from its Windows and Office monopoly on desktop and laptop computers. It had little power on mobile phones. Despite Schmidt's fears about Windows' traction on mobile phones, Gundotra believed the iPhone was such a leap forward, Windows' progress would come to a crashing halt. He thought the initial high price of the iPhone was a red herring. Apple would drop the price if consumers resisted.

All of this seemed obvious to Gundotra in the fall of 2007, but it was not to many other Googlers. "People thought it was crazy," Gundotra said. "Smartphones were a tiny percentage of the mobile business back then [2 percent], so I was accused of believing in the Apple hype. 'If you think people in India and China are ever going to be able to afford a phone that is seven hundred dollars [$499 for the cheapest model], you're smoking dope,' they said." While he had the support of Schmidt, Brin, and Page, many thought he was challenging a foundational tenet of Google's culture—that it was a company that played nice with everyone. Google's success on desktop computers depended on its getting search and other applications to run on *all* software platforms— OS X, Windows, Linux—and all Internet browsers. Getting behind one partner to the exclusion of others was not the way to do that. "I softened the blow a little bit by saying we were shutting down development on all but five smartphones. But it was a very controversial decision. Culturally at Google it was unthinkable that you would not build for every BlackBerry or Windows Mobile phone. Engineers in European Google offices were very angry we wouldn't support various Nokia phones. People had a hard time seeing [that smartphones would become so important], especially the iPhone. People on my staff quit. It was brutal. While [Microsoft CEO Steve] Ballmer was famous for saying that [the iPhone would fail] publicly, *everyone* believed that. They just thought it was going to go away."

• • •

The Android team was particularly troubled by Gundotra's emergence. Its members had not only kept a low profile at Google since the company's purchase in 2005, they'd successfully kept most of Google from even knowing about their project. Now, with Gundotra pushing Google's mobile agenda much harder, with the iPhone actually available for sale and with early prototypes of their own touchscreen phone—the Dream—now visible in the office, they were going to have to acknowledge and defend what they were doing long before they felt ready to do so. If forced into choosing between Gundotra's iPhone apps and Android in 2007, it seemed obvious that Schmidt, Brin, and Page would choose the iPhone. The Android was more than a year from even being a product. "That's when it all [the tension between the two projects] became real," a former member of the Android team told me. "That's when they [Android] started to test-drive phones and talk to T-Mobile about how much they were going to spend on marketing. That's when you started to see that this thing [Android] was going to get bigger and bigger as it went along."

Up until then Android had been like Google's mistress—lavished with attention and gifts but still hidden away. This secrecy wasn't Schmidt's, Page's, or Brin's idea. It was Andy Rubin's. Rubin didn't want anyone to know about his project. Like most entrepreneurs, he's a control freak, and he believed that the only way he could succeed with Android was to run the operation as a stealth start-up inside Google. Google was only nine years old then, but for Rubin, the company was already too slow and bureaucratic. Ethan Beard says he remembers that the (non-Android) part of Google had just spent nine to twelve months negotiating *one* agreement with Motorola—and it was merely a framework for future discussions. "So Andy just tried to do his best to insulate Android from any of that [frustrating bureaucracy]. They didn't interact with anyone else. They were completely separate." Schmidt, Brin, and Page even let Rubin build a café inside the Android headquarters on the Google campus that for a while was open only to Android employees.

The idea of a division inside Google that few even knew about was antithetical to its culture. What made Google different from other corporations was that it avoided silos—separate divisions that didn't interact—at all costs. Schmidt, Brin, and Page had set up the company to actively encourage information sharing. Any engineer could find out what other engineers were working on and even look at the software code with a few clicks of a mouse. Before Google went public—and became subject to SEC rules—Schmidt, Brin, and Page even shared details about Google's revenues and profits in companywide meetings in front of more than a thousand employees.

Rubin respected Google's unique approach. But he also understood that if other companies knew what he was working on, they might beat him to the marketplace. "There were plenty of pissed-off Googlers who said we're not Googley because we're not sharing," a former top Android engineer told me. "We had to turn down some very senior people who wanted to see our source code, and Andy had to be the bad guy. So there was a lot of tension."

Rubin wasn't just driven by his need to make sure Android moved fast. He knew that producing software for smartphones was vastly different from producing software for the web, which was Google's primary business. In Google's web-software world, all products are free and no product is ever truly finished. Juxtaposed against the tyranny of Microsoft and the packaged-software industry in general, this was a truly innovative philosophy. Google would get a product to about 80 percent finished, release it to users, and let their feedback guide the remaining 20 percent of development. Because the software was free, users' expectations were not as high. And because the software was on the web, the refining could be done almost in real time. There was no longer any need to wait a year until the next release went to stores, which was the way most software was still sold back then.

Rubin knew the cell phone industry viewed Google's approach to deadlines with horror. When you make and sell physical things such as cell phones, products that aren't finished in time for the holiday shopping season are catastrophes that waste hundreds of millions in carrier marketing costs, and manufacturer development costs. "I remember some times where Andy would say, 'We need to get this done by this date,' and a part of the engineering team would say, 'We can't get that done by then,' and Andy would say, 'If you can't get it done, I'll fire you guys and hire a new team that *can* do it,'" said another former Android engineer.

At most companies such a hierarchical, even militaristic approach to getting things done would be considered conventional. At Google it was so distinctive that it made the Android team feel as if they were revolutionaries. After the iPhone shock wore off and the Android team saw all the things the iPhone didn't do, its members truly believed that what they were building would be superior in every way, and that they didn't even need Google to pull it off. "I basically thought there was no way the iPhone could compete with us," said Bob Lee, a top Android engineer at the time. "I thought Android was going to turn into Windows [because of its vast distribution across many phones] with a ninety-eight percent market share, and that the iPhone would ultimately end up with just two percent market share."

Rubin encouraged this feeling every chance he got by passing along the perks of his executive-level job to his staff. He was always buying the latest gadgets—cameras, audio equipment, gaming systems, and other electronics—to keep abreast of the latest thinking in his industry. But he rarely kept his purchases long. When he was done, he'd just put them outside his office and send an email to his staff, offering them on a first-come-first-serve basis. Often it was the latest high-end camera or stereo system, worth thousands of dollars. If many on his staff had to be at a conference—say, the Consumer Electronics Show in Las Vegas—he would charter a jet so they could easily get there and back. One year, after Google released the Dream—known by then as the T-Mobile G1—Rubin boosted the Android's team year-end Google bonus with money out of his own pocket. One engineer said it doubled his year-end bonus.

The downside to all this separateness, however, was that it didn't endear Android to the Google rank and file any more than Gundotra had with his decision to throw Google's weight behind the iPhone. As much as the Android team felt as if they could do everything themselves, they couldn't; and when they needed to work with Googlers on the other side of the wall they'd built, their requests were rarely received warmly. "We'd be like, 'Hey, we're doing a phone. Surprise! And we need Gmail on it. Can you help us?'" DeSalvo said. "And they'd be like, 'Well, we have a two-year software road map and you're not on it, so, no, we can't help you.' So initially we had to use the web API [the connection the public uses] rather than a dedicated API [which would be faster and more reliable]. And it was the same thing for Google Talk, Calendar, and all this other stuff. It was just one nightmare after another, just trying to get basic things done, because no one knew that they needed to support us."

It wasn't just the lack of give-and-take between Android and the rest of Google that chilled relations. It was that Rubin's entire effort at information control wasn't working well. Every month in 2007 it seemed there was another rumor that Google was building a phone. Googlers were used to being able to keep their products secret because they were typically developed entirely in-house. While Google management shared more than most companies did with their employees, remarkably little of that information leaked. To build Android, however, Rubin needed to work with a myriad of external suppliers and manufacturers. Googlers couldn't see Android's code, but some of Android's external partners could—and some were clearly talking.

Schmidt, Brin, and Page tried to manage Google so that Android seemed to be more integrated into the rest of the company than it really was. But sometimes their actions actually made Android feel even more separate. For example, the trio was so upset about the leaks that at one of Google's weekly Friday-afternoon gatherings they announced they were launching an investigation to uncover the leakers. For a company that prided itself on a culture of openness and sharing, going after leakers the way U.S. presidents do seemed discordant. Cedric Beust, one of the early Android engineers, said that at some point in the summer of 2007 questions from the staff and the evasive executive responses became so predictable that he and many other Android team members stopped going to the Friday meetings. "It was just too excruciating to have to listen to all this and not be able to say anything," he said. "The hardest part was hiding my phone [when I was carrying a prototype]. It happened a few times where someone [another Googler] would see me with a phone [prototype] and say, 'What is this?' So you would have to have an answer ready. For a while I'd say it was a BlackBerry prototype. Then I'd say it was something we were working on for Nokia. Anything to make it seem as boring and uninteresting as possible."

For the media, the prospect of a Google phone was a delicious story. It made perfect sense—and seemed downright crazy at the same time. Google had been trying to find a way to disrupt the telecom business almost since its founding. Google's purchase of unused voice and data transmission lines over the previous three years had carriers convinced Google was planning to become a carrier itself. An entire team at Google was dedicated to finding wireless techniques of routing around the existing telecom infrastructure. Google had been public about its desire to get its applications running on mobile phones. And everyone knew Rubin was working at Google in some capacity. Why would he be there if not to build a phone? Yet Google had just teamed up with Apple to get its applications on the iPhone. Schmidt was on the Apple board. Jobs would be out of his mind with anger if Google was building a competitor to the iPhone.

. . .

The secrecy, leaks, and backbiting at Google over its mobile strategy in 2007 meant that when the Android team finally *did* have something to announce, it did not impress. The world was expecting something big. And Google pushed hard for attention—scheduling media conference calls, holding briefings with big software developers, and granting advance access to Rubin and his team to writer John Markoff of *The New York Times*. A profile of Rubin appeared the day before the November 5 announcement, under the headline "I Robot: The Man Behind the Google Phone."

But Google hadn't built a phone. It didn't even have finished phone software. Instead, what Google told the world was that it had built . . . a consortium of phone makers, carriers, and developers, the Open Handset Alliance. Together, this group was going to team up and turn Rubin's vision of a better, more unified mobile-phone world into reality. "We are not building a GPhone; we are enabling a thousand people to build a GPhone," Rubin said.

It was bizarre. It was as if the most interesting and innovative company on the planet had been taken over by United Nations bureaucrats. Schmidt and Rubin touted the consortium's size—thirty-four companies—and its global reach. They said the software that would be produced from the effort would be free. Phone makers, carriers, and programmers would be able to modify it at will. They said they hoped, but would not require, that manufacturers and carriers would provide a platform for Google so that its own applications such as search and Maps could prosper. The only definitive thing Schmidt and Rubin said about a product was that work was already well under way, that it was called Android (no one had known what the effort was being called until then), and that phone maker HTC would release a phone with that software on it in a year's time.

It wasn't just dull. The rollout of Android and the Open Handset Alliance seemed half-baked too. The most important players in the mobile-phone world were *not* part of the consortium: Apple, Nokia (the largest phone maker), RIM (the biggest smartphone maker), Microsoft, Palm, and the two largest U.S. carriers—AT&T and Verizon—had all turned Google down. Those *on* the list did not seem super-enthusiastic to be there, either. Most just issued press releases with boilerplate language of support. Most hadn't joined because they thought Google was doing something groundbreaking and revolutionary. They joined because Google paid them to join. Google paid HTC millions to be part of the OHA and to make the first phone.

Up until then HTC had a long and deep partnership with Microsoft, making phones for its Windows mobile operating system. For HTC to join, Google needed to insulate it from all the Microsoft business it was going to lose by partnering with Google, Microsoft's enemy. There wasn't anything nefarious about these transactions, but they were an indication of just how big a hill Google was going to have to climb to make Android and the OHA successful.

Google got more attention a week later when it released a video of cofounder Brin and Android engineering director Steve Horowitz showing off and talking about actual phones, including one that looked iPhone-like. That device had a touchscreen, a fast 3G cell connection, and graphics capabilities that would allow it to run games such as Quake, in which you shoot your way out of a medieval maze; Google Maps, including Street View, worked just as it did on a desktop computer. Most of these were things the first iPhone did not have. Horowitz, who did the demo for that phone, even showed off a little iPhone magic, double-tapping a street-view shot to zoom in. Google was obviously working on some cool things, but strangely, it was going to take another year before the company actually had a product to sell. And it was odd that Google had released a video rather than drummed up excitement with a big press announcement. The Open Handset Alliance had been unveiled on a conference call, but here at least the world had something to look at.

The weirdest part about the Open Handset Alliance announcement was that while the public yawned, it only escalated the tensions inside Google and between Google and Apple. Was Google going to back Android or iPhone? Could it do both? One of the many reasons Rubin had tried to keep Android a secret for so long was so that he could pursue his project without forcing Google to face these questions publicly. At Android's still early stage of development, they would not likely be answered in his favor. Gundotra was already in charge of a negotiated deal with Apple, one that seemed to grow more attractive to both companies by the day. Android was still an experiment without even a finished piece of software someone could get behind.

And Gundotra *was* putting the Android team on the spot. "I said, 'Convince me that this [Android] is something we [Google] should believe in,' and I know they had never had anyone ask those questions, and it was tough for them. 'Who are you to ask these questions again?' they wondered." A former senior member of the Android team echoed this feeling: "In the early days, Google Mobile [the team working with Apple on the iPhone] hated us. I mean, they thought we were the biggest pain in the ass in the world. I know Vic Gundotra [who now run's Google's competitor to Facebook, Google Plus] has come around and been a great advocate of Android, but he really hated it at first. He thought [Android] would be a distraction that would upset his relationship with Steve Jobs. There was a lot of butting of heads and arguments internally about strategy and things like that."

The tension between the two Google divisions got bad enough that Rubin sometimes wondered if he had his bosses' complete support. "We were innovating like crazy [coming up with new features for the iPhone and other platforms]. And Andy said, 'Why are we giving these features away?,'" Gundotra explained. "He wanted to reserve them for Android. And that was a good question." Another executive added, "I remember a hallway conversation at the end of 2007 about Google Maps and whether Google should give Apple a feature it wanted but didn't have, where Andy had to flatly say to Sergey, 'We have to stop giving our best stuff away to Apple if we want Android to succeed.'"

But the conflicts inside Google paled next to the conflict the OHA created between Google and Apple. Steve Jobs felt completely blindsided by the Android announcements, and he was furious. He had known about Android for a while. But he hadn't taken it seriously, according to those who'd talked with him about it. When he saw Horowitz show off the Dream phone in the Google video, however, he exploded with rage. Now he wondered if his partner was building something to challenge the iPhone. "I'm in my car driving somewhere and the phone rings. It's Steve. He was screaming so loud I had to pull off to the side of the road," said someone who talked to him that day. "'Did you see the video?' Steve says. 'Everything is a fucking rip-off of what we are doing.'"

• • •

As angry as Jobs was, he didn't want to believe that Schmidt, Brin, or Page were doing anything nefarious, friends and colleagues say. And Google's triumvirate went to great lengths to reassure him of this: Android was exactly what they always had said it was going to be—an open-source phone-operating system that any manufacturer could use. Google was not making a phone to compete with the iPhone. And Jobs should infer nothing from the prototypes he saw in the video. Google needed phones to test Android on, but it was not getting in the business of making phones. Whatever Google did, it certainly had no intention of copying anything on the iPhone, they said.

Indeed, Schmidt says today that not only had he and Jobs talked about Android, he'd made it clear to Jobs that in terms of Google priorities, iPhone came first. "I think maybe Andy understood the importance of Android back then, but certainly the rest of Google did not. We were busy doing other things," Schmidt said to me in 2011. "When I joined the Apple board [in 2006], Steve and I spoke about this [Android], and I said this thing is coming, and we agreed that we would monitor the situation."

Certainly, Google's other initiatives support Schmidt's recollection. Android's success was dependent on its getting the big U.S. carriers to cooperate, but at the end of 2007 Google was, if anything, going out of its way to make them angry. A giant slice of wireless spectrum was up for auction by the government, and Google, with a $4.71 billion bid of its own, tried to drive the price up for wireless carriers. Google didn't want the spectrum. It just wanted to make sure the government required the winner to play by new, Google-friendly rules. The sanctimoniousness of using money, not to buy spectrum, but to acquire a pulpit from which to lecture carriers on table manners, infuriated them, especially Verizon, the eventual auction winner. When then Verizon CEO Ivan Seidenberg talked to Ken Auletta in early 2008, Seidenberg did not sound like a man rushing to do a deal with anyone with a Google business card. He said Google was in danger of "waking up the bears"—powerful mobile-phone carriers—who would "come out of the woods and start beating the shit out of" the company.

Jobs had a convincing list of reasons to believe Google's explanations too. The two companies' boards of directors and outside advisers were so intertwined they were nearly the same company. Bill Campbell, a longtime Apple board member and one of Jobs's best friends, was one of Schmidt's, Brin's, and Page's closest advisers. Al Gore, the former vice president of the United States, was an adviser to Google and an Apple board member.

Paul Otellini, then the CEO of Intel, was a Google board member but counted Apple as one of Intel's newest large customers. And Arthur Levinson, the then head of Genentech, was a board member of both companies. A fight with Google would force all of these advisers to choose sides. It would cause unwanted media scrutiny. It might spook investors. It might prompt an SEC investigation into the independence of both companies' boards. No one wanted that, especially at Apple, which had just settled a five-year dispute with the SEC over the backdating of Jobs's 2001 options.

While Jobs would never admit this publicly back then, Apple needed Google more than Google needed Apple. When Jobs died, he was arguably the most powerful businessman in the world. But at the end of 2007 that wasn't close to being true. The iPhone was doing well. Apple's stock price had doubled that year. But it was far too soon to call the iPhone a successful product. Jobs had just cut the price of the entry-level iPhone by $100—from $499 to $399—to boost sales, making his most loyal and early iPhone customers angry and feeling duped into paying too much. He was renegotiating his deal with AT&T to drop the price *another* $200 to $199. Meanwhile, Google was paying Apple close to $70 million a year to have its software on the iPhone. That was a lot of money for Apple back then.

Perhaps the most powerful reason that kept Jobs from starting a fight with Google was personal, however: Jobs thought Brin and Page were his friends. Jobs had been their mentor for years, and the three of them were often seen on walks around Palo Alto on weekends or on Apple's campus during the week. Their friendship had started all the way back in 2000, when Google was still a start-up and its financial backers were pressuring Page and Brin to find a CEO with more seasoning than they had. Brin and Page had said the only person they would consider was Jobs. This was a preposterous statement. Everyone knew Jobs would never leave Apple after having just rejoined, and it infuriated Google's venture capitalists. But it was also a genuine expression of admiration from Page and Brin. They had idolized Jobs for a long time, and it helped set their relationship in motion. They thought Jobs typified the kind of leader they wanted to be. Jobs was impressed with what was clearly the next generation of the Silicon Valley elite and was flattered to advise them. "Jobs told me that when he called them [Brin and Page], they just kept downplaying Android," one of his executives said to him. "He basically said to me, 'I believe in my relationships with these guys that they're telling me the truth about what is going on.'"

For a few months it appeared that Jobs's gut feeling about Google might have been right. His relationship with Gundotra blossomed to the point where they were talking weekly. In a blog post a month before Jobs died in 2011, Gundotra recalled this period wistfully:

> One Sunday morning, January 6th, 2008 I was attending religious services when my cell phone vibrated. As discreetly as possible, I checked the phone and noticed that my phone said "Caller ID unknown." I choose to ignore. After services, as I was walking to my car with my family, I checked my cell phone messages. The message left was from Steve Jobs.
>
> "Vic, can you call me at home? I have something urgent to discuss," it said.
>
> Before I even reached my car, I called Steve Jobs back. I was responsible for all mobile applications at Google, and in that role, had regular dealings with Steve. It was one of the perks of the job. "Hey Steve—this is Vic," I said. "I'm sorry I didn't answer your call earlier. I was in religious services, and the caller ID said unknown, so I didn't pick up."
>
> Steve laughed. He said, "Vic, unless the Caller ID said 'GOD,' you should never pick up during services."
>
> I laughed nervously. After all, while it was customary for Steve to call during the week upset about something,

it was unusual for him to call me on Sunday and ask me to call his home. I wondered what was so important.

"So Vic, we have an urgent issue, one that I need addressed right away. I've already assigned someone from my team to help you, and I hope you can fix this tomorrow," said Steve. "I've been looking at the Google logo on the iPhone and I'm not happy with the icon. The second O in Google doesn't have the right yellow gradient. It's just wrong and I'm going to have Greg fix it tomorrow. Is that okay with you?"

Of course this was okay with me. A few minutes later on that Sunday I received an email from Steve with the subject "Icon Ambulance." The email directed me to work with Greg Christie to fix the icon.

Since I was 11 years old and fell in love with an Apple II, I have dozens of stories to tell about Apple products. They have been a part of my life for decades. Even when I worked for 15 years for Bill Gates at Microsoft, I had a huge admiration for Steve and what Apple had produced.

But in the end, when I think about leadership, passion and attention to detail, I think back to the call I received from Steve Jobs on a Sunday morning in January. It was a lesson I'll never forget. CEOs should care about details. Even shades of yellow. On a Sunday.

To one of the greatest leaders I've ever met, my prayers and hopes are with you Steve.

But by spring 2008, it was clear that the warm feeling between the companies was not going to last. The signs were everywhere that Schmidt, Page, and Brin were not going to let their relationships with Jobs get in the way of their ambitions. Google tried to poach a handful of key Apple engineers to work on Google's new Chrome Internet browser. Then talks to renegotiate the Google search and Google Maps agreements between the companies collapsed in acrimony. Google wanted to pay Apple less to be the exclusive search engine on the iPhone and on Macs, and said it wanted more than just basic location data from users' iPhones. In a number of meetings on Apple's campus in Cupertino, Gundotra and Apple marketing boss Phil Schiller actually ended up screaming at each other. Jobs and Schmidt had to step in and resolve the dispute.

Apple was particularly suspicious about the new maps data Google wanted from the iPhone. Google was getting latitude and longitude back from iPhone users. Now it said it also wanted the raw data that went into calculating that position. Was the user on a cell connection or a Wi-Fi connection? What was the location and information about the cell phone tower the iPhone was connected to? "We thought they wanted to use the data to backwards calculate other things the iPhone was doing," an Apple executive said. "Phil's big thing was that that information was proprietary to Apple and a violation of users' privacy because we would be sharing more about our users than our users had agreed to share."

Five years later tempers are *still* hot over this incident. Gundotra says he had never witnessed such high-handed, arrogant behavior anywhere else as during those conferences. "I thought Microsoft was arrogant. It was just unbelievable and very, very painful what happened there. I was optimistic and naive. I thought we could negotiate with Apple, and it would be fine. I had a relationship with Steve so I thought we could make everything work. That's not how it worked out." One of Jobs's executives then is equally cranky about Gundotra. He told me that Gundotra might not have been a fan of Android, but he wasn't a fan of Apple either. "He was trying to be liked by Steve and Phil and by Forstall, and he said he was doing his best to defend Apple inside of Google. But all he was doing was taking the information back to Larry and Sergey and the rest of the teams to get brownie points for himself. It was not about making Android better, necessarily, it was about making Vic better."

Amid this escalating tension and the explosive success of the iPhone 3G in summer 2008, Jobs began concluding that Google's Dream phone was, in fact, going to look a lot more like the iPhone than he wanted. To be released in November 2008, the Dream, to be called the T-Mobile G1, from HTC, would have a handful of multitouch features that Jobs believed belonged to Apple. Schmidt, Brin, and Page had been making Alan Eustace, Google's head of engineering, available for months to answer Jobs's questions and various objections about Android—and to keep Jobs from reaching this conclusion. Eustace was Rubin's boss, and Eustace and Jobs had developed a good dialogue, friends say. But by summer 2008 Jobs felt he was getting nowhere with Eustace—that he and Google were just stringing Jobs along. "I think they [Jobs and Apple's top executives] finally felt that the only way they were going to get this done was not to go through Alan anymore," said someone who talked to Jobs about it. "Alan was translating for Andy [Rubin], and I think they felt like they had to go right to the source to get these things changed."

Another Apple executive said that it was the second version of Android around then that was the final straw for Jobs. "When it started having swipe features and pinch and zoom and double tap, that's when Steve threw down the gauntlet and said, 'We're going over there and we're going to sit down and talk to them.'"

The reports from the meeting with Jobs, Forstall, Page, Eustace, and Rubin in the conference room outside Page's office in Google's Building 43 are varied. But they all agree on one thing: the meeting was nasty and confrontational. Jobs told the three Google executives that Apple had patented the multitouch features that Google was using, and that if they appeared on the G1 when it was released, Apple would sue. The Google team pushed back, saying that while Jobs may have been the first to make a successful product with multitouch gestures, he didn't invent the technology or most of the technologies in the iPhone. One Apple executive who wasn't there but listened to Jobs's briefing about the meeting told me, "It got incredibly personal. Jobs said that Rubin was steamed, telling him that his position was anti-innovation. And this is where Steve was demeaning to Andy, saying Andy was trying to be like him, look like him, have the same haircut, the same glasses, the same style."

No one at Google will talk about the meeting on the record, but off the record they continue to express puzzlement over Jobs's position. They believe that there are very few firsts in Silicon Valley—that all innovations are built on the shoulders of others. There would have been no Intel or Motorola microprocessor without the transistor and the integrated circuit. Without those microprocessors there would have been no personal computer. Without the personal computer there would have been no Microsoft, Apple, or software industry in general. Without the software industry there would have been no Netscape web browser. And without the web browser much of what we take for granted in our lives today would not exist.

One piece of evidence the Googlers used to make their point in their negotiations with Jobs was a 1992 video of James Gosling, a famous Sun Microsystems engineer and inventor of the Java programming language, showing off the Star7. This crude-looking handheld device had a 200 KB radio; a four-inch, LCD, color TV screen; and speakers from a Nintendo Game Boy. Even then, before anyone but the richest executives had a mobile phone or had seen a Newton handheld, Gosling was showing off a machine not only with a touchscreen but with inertial scrolling. The harder you flicked the screen, the faster it scrolled through items. Rubin made the case that, if anything, he and the Android team had been thinking about *those* technologies before Jobs had. Rubin had seen prototypes of the Microsoft Surface—a tabletop multitouch display released in late 2007—when he worked at Microsoft briefly in the 1990s.

But Google's evidence had zero impact on Jobs. "Steve was always of the opinion that Apple invented everything," said one

Google executive involved in the conversations. "And even when you showed him, 'Here, this wasn't invented by you,' he still believes it was. No matter whether you could show him, 'Look at all the places where multitouch was used before, or all these places where scrolling using your fingers was done before, or expansion of things [with your fingers] was done before,' that didn't sway Steve."

5

The Consequences of Betrayal

For Google, the outcome of the meeting with Jobs and Forstall was excruciating. Schmidt, Brin, and Page completely capitulated, and no amount of logic could conceal how painful that was. It wasn't just that Jobs had told them what features to take out of the G1 phone. He'd told them, in some cases, *how* to take them out. Android had long given users the option of creating a pattern on a three-by-three grid of dots to unlock the phone, with a minimum of a three-dot connection. But Jobs insisted that if users could connect the bottom three dots of the grid to unlock their phone, it would mimic the iPhone's patented slide-to-unlock feature. "So to placate Apple we went from a pattern where you could connect three dots to one where you had to connect four," said one senior engineer.

"It was really, really painful. It was almost like he was stealing from us," Android's Bob Lee said about Jobs. He continued,

Pinch to zoom [technically, finger-spread to zoom, pinch to unzoom] is a really very obvious thing, and Apple wasn't the first to do it. Go back, as we did, and look at the stuff Sun did with mobile in the 1990s and the Microsoft Surface. It made me very resentful of Apple that they would play these kinds of games. I loved Apple. I had always developed programs on an Apple. I made it possible for Googlers to develop Google software on Apple machines.

My cat's name is Wozniak. I joined Android in 2006, and most of the stuff we came up with [is] from scratch. Why does it look so much like the iPhone? Well, I think a big part of it is just the technology catching up. Why didn't somebody have a big touchscreen prior to the iPhone? Well, they were too expensive. So it wasn't like the iPhone came along and people said we should start doing that. The whole industry had been thinking about it for a long time. It's just that it finally became a viable thing to do.

No one who was in the meeting with Jobs will talk about it, and it's easy to understand why. All entrepreneurs need to have a thick skin, but Brin, Page, and then Schmidt when he joined Google in 2001, had developed a reputation as being particularly tenacious when challenged. This wasn't good for that image at all. From the moment they came up with a name for the company they had faced down their critics. They were told search was a go-nowhere business. This was considered such conventional wisdom that Schmidt almost didn't interview for the CEO job because of it.

When Google got traction and attracted powerful venture capitalists, Brin and Page often ignored them. The VCs wanted Google to quickly find a professional CEO and settle on a way of making money to support the business. Brin and Page refused to be rushed, and the VCs—Kleiner Perkins and Sequoia Capital—eventually became so angry they almost sued the founders.

Schmidt was hired in 2001. He had been CEO of Novell and a top executive at Sun Microsystems, and he, Brin, and Page have shrewdly managed most doubters and enemies since then. They settled on a business model—search advertising—that remade the economics of media and advertising, online and off. Then, when Google's incredible success led to lawsuits and other broadsides, they gave little ground. Yahoo! sued Google in 2004 for stealing AdWords, the idea for search ads that continues to fuel Google's business. Google gave Yahoo! a few hundred million dollars out of its IPO—Google got a business model that has generated hundreds of *billions*. Media giant Viacom tried to bully Google with a lawsuit in 2006. It charged that YouTube wasn't doing enough to secure Viacom's content from theft. Brin, Page, and Schmidt said Google was doing enough and would do more. They refused to settle and continued to win in court. When Google started hiring top engineers away from Microsoft, Bill Gates and Steve Ballmer tried to block the hires with lawsuits and public ridicule. "Fucking Eric Schmidt is a fucking pussy. I'm going to bury that guy," Ballmer famously said to an employee announcing his departure for Google. Ballmer and Gates had made the world cower for twenty years with threats like this. Brin, Page, and Schmidt laughed at it—and Microsoft's relevance in the tech world has been on the decline ever since. And when the world said Schmidt, Brin, and Page were crazy to get into mobile, they said, "Watch us."

But Steve Jobs threatening a lawsuit was different. No matter how in the right Google felt, the triumvirate apparently believed that an Apple patent-infringement lawsuit would create huge problems for the company, colleagues say. Android was already a long shot. Releasing it to the world under a legal cloud would make those odds almost insurmountable. Android's success depended on partners. Who would partner with Google while the lawsuit was pending? No one.

And they discussed whether an Apple lawsuit might cause broader problems for the whole of Google. Apple was still an underdog back then—not nearly as rich and dominant as it is today. But Google had become so powerful that it was an antitrust target. Regulators, competitors, and columnists wondered if it was becoming the next Microsoft—whether it was using its growing monopoly in search advertising to push other companies around.

Its purchase in 2007 of DoubleClick, the online display advertising company, had barely passed antitrust muster in early 2008. Google already controlled the online search advertising business. If it controlled the biggest company in online display advertising, would that give it control of *all* online advertising? antitrust regulators asked.

Google was in a fight with authors and book publishers over its plan to digitize their books. Making all books ever published searchable sounded like a great public good. But shouldn't authors and publishers be paid for letting Google sell ads against their data in search listings? they asked. Google didn't think so, as it intended to display only snippets relevant to search queries. It believed they would get paid in increased book sales.

And Google's proposed search partnership with Yahoo! in the spring of 2008 had been generating furious criticism from the business and advertising communities. After being allowed to acquire DoubleClick, the Yahoo! deal seemed like a naked power grab. Aggressive lobbying by Microsoft, of all companies, helped convince Justice Department lawyers that they had an antitrust case against Google. They threatened to drag Google into court if it didn't abandon the deal.

In addition, Google's stock price was down. It had had to lay off employees. Because it had become such a large company by then—about twenty thousand employees—its ability to continue to be the innovation machine of the previous decade was being questioned. Big companies' interest in protecting their existing businesses often interferes with their ability to back new and disruptive ideas. An Apple lawsuit accusing Google of stealing its intellectual property was not something they could afford to risk. "Apple made it clear that they were concerned about us violating their UI [user interface], and we agreed. We did not want to violate their UI" is all Schmidt will say about this matter.

The Jobs meeting was particularly difficult for Rubin, friends say. He was indeed as furious as Jobs described, and he almost quit Google over it. He understood what his bosses were saying intellectually. But Jobs had bullied him in front of his bosses, and they hadn't backed him up. For a while thereafter he had a sign on his office whiteboard that read STEVE JOBS STOLE MY LUNCH MONEY.

Jobs's demands that Google pull key features out of the G1 wasn't just infuriating to the Android team on principle. It created an enormous practical problem. By the summer of 2008, the G1 was two months away from launch, but it wasn't close to being ready. Now additionally the engineers were going to have to rewrite its software to exclude all the features Jobs wanted removed. The conventional wisdom about software is that features can be added and removed at will. The reality is that it is much more like writing a book. Chapters can be cut, but only a lot of work makes the cuts invisible.

The final push wasn't made any easier when Page and Brin, who were usually helpful, allowed their personal obsessions to intrude. Page wanted the device to work as fast with his enormous list of more than twenty thousand contacts as it would for any other user. To the Android team that seemed like the perfect becoming the enemy of the good. They suggested that that capability should wait until the second version of Android. Page was not persuaded. Brin, meanwhile, demanded that users be able to scroll through their contact list by tilting the phone and letting its accelerometer decide how fast to scroll based on the angle of the tilt. Erick Tseng, the Android project manager, said, "We actually had an engineer build it. Then we showed Sergey how it wasn't a good user experience," and Brin agreed.

"I personally thought we weren't going to make it," Rubin told Steven Levy for the book *In the Plex*. "Three months before we were supposed to ship, nothing worked. Crashed all the time. Couldn't receive email. Superslow. And over time it got more and more unstable."

• • •

Jobs, not surprisingly, was thrilled with how his meeting with Google turned out. Days after, he portrayed it to his executive team as a big win for all of them—that what was right and good had beaten a bunch of liars, cheats, and scoundrels. An executive who was part of that briefing said that Jobs and Forstall "were kind of gloating about it. They were like, 'Rubin was pissed. You could see it all over his face. We got what we needed to win. And they [Google] said they were not going to do it [multitouch].'" Jobs hated Rubin and told friends he was a "big, arrogant fuck."

None of this made Jobs less angry at feeling forced to go after Google in the first place. He felt Brin and Page, people he once considered friends, had betrayed him. And he felt Schmidt, a member of his board, had dissembled. Jobs's message to his executive team that day was strident: "These guys are lying to me, and I am not going to take it anymore. This Don't Be Evil stuff is bullshit." But he also felt vindicated—that Google was no longer going to be a threat.

Schmidt, while still technically on the Apple board, was effectively no longer a board member. He was now leaving the room during all board discussions about the iPhone, which was increasingly what Apple board meetings were about. Both for appearance and legal reasons, these recusals were happening more and more at Google too. Schmidt did not attend Google Android meetings, for example, and he left the room when Android came up in other contexts, such as among fellow members of Google's board of directors. Schmidt said he did not want to even *appear* as if he could be a conduit for information between the two companies.

Jobs told friends he was tempted to boot Schmidt entirely from the board, but he also understood that that might cause more trouble than it solved. It would attract media attention. It might spook investors. It might distract employees. Jobs may have felt that Google and Apple were no longer allies, but he knew that they still needed each other as business partners. Apple still needed Google search, Maps, and YouTube to sell the iPhone. And since no Android phone was for sale yet, the iPhone was still the only phone powerful enough to run Google's software effectively.

In the coming months Google did little to counteract Jobs's impression that he had thumped it—that the iPhone was going to dominate the mobile-phone world the same way that the iPod dominated the music-player world. The T-Mobile G1 phone "powered by Google" launched in September 2008. It was a good first effort, but comparing it to the iPhone was like comparing a Kia to a Mercedes. It had a touchscreen, but partially because Google had taken out all the multitouch features, it wasn't useful. It had a slide-out keyboard, but users complained that the keys felt mushy. Few were going to dump their BlackBerry for it. And it was difficult to set up if, like most, you used Microsoft Exchange email, contacts, and calendar at work.

But the Gmail, Android browser, and Maps applications were slick, and unlike even the latest iPhone then, the G1 ran more than one application at the same time. It introduced the pull-down notification screen that the iPhone later imitated. It was much more customizable than the iPhone. However, it didn't work with iTunes, the entertainment software of choice. You couldn't even sync it to your computer easily, like an iPhone. Instead, to get your information from your computer to the G1, you had to let the phone sync with Google's cloud, then sync your PC to Google's cloud as well. That may be a virtue today, but back then, before cloud computing was mainstream, it was a hassle.

Googlers were even tougher on the G1 than consumers. That year Google gave G1s to employees instead of the standard companywide Christmas bonus. Employees were not happy about it. I asked a few back then how they liked theirs and got answers such as "Great. Do you want mine?" or "Count how many are for sale on eBay. That's your answer." In subsequent Friday company meetings, Googlers openly asked why the company was wasting its time with Android. Most Googlers by then had iPhones, and the comparison was laughable.

Compared to the iPhone's unveiling, the launch, held in a catering facility under the Queensboro Bridge, was amateurish, according to Levy's account and videos. There were no live demos, only demos on video. Too much time was taken up with boring, self-congratulatory remarks by Rubin, and executives from HTC and T-Mobile. The only sign that this project had backing from the very top of Google came when, toward the end, Brin and Page made an unrehearsed appearance together on Rollerblades. But while their presence added star power, their answers to questions did not. In response to a question about what was the coolest G1 application, Brin said he'd written an app himself that used the phone's accelerometer to automatically time how long his phone stayed in the air when he tossed it. Then he threw the demo phone in the air to illustrate, creating looks of panic on his colleagues' and partners' faces. There were few other phones then, and they couldn't afford to have one break because Brin dropped it.

Juxtaposing the G1 and iPhone launches makes you wonder how Brin, Page, and Schmidt *ever* had more than just a business relationship with Jobs. Their outlook on the world was entirely different. Apple had prospered because of Jobs's meticulous, disciplined search for the best device—the perfect blend of form and function. Google had prospered on the backs of Brin's and Page's zaniness and embrace of chaos. As entrepreneurs the three shared a willingness to reject anything with a whiff of convention and to make big bets when those around them said they were reckless. But that's where the similarities ended.

Brin and Page wound up in front of the media in Rollerblades because they had been at an event with New York's Governor David Paterson at Grand Central Terminal in the morning and thought blading would be a fun and faster way to bypass New York City's gridlock. It didn't matter to them that a car was waiting, that their security detail had planned for traffic, or that they ended up at the G1 launch looking grimy and sweaty. Brian O'Shaughnessy, Android's top public relations aide at the time, says he remembers having to keep his own emotions in check when they arrived. It was his job to make sure the G1 got the widest and most positive media attention possible, and he wondered how to explain to his billionaire founders that they were putting everything at risk. "I was waiting for them backstage when they got to the launch, and I said, 'Guys, don't you want to take your Rollerblades off? You're going out there with the CEO of HTC and T-Mobile executives,' and they said, 'No. No. It's going to be fine.' And they just rollerbladed onto the stage." Can you imagine Steve Jobs ever doing that?

. . .

The way Jobs was handling Google should have made everyone at Apple feel better about the tension between the two companies. Instead, it made many of them feel worse. A handful of executives and engineers had been warning Jobs about Google's ambitions with Android for two years, and they *still* believed Jobs was underestimating Google's resolve. Why had the great Steve Jobs allowed himself to be duped by Google in the first place, and why did it then take him another eighteen months—until early 2010—to respond publicly? One of them put it to me like this: "I kept telling him, 'Steve, we should be paying more attention to those guys. They're hiring like crazy and I know all the guys they are hiring.' But Steve was like, 'I'm going to have my walk [with Larry or Sergey or Eric] and I'll get to the bottom of this.' Then he'd have his meetings with them and come back and say they told him not to worry. 'It's not really serious. It was an interesting idea, but it's not going anywhere,' they'd tell him. Even when Android shipped in 2008, they told him, 'Well, it's not really stable. It's not great. We don't know if we are going to continue it.' And I was just like, 'I don't believe this is happening.'"

Another recalled his and his colleagues' panic in 2007 when Google's Schmidt and the rest of the Apple board got iPhones to carry around months before they went on sale: "You have to know that there were a lot of people at Apple working on the iPhone going, 'What the fuck? They are handing our phone to a guy in charge of a company that we're competing with. They'll take the phone, tear it apart, and steal all our ideas.'"

Some at Apple have speculated that Jobs's blindness could simply have been because of what he considered his great friendship with Brin and Page. It is human nature to believe we are good judges of character. Successful founders and CEOs such as Jobs think they are particularly good at it. Being able to find and hire the most talented, reliable, and trustworthy people is, after all, a critical part of building and running a successful company. But others also wonder if Jobs's cancer had started to become a factor by then too. By the middle of 2008 Jobs was obviously not well. Most of the time his voice was strong and his energy was good—but he looked emaciated, as if he had lost fifty pounds in six months. At times he was also obviously in pain. "I'd see him double over in meetings. I'd see him get in a corner and just sit there with his knees pressed against his chest. We're all in the executive boardroom. It was terrifying to watch," an executive said.

No one asked if Jobs was sick, even though his appearance had become the elephant in the room in most meetings with him by 2008. "We never wanted to admit it. We just didn't go there. You just don't do that to somebody. You wouldn't want it done to you. And he would always say, 'Don't worry. I just got cleared by the doctors' or 'I'm fine,'" one executive said. But no one knew then what everyone knows now—that Jobs was not only sick but terminally ill. His pancreatic cancer had spread to his liver, and he needed a transplant, which he got when he was near death in early 2009, according to Walter Isaacson's 2011 biography of Jobs. Now some who were in those meetings with him back then wonder if his illness wasn't starting to take the fight out of him. "Put yourself in Steve's shoes," said one. "You're sick, and some days you're just irritable, but on others you say, 'I give up. I've heard what I need to hear. Let's move on.'"

Another Jobs confidant thinks Jobs was simply blinded by overconfidence. "I just don't know that anybody really focused on the fact that there was going to be a full-fledged licensed operating system that they [Google] were going to provide to manufacturers. There were a lot of rumors about a phone and about how they were going to do a phone OS; but I don't think Apple gave two shits about that because I think they felt that they were so good and so far ahead of everyone else that it didn't matter. So if they [Google] were going to do a Nokia-like OS or something like that, nobody was going to worry. [Even in 2008] I don't think anybody focused on that fact—that this was going to be a knock-down, drag-out Apple competitor."

This person initially rejected Jobs's health as being part of the problem. Upon further questioning, however, he reconsidered and said, "Look, I think you're right. Would he have been more combative during that period [if he hadn't been sick]? Probably, yes."

. . .

As in any divorce, Googlers and Appleites may never agree on how the two started fighting, at what point Apple began cutting business ties with Google and why it is now spending hundreds of millions of dollars suing members of the Android community around the world. Was Jobs truly betrayed by allies who shamelessly copied his work, as Apple still alleges years after Jobs's death? Or is Apple just perpetuating a cover story to hide the fact that illness and/or personal relationships, and/or overconfidence, had allowed him to miss signs that his relationship with Google was changing? Was Google sucked into fighting with Jobs when all it really wanted was to find a way to get along? Or was its behavior more premeditated and nefarious?

What *is* clear is that after Jobs forced Google to capitulate to him in the summer of 2008, Google privately began dropping all pretense of friendship too, and with single-minded ferocity it focused its energies on competing with Apple. Throughout the winter of 2008 and spring of 2009, as Jobs took a six-month leave from Apple for a liver transplant, Google didn't just invest heavily to build a second Android phone—the Droid—but started working on a third Android phone it would design, market, and sell itself. More immediately, Gundotra geared up his mobile-software team to build an iPhone app that Google might use as a Trojan horse.

Gundotra's falling-out with Jobs earlier in 2008 had, by the end of the year, made him a staunch Android ally, and he focused his team on not only building basic Google apps for the iPhone—such as search, Maps, and YouTube—but on developing a mobile version of software called Google Voice. Like Android, Google Voice grew out of the acquisition of a start-up in August 2007. The company, GrandCentral Communications, seemed like a weird purchase at first. It was like Skype. It made software to enable telephone calls that traveled over the Internet instead of via a telephone company. But to many Google engineers that was like owning a fancier buggy whip. Telephone conversations were something their parents did. To them it was old, increasingly obsolete technology. When Google had moved to its current office complex, Brin and Page had looked into not installing telephones at all—until they were told that would be a violation of the fire code.

GrandCentral's internal sponsor at Google, Wesley Chan, saw its potential differently: Google Voice was like Gmail. It was yet another application that made Google the center of users' world, another application that gave Google information about those users' interests, another application that could help Google sell more advertising. According to Levy's book, Page liked the disruptive potential lurking within GrandCentral's software. It could run on Android, and the carriers were not innovative enough to offer it to their customers. It offered the possibility of making Google a stealth phone company.

Google started rolling GrandCentral out to new users in 2008 under the new name Google Voice. The premise was powerful: Consolidate the various telephone numbers and email addresses we use into one communcations hub that anyone could set up. Google issued you a single phone number. You then linked that to all your other phones. When someone dialed your Google Voice number, the software automatically forwarded the call to all of your other phone numbers (or as many as you said it should) for free. It kept track of all those numbers and synced them with names in your Gmail contact list. It transcribed voice mails—albeit badly—and emailed them to you. It stored your cell phone's text messages. It offered free conference calling that anyone could set up. Phone companies offered some of these services too, but they often cost money and were harder to set up. Gundotra believed that Google Voice would be particularly useful as an iPhone application. Not only would it add features that the iPhone did not yet offer, but it would essentially wrest the most important functions of the iPhone—calls, contacts, and email—away from Apple and, instead, connect them to Google's servers. *Hostile takeover* is Wall Street terminology. It is hardly ever used in Silicon Valley. But when you cut through all the engineering subtleties, that is exactly what Google was doing.

What made Gundotra's strategy so brilliant was that Google couldn't lose. By then the Apple app store was a year old and an enormous hit. It not only was generating billions of dollars in new revenue, it was creating platform lock-in similar to the way Microsoft had done with Windows in the 1990s. The more software you bought for your iPhone, the more costly it became to replace those apps on another platform, and the more locked into buying another iPhone you would be. But Gundotra also understood that all that power came with an enormous responsibility: How would Apple decide which applications were allowed into the app store and which would be rejected? Deciding what music, movies, and TV shows to sell on iTunes was easy. If consumers didn't like Apple's selection, they could typically get that content in many other ways. But the app store was the only outlet for the new industry of software developers the iPhone created. Developers who spent money and time developing an application for the iPhone had little recourse if Apple rejected it. Apps that were obviously political, pornographic, or violent were easy calls. But dozens fell in gray areas and had already become an nettlesome public relations problem for Jobs and Apple. An app that allowed users to read classic books was rejected because it included the *Kama Sutra*. The political cartoonist Mark Fiore won the 2010 Pulitzer Prize for his work, but his app of cartoons was rejected because it made fun of political figures. If Apple rejected Google Voice—if it felt that it could reject the app of a big company and business partner—it would confirm Silicon Valley's worst fears about Apple's growing power in the mobile-phone business.

Nothing goes exactly as planned in business, but Gundotra's Google Voice gambit worked pretty close to the way he hoped. On July 28, 2009, two weeks after announcing Google Voice for all mobile phones *excluding* the iPhone, but assuring the world that the iPhone app would soon be available, Google announced that Apple had completely rejected Google Voice. Days later, Apple announced that Schmidt was leaving its board of directors because of his conflicts of interest, and the FCC leaked word that it was looking into the whole affair.

Almost all the media coverage focused on Apple's unreasonable and possibly unlawful control over its app store, portraying Jobs as a power-mad despot. In an effort *not* to look despotic, Apple tried to lead journalists into concluding that AT&T, not Apple, was behind all the rejections. But that made things even worse. It made the FCC wonder if Apple and AT&T were in some kind of improper collusion.

Two months later, in response to Freedom of Information Act requests by the media, the FCC released its correspondence with the three companies. It did not make Apple look good. Google's letter said, "Apple representatives informed Google that Google Voice was rejected because Apple believed the application duplicated the core dialer functionality of the iPhone. The Apple representatives indicated that the company did not want applications that could potentially replace such functionality." Meanwhile, Apple's letter stated, "Contrary to published reports, Apple has not rejected the Google Voice application, and continues to study it. The application has not been approved because, as submitted for review, it appears to alter the iPhone's distinctive user experience by replacing the iPhone's core mobile telephone functionality and Apple user interface with its own user interface for telephone calls, text messaging and voicemail."

Apple later allowed Google Voice and other voice applications into the app store. But executives at both Apple and Google said that everyone at the top of the two companies knew that Jobs himself had demanded Google Voice be rejected. "By 2009 people were already screaming that we were being censors," one Apple executive said. "So [which apps we approved] was important for Apple's image to get right. No one wanted to make these tough calls, so it wound up being up to Steve to do it."

. . .

The Google Voice skirmish generated a lot of media coverage and gave Silicon Valley its first true glimpse into something it had been speculating about for more than a year: that the Apple-Google partnership to protect the world from Microsoft was unraveling—that they were a lot more angry at and scared of each other than either of them were of Microsoft. But the Google Voice fight would quickly have become insignificant if Android didn't prove to be the threat that Jobs and Apple feared—if Rubin and the Android team didn't produce a phone consumers wanted to buy. That threat seemed far-fetched by year-end 2008 after the G1 had been out three months. The G1 was such a flop with consumers that it seemed that it would make building the next phone *harder*, not easier.

But the opposite happened. Instead, the stumbling start of the G1 galvanized manufacturers and carriers to help Android succeed. The iPhone revolution didn't just have Google and Android scrambling, it had the entire mobile industry figuring out how to compete with Apple. Motorola and Verizon, two partners that had been unavailable or uninterested in Android the year before, were suddenly and particularly intrigued.

Sanjay Jha had just taken over as Motorola CEO in August 2008. The company had made so many mistakes before and after the iPhone was released that many believed it was headed for bankruptcy protection without a Hail Mary pass. So Jha, who had a long relationship with Rubin dating from Jha's days as a top executive at chip maker Qualcomm, took the immediate and controversial step of declaring that Android would be the only operating system to ship with Motorola phones. Before that Motorola had roughly half a dozen operating-system teams. Thousands lost their jobs.

Meanwhile, Verizon, which at the end of 2007 had made clear that it hated Google, was now beginning to realize that maybe it needed Google more than it hated it. Verizon executives had wanted to believe that AT&T's deal with Apple—which gave Apple all design, manufacturing, and marketing rights—was an aberration. They spent $65 million marketing the LG Voyager in 2007 and another roughly $75 million marketing the BlackBerry Storm in 2008 in hopes of proving that point. But both were critical and commercial disappointments, and by the end of 2008, Verizon COO John Stratton was starting to worry about AT&T and the iPhone's taking his best customers. "We needed to get in the game," Stratton said. "And we realized that if we were going to compete with the iPhone, we couldn't do it ourselves."

The shared need—even desperation—of all three companies to come up with a response to the iPhone allowed all manner of fresh thinking by their top executives and engineers. Schmidt, who had viewed carriers as evil incarnate, was taken by Verizon's seemingly sincere commitment to opening up its network so that others besides Verizon could use its bandwidth to fuel new ideas. Stratton was impressed by Schmidt's reasonable attitude in person; he was nothing like the bomb thrower he seemed to be in his public statements. Jha was desperate to work with both companies to save his own.

Meanwhile, it wasn't just Jha's engineers who had come to understand and respect Android, Verizon's engineers had come to the same conclusion. They had been poring over every smartphone operating system on the market—and even tried building their own—and had concluded that Android was one of the best. This was a big statement from a carrier such as Verizon, notorious for wanting to control everything on its phones. In 2005 Verizon had been so convinced of its dominance in the wireless business that it had turned down Jobs's offer of a partnership to build the iPhone. AT&T had been Apple's second choice. What Verizon engineers liked was that Android was written with the future in mind. Most smartphone software—including the iPhone's—was designed to require regular connections to a PC. But from the beginning, Android was written with the assumption that one day this would not be necessary—that everyone would use their smartphone as their primary Internet and computing device.

And Rubin had designed a partnership that was much more carrier-friendly than anything Apple had come up with. On both Apple and Android platforms, app makers get about 70 percent of the revenue from selling their software. But Apple takes the remaining 30 percent, whereas Rubin decided to give what might have been Android's share to the carriers. Some thought he was crazy to leave that kind of money on the table. Rubin thought it was a small price to pay to give the Droid every possible chance of succeeding. A carrier's commitment to a device could mean the difference between its success and failure, and Rubin wanted to give carriers every incentive to strongly back the Droid. If the Droid succeeded, Android and Google would benefit in so many other ways—higher search traffic, improved advertising revenue, increased customer loyalty—that it would be worth it in the end.

The potential of the Droid partnership was exciting. But Rubin said the work to produce an actual phone made the stress levels of the G1 seem tame by comparison. At the end of 2008, Jha had promised Rubin a device far faster than any other smartphone. He'd said its touchscreen would have a higher resolution than the iPhone's; that it would come with a full keyboard for customers who didn't like the iPhone's virtual keys. And he promised a phone that was thin and sleek, one that could compete with the iPhone on pure aesthetics. But when the first prototypes started showing up at Google in the spring of 2009, they looked nothing like the designs Jha had presented. Indeed, they were hideous. There was no way to sugarcoat what had happened: Rubin and his team had had so much faith in Jha that they hadn't questioned him closely enough. Now it appeared that faith was going to cost them enormously.

Despair set in. "It looked like a weapon. It was so sharp and jagged and full of hard lines. It looked like you could cut yourself on the edges," says Tom Moss, who was Rubin's head of business development. "We were really concerned. There were a lot of conversations where we asked, 'Is this really the device we want to do? Should we try to talk Motorola out of it?'" The implications of canceling the project were huge. Another dud, right on the heels of the disappointing G1, might cement the public's perception of Android as a flop. Executives at Verizon would look inept. They were still taking heat for passing on the iPhone. And a failure would likely mean the end of Motorola, the company that had invented the cell phone. "There was a lot riding on it," Rubin said to me in 2011. "I was betting my career on it."

A sense of doom—and panic—hung over the project all summer. The phone needed to be delivered to stores by Thanksgiving, but that now felt more like an execution date than anything to look forward to. Android engineers worried the phone wouldn't sell, but still needed to work weekends and holidays to develop the software. Meanwhile, Jha, Rubin, and Stratton spoke almost every day trying to figure out a way to tweak the design without having to reengineer all the electronic components. And the phone still didn't have a name. McCann, Verizon's longtime ad agency, had come up with a list of possibilities—including Dynamite—that few liked. As late as Labor Day, the phone still went by its code name, Sholes—the last name of the man, Christopher Latham Sholes, who invented the first commercially successful typewriter in 1874. Feeling cornered, Stratton reached out to McGarryBowen, a young ad agency known for its unconventional thinking. "We told them they had a week," said Joe Saracino, who was Verizon's executive in charge of the new phone's marketing. "A few days later, cofounder Gordon Bowen comes back and says, 'What do you think when I say *Droid*?'"

In retrospect, what the agency had done was simple: it turned the phone's menacing looks into its biggest asset by marketing it as an anti-iPhone. The iPhone was smooth and refined, so they would pitch the Droid as rough and ready for work. The iPhone's electronics and software were inaccessible, so they'd market this phone's hackability. "If there had been a phone in the movie *Black Hawk Down*, it would have looked like the Droid," Bowen told the executives. A few weeks later, in early October 2009, Verizon and its new agency presented the Droid campaign to a group of two hundred Android staffers. One ad featured stealth bombers dropping phones on a farm, in the woods, and by the side of a road. Another attacked the iPhone as a "digitally clueless beauty pageant queen." A third listed all the things the Droid could do that the iPhone couldn't. When the ads were over, the room erupted in applause. The Android team had been demoralized, but "when they decided they were going to do this full-on attack on the iPhone— that we were going to war—we got really excited," Tom Moss said.

When the Droid launched, on schedule, it was a tremendous hit, outpacing sales of the original iPhone in its first three months. In January 2010, Google launched another salvo at Apple with a phone it had developed itself called the Nexus One, which was a commercial failure because Google tried to market and sell the phone itself, instead of through a carrier. But it was a technical triumph. It had a bigger touchscreen than the iPhone. It had a noise-canceling microphone so that users could talk in a busy street without annoying their callers with background noise. It used a phone chip that worked on every carrier frequency so users could switch carriers without buying a new phone. It had a better camera, and it allowed users to talk longer on a single charge. Most significant, it had all the multitouch features Jobs had demanded Google remove from the G1 roughly eighteen months before. Motorola had released the Droid without those features. But a week after launching the Nexus One, Google released a software update for the Droid that added multitouch there too.

. . .

For Jobs, it was the final straw. He had told Google that if it included multitouch on its phones, he would sue, and true to his word he sued the Nexus One maker, HTC, a month later in Delaware

Federal District Court. More noticeably, he began seeking out public opportunities to attack Google and Android. A month after the Nexus One was released—and days after Jobs announced the first iPad—he tore into Google at an Apple employee meeting. "Apple did not enter the search business. So why did Google enter the phone business? Google wants to kill the iPhone. We won't let them. Their Don't Be Evil mantra? It's *bullshit*."

In October, at the end of the quarterly earnings conference call with investors and Wall Street analysts, Jobs spent five minutes laying out in detail why Android was an inferior product in every way. He said Android was hard for consumers to use because every Android phone operated differently. He said the Android was hard to write software for because of that. He said that meant Android software would not be very good and would not work well. He said the argument that Android was better than the iPhone because the Android platform was open and Apple's was closed was "a smoke screen to hide the real issue: What's best for the customer?" He said the marketplace supported those claims. "This is going to be a mess for both users and developers."

His strongest comments, which he made a week after Apple sued HTC, have been repeated hundreds of times since they appeared in Isaacson's biography at the end of 2011:

> Our lawsuit is saying, "Google, you fucking ripped off the iPhone. Wholesale ripped us off." Grand theft. I will spend my last dying breath if I need to, and I will spend every penny of Apple's $40 billion in the bank to right this wrong. I am going to destroy Android because it is a stolen product. I'm willing to go to thermonuclear war on this. They are scared to death because they know they are guilty. Outside of Search, Google's products—Android, Google Docs—are shit.

Privately, Jobs was just as animated. In public he had a long history of fibbing to hide his true intentions. In 2004 he said

Apple would never make a phone while Apple was working on—a phone. Some therefore wondered if Jobs's public trashing of Android also had ulterior motives. But during Apple executive-team meetings, Android was almost an obsession for him. It was one of the reasons why he bought Quattro Wireless at the end of 2009, for $275 million. Quattro was one of the early companies with expertise in selling, creating, and distributing advertising for smartphones. Google controlled online advertising on desktops and laptops. Jobs didn't want Google extending that control to the smartphone too. "I think he felt that content [games and other apps on phones and tablets] was going to be ad supported, and that those developers needed to make money," said Andy Miller, Quattro's CEO and cofounder. "He thought that if Apple didn't have a home team providing them with a check, and all their advertising dollars came from Google and AdWords, then they would think about developing for Android first. So he set out to do that when he went out on leave [to get a liver transplant]. He told Scott [Forstall] that that was what he wanted to do, and Scott met with us."

Miller said it was an amazing experience working for Jobs, but that it was quickly clear to him that Apple wasn't set up to be successful as an advertising company any more than Google is set up to be a consumer-products company. iAd now probably generates roughly $200 million a year in revenue for Apple, Miller said. It is what Apple is using to finance its newly launched free Internet radio service. But at the beginning of 2010 it was difficult to integrate ad sales into Apple's "We make and sell the most beautiful things on earth" culture. Miller remembers it as being one of the most exciting and exhausting experiences of his career. "I was a VP reporting directly to Steve, and I had to do a presentation to him, Forstall, Eddy Cue, and Phil Schiller every Tuesday. I was doing a presentation every week for the leader of the free world, so that was a huge amount of stress. Meanwhile, Steve got sicker and sicker. We started to do meetings at his house. Nobody would make a[n advertising] decision without Steve because he understood advertising better than anyone at the company. I mean, he was the miracle man. He kept coming back and coming back. But [he was obviously so sick that] you just couldn't look at him after a while. It was awful. But he was really incredible. I think he was doing stuff until two days before he died. The worst part about it all was that he was almost always right."

. . .

An irony that is often lost in discussions about the Apple/Google fight is that for all the lawsuits that now have been filed, Apple has not yet actually sued Google itself. It has only sued the *makers* of Android phones, such as Samsung, HTC, and Motorola. The private assumption by Google, and the phone makers as well, is that Apple understands it's easier to convince a judge and/or a jury of theft if lawyers can put two phones side by side, as Apple did successfully in front of a jury in 2012 in its suit against Samsung. It's much harder to prove theft with software—especially software such as Android, which carriers and manufacturers can modify at will, and which Google gives away for free. This has created a strange dynamic in the Apple/Google fight. It has allowed Google—especially Schmidt, who is still Google's most public face—to remain oddly removed from a battle that is really about him and Google's executive team. The Apple/Google fight is now one of the nastiest, longest, and most public corporate battles in a generation. But when you listen to Schmidt or any other Google executives talk about it, they sound almost as if Google were a bystander. Schmidt has been so good at staying above the fray that he has at times sounded like a parent talking to a child in the midst of a tantrum when he talks about Apple and Jobs.

On Android's evolution, he said to me in the middle of 2011, "Larry and Sergey and I understood the strategic value of Android, but none of us I think foresaw how strategic it would become. Every once in a while a perfect storm occurs. Your competitors make some mistakes. You end up with the right product at the right time. There are really no other good choices of products. It all sort of happens in a moment. That's what happened with Android."

In the middle of 2012 I asked him to explain how it took so long for Jobs to understand Google was a competitor, and Schmidt said, "Remember this [Android] was a small business for Google [in 2008]. This was not a big deal. So we [Jobs and I] monitored it."

He wouldn't answer my questions about Jobs, saying it was unseemly to talk about him in this context now that he is dead. But in 2010 he said to Isaacson, "Steve has a particular way that he wants to run Apple, and it's the same as it was twenty years ago, which is Apple is a brilliant innovator of closed systems. They don't want people to be on their platform without permission. The benefit of a closed platform is control. But Google has a specific belief that open is the better approach because it leads to more options, competition, and consumer choices."

And at the end of 2012, Schmidt told *The Wall Street Journal*, "It's always been on and off [our relationship with Apple]. Obviously, we would have preferred them to use our maps. They threw YouTube off the home screen [of iPhones and iPads]. I'm not quite sure why they did that." But he said whatever their disagreements, none of Google and Apple's conflict was nearly as bad as the media made it out to be. "The press would like to write the sort of teenage model of competition, which is 'I have a gun, you have a gun, who shoots first?' The adult way to run a business is to run it more like a country. They have disputes, yet they've actually been able to have huge trade with each other. They're not sending bombs at each other."

Schmidt is an old hand at these kinds of interactions, and he is good at it. Anyone who has ever worked for Schmidt will tell you that he is one of the toughest, most competitive executives walking. Ask Rubin what it was like to be on the receiving end of a few "Don't fuck it up" lectures from Schmidt. "Not fun," Rubin says. But in public Schmidt comes across as anything but the ambitious, competitive Silicon Valley tycoon that he is. He looks and sounds like an economics professor. Dressed typically in khakis and either a sweater or a blazer and tie, he goes out of his way to make journalists feel comfortable in his presence. He often solicits follow-ups to make sure, as he often says, that he has answered your question "crisply." He is one of the rare executives unafraid to answer questions head-on. His answers are filled with facts, data, and history. He always has an agenda, but he rarely appears evasive. Most CEOs avoid detailed discussions with journalists at all costs. They'd rather seem evasive than miss an opportunity to repeat a talking point. Schmidt prefers to overwhelm with facts and knowledge. He's not afraid to talk about facts that don't support his thesis. He just supplies other facts that do.

Schmidt's public diffidence serves many goals. Many still don't understand how Google works—how it makes money and what it does and doesn't do with all the information about the Internet and its users that it sees. Schmidt is so good at explaining it all that even after handing over CEO duties to cofounder Page, Schmidt has been called Google's explainer in chief. These explanations solve two problems: They truly keep the debate about Google focused on facts. They also make Google seem less ambitious and competitive than users, customers, and competitors are being tempted to believe.

It's been astonishingly effective—especially on Microsoft. For five years, Schmidt denied that Google was competing with Microsoft Windows for control of desktop computing, and Microsoft sounded as if it believed that for a while. By 2005, however, Google, not Microsoft, had more influence over what users did with their computers. Schmidt denied that Google was building an online version of Microsoft Office, and Microsoft believed that effort wasn't much of a threat either. By 2010, however, big commercial customers such as the City of New York started using Google's applications to force Microsoft to lower its Office prices. And Schmidt denied that Google was building its own Internet browser—to compete with Microsoft, Apple, and its open-source partner Mozilla, which makes Firefox. Then, in 2008, it released Chrome, its own Internet browser. Schmidt said, quite reasonably, that over time it had become clear to him that a company such as Google that depended on Internet-browser access for people to use its products should not cede control of the browser to anyone. But it would have seemed less Machiavellian if he hadn't been denying Google's plans so forcefully for so long.

Google has seemingly played a similar game with Apple over its mobile ambitions. It told Apple and Jobs that it wasn't serious about Android, that it might scrap the project, that it would never compete with the iPhone, until one day they were the fiercest of rivals. Schmidt consistently denies that he or anyone else at Google has done anything improper in dealing with Apple, and that is probably true. As Schmidt has said, innovation is messy; it wasn't clear for a while that Android was going to be successful; Google needed to get its software onto mobile devices; and the iPhone and Google's relationship with Jobs were transformative. But it is also true that by 2008, Schmidt along with the rest of the senior executive team at Google talked privately about what Google would do if the iPhone became as dominant in mobile as the iPod was in music—if the gateway to the mobile Internet ran through Apple. "It was the elephant in the room of all our Android meetings," Cedric Beust, the Android engineer said. "An iPhone-dominated world could threaten Google financially [by perhaps forcing Google to pay Apple a toll for mobile Internet access through the device]. But also the model Apple pushes was not the one engineers and everyone at Google are comfortable with. It's not the kind of future they want to live with. I think those people saw that Apple might even be worse than Microsoft—the way they curated out everything they didn't like from their app store and all that. I think we came close to that [problem], but I think the timing of Android prevented it and forced Apple to become a bit more humane and bit more humble."

Other Google executives say said that Page was even more aggressive than Schmidt in pushing Android to become Google's mobile solution and then, in early 2007, to compete with the iPhone. Executives closest to Page say they are not surprised by this. "Larry's not actually that thrilled at being a technology provider to anybody," one of them explained. "He wants to build products and have users and be in control of our destiny as a company. So [only being a technology provider to Apple on the iPhone] wasn't really optional, though I'm sure that's what Apple would have preferred." Schmidt surely didn't tell Jobs about all this—that Google had become more worried about Apple than Microsoft, and that Google was a lot more serious about Android than he let on. Nor should he have. But it *does* make you wonder about the prospects for a settlement between the two companies. Every time Schmidt talks about the Apple/Google fight as if he can't understand why it got so nasty, it must feel to Apple as if he is picking a scab.

6

Android Everywhere

By 2010 Apple and Google were attacking each other on every possible front: in the courts, in the media, and in the marketplace. Android's surge in popularity was astonishing, and Rubin, Schmidt, and the rest of Google made no secret of their glee. It seemed that every chance they got during 2010 they would expound on how many monthly activations Android had racked up and how mobile devices were going to change the future of Google and the world. In an April 2010 interview with *The New York Times*, Rubin even predicted that Android was going to rule the entire mobile universe. The year before he had been worried that Google would abandon Android and that he and his team would need to job hunt. Now he confidently proclaimed, "It [Android] is a numbers game. When you have multiple OEM's [phone manufacturers] building multiple products in multiple product categories, it's just a matter of time" before Android overtakes other smartphone platforms such as iPhone and the BlackBerry.

It was as if little else about Google mattered anymore. That wasn't really true, but it wasn't a huge exaggeration either. In 2010, Android started the year with 7 million users. By year-end it had grown to 67 million and was adding three hundred thousand new customers a day. Android itself wasn't making money yet, but it was heading there fast. More important, it was accelerating the revenue and profit growth of other Google applications such as search and YouTube, and it was getting more people to sign up

for Google accounts and give Google their credit-card information. The more people used Android, the more Google searches
they did and the more ads they clicked on.

Google still made most of its money from searches on laptops
and desktops. But everyone at the top of the company knew they
wouldn't be the dominant source of revenue forever. Soon, fewer
and fewer people would be buying those devices, and more and
more would be buying smartphones and other mobile gadgets
with Internet access. The growth and profits for Google lurking in
these numbers were eye-popping. Each mobile-phone ad might
sell for less than a desktop ad, but its potential audience and,
therefore, total revenue potential were enormous. Consumers buy
five times more cell phones every year than PCs—1.8 billion versus 400 million. Google had barely penetrated this market.

Thanks to Android, Google's potential audience for its ads
and applications had quintupled.

It had all worked almost exactly the way Rubin had envi-
sioned it would too: manufacturers and carriers wanted to compete with the iPhone, and Rubin's success with the Droid had
convinced them that Android was their best chance of doing
that. Rubin took full advantage of the opportunity, pushing his
engineers to deliver three major updates to the Android software in 2010—a relentless pace. By the end of 2010 Android
didn't just have monster hits such as the Droid, but a handful of
others such as HTC's Evo 4G and Samsung's Galaxy S. In all,
by the end of 2010, nearly two hundred Android phone models
were available in fifty countries, and carriers and manufacturers
worldwide were lining up to throw their multimillion-dollar
marketing budgets behind them. An electronic poll of the audience at a *Fortune* magazine technology conference in July 2010
asked, "Who will have the dominant smartphone in five years?"
The verdict was clear: 57 percent picked Android; 37 percent
picked iPhone.

By early 2011 Schmidt was marveling not only at how smartphones had changed technology, but how they had become one

of the most important advancements in human civilization. In a speech he gave in Germany he said:

> We have a product that allows you to speak to your phone in English and have it come out in the native language of the person you are talking to. To me this is the stuff of science fiction. Imagine a near future where you never forget anything. [Pocket] computers, with your permission, remember everything—where you've been, what you did, who you took pictures of. I used to love getting lost, wandering about without knowing where I was. You can't get lost anymore. You know your position to the foot, and by the way, so do your friends, with your permission. When you travel, you're never lonely. Your friends travel with you now. There is always someone to speak to or send a picture to. You're never bored. You're never out of ideas because all the world's information is at your fingertips. And this is not just for the elite. Historically, these kinds of technologies have been available only to the elites and not to the common man. If there was a trickle down, it would happen over a generation. This is a vision accessible to every person on the planet. We're going to be amazed at how smart and capable all those people are who did not have access to our standard of living, our universities, and our culture. When they come, they are going to teach us things. And they are coming. There are about a billion smartphones in the world, and in emerging markets the growth rate is much faster than it is anywhere else. I am very excited about this.

The telecom industry had been desperately worried that Rubin planned to marginalize it the way Bill Gates had tried to marginalize PC makers with Microsoft Windows in the 1990s. But Rubin had insisted that was not his plan, and it appeared that he was keeping his word. Rubin allowed each carrier and manufacturer to add their own software and applications on top of Android to differentiate themselves from one another. And he gave to the carriers the 30 percent cut of app store revenues that Apple took for itself.

For the hidebound cell phone business, Rubin's strategy was truly innovative. It was: Create as much competition among carriers and manufacturers as possible. By scrambling to compete with the iPhone they would also be competing with each other. Manufacturers previously made phones to please carriers more than consumers, because in the United States, at least, they depended upon carrier subsidies and marketing support to sell their phones. But it became clear that to compete with the iPhone, they would have to jettison these old ways. Verizon and Motorola learned that lesson with the Droid. What was essential now was to make phones that consumers wanted to buy.

Carriers and manufacturers didn't talk much about this, but their actions spoke loudly. HTC bought a design firm, One & Co, to help it make cooler-looking phones. Samsung's design approach so closely resembled Apple's that it became the center of their ongoing patent lawsuit. And carriers listened to consumers when they complained. In the fall of 2010 Vodafone tried to foist a slew of its own apps onto customers of certain HTC Android smartphones. When consumers realized they couldn't remove them, the reaction was so virulent that within a week Vodafone had backtracked. It pushed out a software update that removed all the apps, restoring phones to their previous condition.

When Rubin explains this to me in the conference room down the hall from his office, he talks like a man who has been thinking about this evolution for a long time.

> So the thing that disappeared in 2008 [that made the industry rethink] was the walled garden—it completely disappeared. And [despite what most say], it wasn't because of the iPhone. It was because of the Internet. It's because the killer application that consumers wanted was that they wanted to take the Internet with them. You'd be stupid to

try to compete with the Internet [if you were a carrier or a manufacturer]. How could you? So Android enabled both of them to take advantage of the Internet in a controlled way. Our pitch was "You have costs. We understand what those costs are. You want to be differentiated and don't want to be commoditized. So we're going to give you this, this, this, and this—the hook to solve that equation."

Translation: None of us can beat Apple on our own. But if we work together, each of us focusing on what we are truly good at, we can not only beat Apple but make all our businesses stronger and more profitable than they were before.

The market forces Rubin channeled and the incentives he set up didn't always work perfectly. Despite his best efforts, carriers and manufacturers were slow to roll out Android software updates. One phone would have the latest version of Android, but another would have the previous version or even the version before that. This meant that not all apps in the Android app store worked on all phones, and it meant that consumers sometimes thought they were buying a phone with the latest and greatest Android software, only to find out that that wasn't the case.

But the market pressure on the industry was a lot greater than it had been in the past. Rubin made sure that each year there was at least one phone model that carriers and manufacturers weren't allowed to customize with their own software, such as the HTC Nexus One and Samsung Nexus S in 2010. That way, if consumers didn't like HTC Sense, Samsung TouchWiz, or any of the other carrier and manufacturer customizations they used to distinguish themselves in the market, they always had alternatives.

Most important, Android was good enough by 2010 to offer consumers something they had begun to crave: choice. Apple had completely controlled the high-end smartphone market for three years. But it made only one phone, with a fixed set of capabilities and customizations available with, in the United States, only one carrier, AT&T. By 2010 a few Android phones were not only as cool-looking as the iPhone but were better devices in some ways. They had replaceable batteries, upgradable memories, and more customizable software. Most Android phones had bigger screens than the iPhone. They all supported multitasking [the ability to run more than one program at a time], which the iPhone did not. Any software developer with an idea could get his program listed in the Android app store without advance approval, unlike in Apple's store. Android phones were better for watching video because they had a video player that ran Adobe Flash. Apple had banned it as bad technology, but it had become the standard for video on the Internet. And in the United States, Android phones ran on both the T-Mobile and Verizon networks, which to many was a competitive advantage in itself. AT&T had the iPhone, but it was so popular that the reliability of its network was suffering, with slow Internet speeds and higher-than-normal call drops.

Rubin did what he could to make the Android pitch everywhere he went. In 2010, for the first time in his career, everyone wanted to listen to him. He was inundated with requests for media interviews, mobbed at conferences, and enjoyed access to the CEO of every cell phone maker and carrier in the world, all of whom wanted Rubin to help them hone their own messages.

It was his good fortune that his competitors Apple and AT&T seemed to do everything in their power to help him. Weeks before Jobs was to unveil the iPhone 4, gadget site *Gizmodo* spoiled the valuable surprise quotient Apple builds into every product launch. An Apple engineer, doing legitimate bug-testing outside Apple, had left the prototype in a Redwood City bar. *Gizmodo* got its hands on it and published pictures. Then, after the new iPhone had been released in June, reviewers discovered the iPhone 4's new wraparound antenna had a dead spot. It forced Jobs to call a damage-control press conference. On top of all this was the growing customer dissatisfaction with the iPhone's U.S. network operator, AT&T. AT&T had been unable to handle the explosion of traffic the iPhone caused on its network, and by 2010 its customers had become furious and vocal about it. All three stories became international news in 2010 and fodder for late-night comedians. The stories gave Rubin and other members of the Android community almost unlimited opportunities to highlight the differences between the Apple way and the Android way. And they took full advantage of the openings.

Intellectually, it's easy to understand why Jobs was so angry about the lost prototype. He felt Apple itself had been burglarized. When the prototype was found by other bar patrons, they first called Apple. But when they couldn't get Apple to respond immediately, they called a few media outlets. *Gizmodo* bought the prototype for $5,000, saying that it did not know whether it was real. Jobs cared because *Gizmodo*'s photos would likely cost Apple millions in lost sales and marketing buzz. Few would buy the iPhone that was currently on sale now that they knew what the new one looked like and when it was likely going to be released. And Apple might get less coverage for the iPhone 4's actual unveiling since it was no longer a surprise. But Apple and Jobs had become so rich and powerful by then that instead of looking like the victims, they looked like bullies. The San Matteo sheriff's office opened a criminal investigation into whether *Gizmodo* had illegally received stolen property. They got a search warrant for the *Gizmodo* journalist's home and seized his computer equipment. Jobs looked as if he had orchestrated it all because he publicly supported the investigation. The *Gizmodo* journalist wasn't charged with a crime, and he got his computer equipment back. But journalists couldn't wait to ask Rubin about it all, and he happily obliged. When a *New York Times* reporter asked him what he would do if one of his Android prototypes had been found in a bar, he said, "I'd be happy if that happened and someone wrote about it. With openness comes less secrets." The implicit advertisement was clever: *If owning an iPhone makes you feel part of a totalitarian state, that's because the company that makes it is run by a despot. Try Android.*

In June came "Antennagate," and with it, the question of whether the iPhone truly *was* the best designed and most beautiful phone in the world. Apple had figured out a way to put all the iPhone's antennas on the outside of the device—three thin, shiny pieces of metal wrapping around the edge of the phone. It was supposed to improve the iPhone's cell reception. Jobs touted it hard when he announced the phone as the perfect example of complementary form and function. But reviewers discovered that if it was held a certain way—especially by left-handed users—a finger could easily cover a spot where two pieces of antenna met and degrade the signal. Jobs was ultimately forced to call a press conference to explain the problem, and to offer a fix—a free case.

But Jobs also couldn't resist pointing out that Android phones had similar problems, and the dig backfired. Members of the Android community collectively and publicly made fun of Jobs's well-known arrogance about the beauty of Apple products. "You know, I heard that the most popular voice message on iPhone 4 was 'Sorry I can't answer your call because I am holding my phone.' I don't think this is an issue with Droid X," said Sanjay Jha, Motorola's CEO, at a technology conference put on by *Fortune* magazine. He and other members of the Android community gleefully named the problem "the iPhone death grip."

But the Android community had the most fun of all with "Connectiongate"—the iPhone's reliability problems on AT&T's wireless network. Carriers love to trash one another's networks, and consumers love to trash their carriers, but historically the real differences among wireless services have been marginal. With AT&T and the iPhone, connection and call quality were enormous problems compared to reception for other carriers, and they seemed to get worse and worse through 2009 and early 2010. The difficulty was simple: Before the iPhone, no one had built a pocket computer that could not only surf the Internet but stream video. That meant AT&T's projections for data traffic were way off the mark. The solution, on the other hand, was complex. It was going to take two or three years and nearly $50 billion for AT&T to upgrade its network to handle all the new traffic. That isn't a satisfactory explanation to consumers locked into two-year contracts and paying at least $100 a month for service.

Few could have handled it well, and AT&T and Apple handled it less than well. Apple blamed all the problems on AT&T even though the iPhone itself was the source of some connection problems. Apple refused to modify the way the iPhone consumed data even though that might have helped matters. Meanwhile, AT&T—at least initially—responded defensively rather than proactively. By the end of 2009 Verizon was pummeling AT&T with a series of "map" ads, claiming that AT&T's spotty 3G network was to blame for poor service. AT&T customers began posting news of dropped calls on the Twitter hashtag #ATTFAIL. AT&T made this debacle worse by suing Verizon rather than parrying with their own advertisements.

By 2010 many consumers in the United States were buying Android phones just so they didn't have to have AT&T as a carrier. Jobs had been leaning on AT&T executives to speed up its network upgrades since the iPhone had launched in 2007. But he had limited leverage until the start of 2011, when the exclusivity period with AT&T expired and Verizon could also offer the iPhone. He'd considered dropping AT&T and switching to Verizon more than half a dozen times, but concluded the move was too risky. It would have required redesigning the iPhone, because Verizon phones used bigger cell radios than AT&T phones, and there was no additional room in the iPhone case. Verizon cell radios were well known to be battery hogs. Lastly, it wasn't clear at the problem's peak in 2009 that Verizon would be able to handle the iPhone traffic any better. "There were plenty of conversations along the lines of 'Why are we sticking ourselves with this boat anchor [AT&T],'" Bob Borchers said. "But every time we had that conversation, it always came down to the fact that the technology challenges were too high to warrant doing the work."

• • •

Jobs did little to hide his fury at all these problems in 2010. He was *so* vocal that by the fall he was starting to sound defensive, petulant, and pedantic. By then he was not only trashing Android as bad for consumers but publicly questioning the veracity of Google's sales and activation numbers. It wasn't just that he felt Google had stabbed him in the back or that maybe he was embarrassed for having misjudged Android's appeal. He felt that if Android wasn't stopped, the future of Apple itself was in peril, he told executives. One executive who heard Jobs talk about the issue described Jobs's feelings this way: "It [Android] was an existential threat. Apple's business depended on it selling its devices for a lot more than it cost to make them, and then using that money to develop new products. Android's approach was completely the opposite of this. Google was about growing the platform, without regard to the cost or profit on the devices. It made money off advertising, not hardware." In Jobs's opinion the two approaches could not coexist.

Jobs had launched the iPhone in 2007 thinking he'd not only created a beautiful, revolutionary device, but that he was leveraging the dominant content platform in the world, iTunes. Because of the iPod—which by 2007 had sold more than 100 million units—virtually everyone with a computer managed and purchased their music through that software. There was little incentive to use any portable music player other than an iPod, with huge incentives for families to buy more than one. Apple had three different iPod models that came in a variety of colors and capacities. And Apple made sure it was a pain to use competing hardware or software. The only easy way to get music onto an iPod was through iTunes. The best music selection was in the iTunes store, if you didn't want to rip from your own CDs. And many non-Apple devices wouldn't connect to iTunes and wouldn't play all songs purchased through the store.

The iPod-iTunes symbiosis was a powerful thing to behold. Like Microsoft Windows in the 1990s, it was self-reinforcing and in 2007 seemed to be an unassailable fortress. Apple effectively had a monopoly in music players—in excess of 70 percent market share—because of it. Everyone at Apple knew the dynamics of the global cell phone market were different from those driving music players. It was many times larger, and it was dominated by some of the biggest corporations in the world. But when iPhone sales took off, it was hard for Jobs and the rest of Apple not to wonder if history was repeating itself—if the iPhone wouldn't quickly become just as dominant as the iPod.

For years Apple had worried about every potential competitor in the marketplace—RIM, Nokia, Walmart, Amazon, Dell, Microsoft, and various wireless carriers—breaking the iPod's dominance. Instead, the reverse had happened. Every competitor made a run at Apple and failed. Meanwhile, the iPhone made Apple even more dominant. It had tied consumers to the iPod by sucking all their music into iTunes. Now something similar was happening because of iPhone owners' love affair with the app store. Before long, many users had shelled out $50 to $100 in apps, meaning they would have to spend all that money again if they wanted the same applications on Android or another smartphone platform.

But by 2010 it was also clear that Rubin and Android were playing a much more sophisticated game than Apple's previous competitors. To them the hub wasn't the laptop or the desktop computer, but the millions of faceless machines running 24-7 in Google's giant network of server farms—now often referred to as the cloud. Connecting and syncing with a personal computer— the way iTunes was set up—was necessary when devices didn't have wireless capability or when wireless bandwidth was too slow to be useful. But in 2010 neither was true, prompting Rubin and the Android team to ask, Why tether users to one machine when the Wi-Fi and cellular chips inside smartphones are fast enough to let them have access to their content on *any* machine?

Android now wirelessly synced with virtually all mail, contact, and calendar servers—whether stored at Google, Microsoft, or Yahoo!, or at a worker's company. Music and movies could be downloaded from Amazon in addition to the iTunes store. Spotify and Pandora offered music subscription services for small monthly fees. Developers were scrambling to make sure that all of the programs inside the Apple app store could be found inside the Android app store too. As for all that content trapped inside iTunes, Google and the rest of the software industry were writing programs that made it easier and easier to get it out and uploaded to Google—or anywhere.

With many new ways to download and enjoy content on Android devices, the penalty for using a non-Apple device that wouldn't connect to iTunes was diminished. Freed from this control, users were choosing Android devices in droves, and Jobs was desperately worried this trend would accelerate, Apple executives at the time recalled. The monopoly power of iTunes as a content hub had begun to evaporate.

It all exposed an often overlooked component of Jobs's genius: his basic worldview about technology had not changed since he started Apple in 1976 and built the Macintosh in 1984. While most high-tech executives struggled to adapt to a world that was in constant flux, Jobs had never faltered in his belief that consumers would gravitate to the best designed and most beautiful products. He continued to believe that he alone knew what this incredibly subjective thing was. And he continued to believe that the only way to ensure his vision's success was to control the entire user experience—the software, the hardware, and the content users accessed. But Android's rise was now calling all that into question.

* * *

Jobs said he never saw the similarity between his fight with Android and his fight with Bill Gates and Microsoft in the 1980s. But just about everyone else inside and out of Apple did. Android and iPhone were in a platform war, and platform wars tend to be winner-take-all contests. The winner ends up with more than 75 percent of the market share and profits, and the loser ends up scrambling to stay in business.

In the Microsoft/Apple fight, Microsoft won by more widely distributing its software, which created a bigger selection of applications to buy, which attracted more customers. Once customers had spent hundreds of dollars on applications that ran on only one platform, it was much harder to get them to switch. Ultimately, everyone started using computers running Microsoft DOS and then Windows because everyone else was doing it. This wasn't lemminglike behavior but completely rational. Computers were only useful if work performed on one machine could be used on another machine.

This was almost precisely the Android strategy. In 2010 the Android ecosystem was still far from robust. The Android app store was badly organized, and developers had a tough time making money there. Apple's three-year head start had allowed it to sell nearly 60 million iPhones, create a store with more than 200,000 applications, and establish a developer ecosystem that had been paid more than $1 billion over two years. But because any phone manufacturer could make an Android phone, the size of the Android platform was exploding. By the end of 2010 it was as big as the iPhone's. And it seemed like only a matter of time before Google fixed the problems with its app store.

More worrisome to Apple was that Rubin could succeed without having to convince many iPhone customers to switch. The number of people worldwide switching from cell phones to smartphones in the coming years was going to be so enormous that he just needed to focus on that group—not necessarily on iPhone customers—to get a dominant smartphone market share. It seemed unfathomable that Jobs would lose two battles the same way a generation apart. But with so many similarities between the two dogfights, it was hard not to think about it.

There have always been good reasons to believe that the Apple/ Google fight might not play out like Apple versus Microsoft. Developers seem more capable of writing software for two platforms than they were in the 1980s. The platform-switching costs remain much smaller too. Back then PCs cost more than $3,000 and each software title cost more than $50. Now the costs are less than a tenth of those. A new phone with a carrier subsidy costs

$200, and each app costs less than $3 and is often free. Also, third parties—the carriers—continue to have a vested interest in making sure consumers have as many ways to connect to their network, and pay them money, as possible.

But what Google and Apple executives have always understood is that if the battle turns out that way—if somehow their mobile platforms can harmoniously coexist—it will be a historical aberration. Because of the press coverage surrounding the Microsoft antitrust trial fourteen years ago, a huge amount of analysis has been done on how Microsoft built its Windows monopoly in the PC business: if you get enough people using your technology platform, eventually it creates a vortex that forces almost everyone to use it. But these economic forces have not been unique to Microsoft. Every major technology company since then has tried to create the same kind of vortex for its business.

It was, of course, how Jobs had dominated the music-player business with the iPod. It was also how Google in 2004 started to embarrass and challenge Microsoft for dominance in high tech and pushed Yahoo! to the brink of implosion. Google's top-quality search secured the most search traffic. That gave it the best data about user interests. That data made its search advertisements appearing alongside the search results the most effective. That virtuous circle encouraged more search traffic, more data, and even better search ads. No matter how much Microsoft and Yahoo! tried to attract traffic with lower ad rates and improved search results, Google was always able to offer a better deal.

eBay did the same thing to the roughly two dozen other online auction companies, such as OnSale and uBid. By allowing buyers and sellers to easily communicate and rate one another, it built a self-policing community. That fueled a rapid growth in bidders. The more bidders eBay acquired, the more reliable its prices became. The more reliable eBay's prices became, the more new bidders wanted to use it. The more bidders wanted to use eBay, the less they wanted to use competitors' sites. Facebook's social media platform is the most recent example of the power of platform economics. Its superior technology allowed it to offer users better features than competitor MySpace. Better features made Facebook more useful. The more useful it was, the more data users shared. The more data users shared, the more features Facebook could offer. Soon people were joining Facebook just because everyone else was joining Facebook.

As the mobile platform wars go forward, Google's and Apple's ecosystems might be able to coexist long term and generate big profits and innovation for both companies. But given recent history, they will have to fight it out as if it *won't* happen that way. "It's like the battle for the monopolies that the cable guys and the phone guys got thirty to forty years ago," said Jon Rubinstein, the longtime top Apple executive and former CEO of Palm. "This is the next generation of it all. Everyone—Apple, Google, Amazon, and Microsoft—is trying to build their walled garden and control access to content and all that. It's a really big deal." In other words, it's not the kind of thing Apple or Google can afford to be wrong about.

7

The iPad Changes Everything—Again

Jobs's solution to Google's Android-everywhere strategy was simple and audacious: he unveiled the iPad. If Google was going to try to win the mobile-platform war on breadth, Jobs wanted the world to know that he was going to win it on depth. Maybe more people in the world would own Android phones than iPhones. But the people who owned iPhones would also own iPads, iPod Touches, and a slew of other Apple products that all ran the same software, that all connected to the same online store, and that all generated much bigger profits for everyone involved.

Only someone with the self-confidence of Jobs would have the guts to set such a high bar. But then, that was what made him so captivating to watch. All Rubin had to do to expand Android was to get it on more and more machines. Like Gates with Windows, he didn't care which products were hits and which were not as long as in the aggregate the Android platform was growing. For Jobs to make Apple's strategy work—to grow the iOS platform vertically—he needed to hit it out of the park every time. Every new product Apple released needed to be a success, along with every update of its older products. Indeed, when executives inside and outside Apple wondered if Jobs was making the same mistake against Android that he made against Microsoft—if he was keeping his platform too rigid—it seemed that, if anything, Jobs was *increasing* its rigidity. Starting in 2010 Jobs had more and more Apple products assembled with special screws to make it difficult for anyone with typical screwdriver heads to open the cases of his machines. It seemed like a small thing, but to those inside Silicon Valley its symbolism was large: One of Android's pitches to consumers was the flexibility of the software and the devices. Jobs was making it clear that Apple was not interested in customers who were tinkerers.

Minutes after Jobs unveiled the iPad on January 27, 2010, it appeared as if he'd cleared the bar he'd set for Apple by a mile. When he took the stage, he still looked gaunt from his liver transplant nine months earlier; but the presentation was every bit as polished. It was remarkable, really. Many knew Jobs was going to unveil a tablet despite what he had told Walt Mossberg of *The Wall Street Journal* seven years before. "It turns out people want keyboards . . . We look at the tablet and we think it is going to fail," Jobs had said. But he'd clearly reconsidered this. Rumors about Apple making a tablet had been around for months, and the CEO of one of Jobs's publishing partners had actually confirmed its unveiling on television the day before. Yet the iPad was so meticulously designed that people were still surprised.

Jobs took full advantage of the world's shock. He laid out his new invention for the world more slowly than usual, as if he were helping his audience complete a vast jigsaw puzzle. He put up a slide with picture of an iPhone and a Macbook laptop, put a question mark between them, and asked a simple question: "Is there room for a third category of device in the middle? We've pondered this question for years. The bar is pretty high. In order to create a new category of device, it's going to have to be *far* better at doing some key tasks. Better than the laptop. Better than the smartphone . . . Otherwise it has no reason for being."

He then raised and crushed what had become the usual answer to this question: "Some people have thought that's a netbook. The problem is that a netbook isn't better at *anything*. They're slow. They have low-quality displays. And they run clunky, old PC software [Windows]. They're not better than a laptop at anything. They're just cheaper."

Then and only then—after more than two minutes of buildup—did he say what the world was waiting for: "We think we have the answer." With that, a picture of the iPad dropped nicely into place between the iPhone and the Macbook on the slide.

It wasn't just the iPad's looks that had everyone rapt. Many wondered if they were watching the world's greatest entrepreneur make a huge mistake. The tablet computer was the most discredited category of consumer electronics in the world. Entrepreneurs had been trying to build tablet computers since before the invention of the PC. They had tried so many times that the conventional wisdom was that it couldn't be done.

Alan Kay, who is to certain geeks what Neil Armstrong is to the space program, drew up plans for the Dynabook in 1968 and laid out those plans in a 1972 paper titled "A Personal Computer for Children of All Ages." It never got built, though Kay went on to do something arguably even more important. He became one of the inventors of the graphical user interface at Xerox PARC. The first Macintosh and later Microsoft Windows were rooted in Kay's work. Apple prototyped something it called the Bashful in 1983 but never released it. The first tablet to get any consumer traction came from Jeff Hawkins, the entrepreneur behind the PalmPilot in the late 1990s. He built the GRiDPad from Tandy, which was released in 1989. It worked with a stylus, weighed about five pounds, and cost about $2,500. Bookkeepers in the U.S. army used it to fill out electronic forms and keep better track of inventory. It was shortly followed by competitors such as the NCR 3125. But none of the devices did much more than that, and they were just as expensive as a PC. The NCR machine cost $4,700.

GO Corp. took the next whack at tablet computing with the EO in 1993. The company had been founded in 1987 by Jerry Kaplan, an early Lotus Development Corporation executive; Robert Carr, a chief scientist at Ashton-Tate (a top software company); and Kevin Doren, who had, with Kaplan, built one of the first digital music synthesizers. GO Corp. is still well known in Silicon Valley because of the caliber of people it hired and the sophistication of its software at the time. The EO came with a cell phone, a fax machine, a modem, a microphone, a calendar, and a word processor. Users accessed all these functions on a touchscreen using a special pen. Back in the days when few people had laptops and few executives knew how to type, the idea of a portable electronic tablet that users could navigate with a pen seemed exactly what the business world was looking for. GO Corp.'s early employees included Omid Kordestani, Google's first business executive, and Bill Campbell, Apple's vice president of marketing in the 1980s. But persistent funding problems forced GO Corp. to sell to AT&T, which shut it down in 1994.

Apple unveiled the Newton in 1994. This groundbreaking PDA, or personal digital assistant, turned out to be Silicon Valley's Edsel, a one-word explanation for why tablets could never sell. It also became emblematic of Apple's Jobs-less era, when the company was run by a series of increasingly unsuccessful executives—John Sculley, Michael Spindler, and Gil Amelio—until it nearly went into bankruptcy. The Newton was affordable—less than $1,000—but it was marketed as a pocket device and was too heavy. Its battery life was terrible, and its most hyped feature, handwriting recognition, didn't work well. It was, fittingly, one of the first projects Jobs killed when he returned in 1997. By then, if you wanted computing power that was portable, you could buy a laptop. Everything else involved too much compromise. Indeed, the PalmPilot and devices like it became so popular for the next half decade because they didn't try to do too much. They were small, inexpensive, and ran for a long time on AAA batteries. But they were really electronic calendars and address books, not tablet computers.

The most recent effort in tablets had been made by Bill Gates and Microsoft in 2002. Working with most of the companies that made Windows desktops and laptops, it released machines with software that—among other things—allowed you to take notes while recording a speech that would be synchronized with the speaker's recorded voice. Touch a part of your notes with the stylus and the device took you to the proper part of the recording. But the machines were no lighter than a laptop. Their battery life was no better. They weren't cheaper. And they all ran Windows, which, while modified for the tablet, wasn't written originally with tablets in mind. By 2009—even though tablet PCs were still being sold—it felt as if the Amazon Kindle were the only thing available that even resembled a tablet. Amazon had come out with the clunky electronic reader at the end of 2007, and it was increasingly popular. But it wasn't really a tablet. It had a black-and-white screen that was great to read text on. But that's all it effectively did. It displayed graphics and photos badly, and its Internet connection was only useful for downloading books.

All of this made doing a tablet risky for Jobs, especially with Google breathing down his neck. Some wondered if it didn't make it *too* risky. But it also made a tablet the perfect project for Jobs to tackle. He had already reimagined the personal computer, the portable music player, and the cell phone. He made them better and more mainstream—the way Henry Ford had reimagined the automobile.

And Jobs did truly reimagine the tablet with the iPad. It did almost everything a laptop did. In addition, it was a quarter the weight—one pound eight ounces. It had three times the battery life—ten hours. It had a touchscreen like the iPhone and turned on like one too—without booting up. Because it came with a cell phone and Wi-Fi chip, it was always connected to the Internet. Cell phone connections for laptops were typically expensive add-ons. The iPad did all this for $600, when many laptops cost twice that. And there was no learning curve for consumers because it came with almost the same software that was on an iPhone. It ran iPhone apps. For those who didn't want to use its virtual keyboard, it connected flawlessly to physical wireless keyboards. Apple also said it had rewritten its own office software—Pages, Numbers, and Keynote—to take advantage of the touchscreen.

The foundation of Jobs's iPad pitch was counterintuitive. But most don't buy a laptop for the tasks they were originally designed for—heavy office work, such as writing, crafting presentations, or financial analysis with spreadsheets. They use it mostly to communicate via email, text, Twitter, LinkedIn, and Facebook; to browse the Internet; and to consume media such as books, movies, TV shows, music, photos, games, and videos. Jobs said that you could do all this on an iPhone, but the screen was too small to make it comfortable. You could also do it all on a laptop, but the keyboard and the trackpad made it too bulky, and the short battery life often left you tethered to a power outlet. What the world needed was a device in the middle that combined the best of both—something that was "more intimate than a laptop, and so much more capable than a smartphone," he said.

As the father of the Macintosh, Jobs had more credibility than anyone else to reimagine the PC and challenge the conventional wisdom about tablets. But he still spent the first five minutes of his presentation making sure the world understood that he'd assessed that issue from every angle. Then he plopped into the Le Corbusier chair he'd had set up on the stage and, for the next fifteen minutes, as if he were in his living room, showed the world how he read *The New York Times* and *Time* magazine, bought movie tickets, looked at animal pictures on *National Geographic*, sent email, looked through a photo album, listened to the Grateful Dead and Bob Dylan, navigated to a satellite picture of the Eiffel Tower, found a San Francisco sushi restaurant with Google Maps, watched the famous surfing-dog video on YouTube, and watched scenes from the movies *Up* and *Star Trek*. Later he unveiled the iBooks store and showed how it was better and easier to read a book on an iPad than on a Kindle—saying that Amazon had created a fine device but that "Apple was going to stand on their shoulders and go a little further."

Technically, one navigated an iPad the same way as an iPhone, but the difference in user expectations was vast. Jobs and others involved in the unveiling, such as iPhone/iPad boss Scott Forstall, hit this point over and over. Cell phones were always designed to fit in a pocket and be navigated with fingers. But navigating something like the iPad with a screen the size of a laptop's had always required either a stylus or a trackpad/mouse and a keyboard. "If you see something, you just reach out and tap it. It's completely natural. You don't even think about it. You just . . . do," Forstall said.

· · ·

The immediate reaction to the iPad was full of oohs and aahs. *The Economist* famously put a picture on its cover of Jobs in religious garb holding the device. THE BOOK OF JOBS. HOPE, HYPE AND APPLE'S iPAD said the headline. But the reaction to it in the days and months thereafter was, remarkably, tepid. There were widespread gripes about the iPad's lack of a camera, its lack of multitasking, and the images of feminine protection some said its name conjured.

The biggest criticism, however, was the one Jobs thought he had answered in his presentation: What do I need it for? It looked like an iPhone, only four times bigger. Competitors such as Schmidt, amid his standard "I won't comment on a competitor's products," said snidely, "You might want to tell me the difference between a large phone and a tablet." Gates said, "I still think some mixture of voice, the pen, and a real keyboard will be the mainstream. It's a nice reader, but there's nothing on the iPad I look at and say, 'Oh, I wish Microsoft had done it.'" He said he *had* felt that way with the iPhone. It wasn't just competitors who trashed the iPad. *Business Insider,* a well-read online news site, ran a commentary that said, "Apple's iPad Is This Decade's Newton." *MacRumors*, another well-read online news site, pointed out that the iPad TV commercials bore a striking resemblance to those for the Newton in 1994.

With so much at stake in his battle with Google, Jobs was furious at the initial reception the iPad got. The night after the presentation he told Isaacson, "I got about eight hundred email messages in the last twenty-four hours. Most of them are complaining. There's no USB cord. There's no this or no that. Some of them are like 'Fuck you.' How can you do that? I usually don't write people back, but I replied, 'Your parents would be so proud of how you turned out.' And some don't like the iPad name and on and on. I kind of got depressed today. It knocks you back a bit."

But the skeptical public reaction had a simple explanation. No one had ever seen a device like the iPad before, and the first ones would not go on sale for two months. Consumers knew instinctively that they needed a phone and a laptop because they had been around for a long time. The only tablets they had ever seen were devices they didn't want. Even those who worked on the iPad at Apple were dubious about it at first. "I remember when I first saw it, I thought it was a rock fetch [a pointless endeavor], to tell the truth," said Jeremy Wyld, an Apple engineer who worked on the software for it and the iPhone. "I thought, 'This thing is ridiculous.'" Wyld wasn't just shooting his mouth off. He was one of the earliest engineers on the Newton in the 1990s, before leaving Apple for engineering jobs at Excite and Pixo. When he looked at the first iPad, all he saw was a bigger iPhone that now no longer fit in your pocket. "I saw that when we made things bigger, people didn't like it."

When Wyld played with one of the prototypes, the experience instantly changed his mind, however. "They gave me one to play with, and I started checking email or something . . . and right then I said, 'Now I get it. I am sick and tired of looking at a laptop to read my email in the morning. This is so much more personable than a laptop. A laptop is very cold. You get this much warmer feeling working with email on an iPad with your cup of coffee.'"

What Wyld discovered was that while the iPad looks like an overgrown iPhone because it runs the same software and has a touchscreen, it was really a new kind of laptop. You'd never give up a smartphone to own an iPad, but you would certainly dump your laptop to own one. That it looked like a large iPhone was initially something to be criticized. It turned out that the bigger screen, as simple a tweak as this was, was exactly what made it such a new and powerful device.

The importance of screen size seemed so obvious to Joe Hewitt—who had written the Facebook iPhone app in 2007 and had helped conceive and build the Firefox Internet browser in 2002—that the day after the iPad's unveiling he wrote a nine-hundred-word blog post saying the iPad was the most important thing Apple had ever done. The year before, Hewitt had been fiercely critical of Apple for its restrictive app store policies. But his years of developing software for many different devices and platforms told him that the iPad had solved a fundamental problem.

"I spent a year and a half attempting to reduce a massive, complex social-networking website into a handheld, touchscreen form factor," he said of the challenge of making Facebook work on the iPhone.

My goal was initially just to make a mobile companion for the Facebook.com mother ship. But once I got comfortable with the platform, I became convinced it was possible to create a version of Facebook that was actually better than the website! Of all the platforms I've developed on in my career, from the desktop to the web, the iPhone OS gave me the greatest sense of empowerment and had the highest ceiling for raising the art of UI design.

Except there was one thing keeping me from reaching that ceiling: the screen was too small . . . It needed to support more than one column of information at a time. I couldn't fit enough tools on the screen to support any kind of advanced creative work. Photos were too small to show off to my farsighted parents. The web required too much panning and zooming to enjoy reading. Beyond just Facebook, most of the apps I used most on my iPhone also suffered from these limitations, like Google Reader, Instapaper, and all image, video, and text-editing tools. The bottom line is, many apps which were cute toys on iPhone can become full-featured power tools on the iPad, making you forget about their desktop/laptop predecessors. We just have to invent them.

. . .

Unlike the iPhone, which got developed faster than it should have been, the iPad's journey through Apple's hardware, software, and design teams was long. Jobs told Isaacson that it started in 2002 at a birthday dinner for the spouse of a friend. The spouse was one of the engineers on Microsoft's just-released tablet software, and he boasted about how the device was going to change the world. It angered Gates, who was there, because he worried the engineer was giving away company secrets. And it angered Jobs because he wasn't about to let anyone from Microsoft show him up.

"This guy badgered me about how Microsoft was going to completely change the world with this tablet PC software and eliminate all notebook computers and that Apple ought to license his Microsoft software," Jobs told Isaacson. "But he was doing the device all wrong. It had a stylus. As soon as you have a stylus, you're dead. This dinner was like the tenth time he talked to me about it, and I was so sick of it that I came home and said, 'Fuck this, let's show him what a tablet can really be.'"

The man Jobs turned to, Tim Bucher, was someone he'd known for years, but who'd just joined Apple the previous year to run Apple's Macintosh hardware division. He had a reputation as a creative thinker and master tinkerer. He'd already run engineering for WebTV for three years and been the vice president in charge of consumer products at Microsoft after it bought WebTV in 1998. Before joining Apple he'd started his own successful online consumer storage company. He made an impression at Apple immediately. One day in a meeting with Jobs he pulled out a bunch of parts he'd been carrying around in a shopping bag and assembled a prototype of a Mac mini before Jobs's eyes. He'd gotten chief designer Jony Ive to design the case and, using spare laptop parts, built the innards in his garage. He'd carried all this around with him for weeks until the right moment to show Jobs presented itself.

After Jobs told Bucher to investigate building a tablet, he quickly found himself buying dozens of Windows-based tablets made by various PC manufacturers and spending hours in Ive's design studio with Ive and Jobs critiquing them. "His main mantra was 'I want to read the newspaper,' and he would always use the restroom as an example. He would never say, 'I want to show Bill Gates.' It was more, 'This is a piece of shit. We can do so much better. Why did they do this? Why did they do that? Let's make something completely different from the ground up.'"

Perversely, the work that seemed technically hardest—building the multitouch display that is now on every tablet and smartphone—got the furthest, while seemingly the most straightforward work—figuring out a way to build the rest of the device—quickly ran aground.

Part of what gave the multitouch work traction was that one of the engineers on the project, Josh Strickon, had built a crude multitouch display for his MIT master's thesis. And by 2003 he had, with Steve Hotelling and Brian Huppi, who both are still at Apple, figured out a way to show off a much more refined version of the technology to Fadell. Visually it was messy looking. It used the screen of one of the tablet prototypes. But the chips that would tell the screen to respond to finger inputs sat on a separate two-by-two-foot circuit board that was hardwired to the screen. To power all that and give the gestures something to navigate, it all needed to be connected via USB cables to a powerful Mac Pro desktop computer. To enable all that to be seen by a crowd in a conference room, the Mac Pro had to be connected to a projector. The point of the demonstration was to position the multitouch team—known then only as the Q79 group—to get $2 million in Apple funding to turn the big circuit board into a single chip that could go inside a device.

The demo went well. They showed off the virtual keyboard and the pinch and spread features that are so strongly associated with the technology today and got Fadell's approval. The problem was that the tablet hardware was unusable. The energy-efficient ARM processors that would eventually drive the iPhone and the iPad were not yet powerful enough to run software that would appeal to consumers. The tablet needed a hard drive, which took up too much room in the case because flash storage was still too expensive in the capacities they needed. What that left was a machine without a keyboard that was not much lighter, cheaper, or better powered than a laptop.

Jobs had hoped to show Gates that he could build a better tablet—one that didn't need a stylus. But he discovered Gates's problem had less to do with a lack of imagination and more to do with the idea's being ahead of the technology necessary to make it a reality. "We had this idea for a device and we had the interface [multitouch] and all that, but there wasn't a viable platform," Strickon said. Indeed, it seemed so clear to him that the project would go nowhere that he left Apple for a mobile marketing start-up and then an engineering post at *The New York Times*. He wasn't wrong. Apple shelved the project for a year before Jobs revived it to build the iPhone.

Only after the iPhone came out in 2007 did Jobs start to reconsider a tablet. Chief designer Jony Ive had been exploring netbook designs. He was stuck on how to build a machine that small with a keyboard hinge that was both good-looking and functional. According to Isaacson's account, Ive asked Jobs if they could just do away with the hinge and put the keyboard on the screen as they had done with the iPhone, and quickly Jobs's dalliance with netbooks turned into Apple's tablet revival.

But it wasn't until the fall of 2009—months before unveiling—that Apple settled on what kind of product the iPad would be. Apple was going to build a tablet no matter what. Jobs had been trying to build one since 2003, and he had been thinking about building one since the 1980s, according to videos of him then. Also, the technology was finally ready: there were finally enough bandwidth, powerful enough processors, and strong enough batteries to make a tablet useful. Multitouch had proved to be hugely popular in the iPhone, so the idea of using a virtual screen to write emails or type in web addresses was no longer foreign. And because Apple was selling so many iPhones, it had driven the price of components for a tablet down to affordable levels.

The question that remained unanswered when Jobs returned to Apple from liver transplant surgery in the summer of 2009 was what kind of device the tablet would be. Would it be just an iPhone with a bigger screen or would it have its own set of apps that set it apart? Initially Jobs was leaning toward its being just a bigger iPhone. He thought of it purely as a consumption device, a confidant said. You wouldn't be able to edit documents or spreadsheets on it. And he was leery of having it become an e-book reader like the Kindle, which had been out for nearly two years. He thought people were reading less and less anyway, and that those who still did read books would prefer the physical over the electronic versions.

Eddy Cue, Apple's iTunes boss, and Phil Schiller, Apple's head of global marketing, were among those who made it their mission to help Jobs clarify his point of view. Schiller pushed Jobs to modify his view of what a "consumption device" really meant. If someone sent a document or a spreadsheet or a PowerPoint presentation, iPad users needed to be able to edit it. Cue, meanwhile, made it his mission to get Jobs to rethink his view about e-books. Amazon's Kindle was getting much more traction than they expected. An estimated 1.5 million had been sold by mid-2009. And readers were downloading e-books at an astonishing rate.

Cue was keenly aware of the competitive threat this posed. For two years Apple had been increasingly competitive with iTunes in music, movie, and TV show downloads. If Apple passed entirely on selling e-books or e-magazines, that would give Amazon a huge competitive boost. "The fact is that if we didn't have those book agreements, there would be a lot of people saying, 'Oh, well, this is not a competitor to the Kindle.' We needed the publishing agreements so people could legitimately say, 'I can get something better than a Kindle if I buy an iPad,'" a Jobs confidant told me.

In testimony during the Department of Justice's antitrust trial against Apple in June 2013, Cue explained the evolution of the e-books on the iPad this way: "When I got my first chance to touch the iPad, I became completely convinced that this was a huge opportunity for us to build the best e-reader that the market had ever seen. And so I went to Steve and told him why I thought [the iPad] was going to be a great device for e-books . . . and after some discussions he came back and said, you know, I think you're right. I think this is great, and then he started coming up with ideas himself about what he wanted to do with it and how it would be even better as a reader and store."

Cue said the "page curls" in the iBooks app, which show up when you flip an iBook's page, was Jobs's idea. It also was Jobs's idea to pick *Winnie-the-Pooh* as the freebie book that came with every iBooks app. He thought it best showed off iBooks's capabilities. "It had beautiful color drawings that had never been seen before in a digital book," Cue said.

The problem, Cue said, was that this conversation happened in November 2009. "We were launching the iPad in January. And so Steve said, 'you can go do this, but you've got to get it done by January . . . I want to be able to demo it onstage.' And so that was the sort of challenge presented to me."

The challenge had special meaning for Cue. "Steve was near the end of his life when we were launching the iPad, and he was really proud of it," he said. "I wanted to be able to get that done in time for [the event] because it was really important to him . . . I like getting my work done and I pride myself on being successful, but this had extra meaning to me."

When the first iPads went on sale in early April 2010, it became clear that the initial tepid public reaction to the device had been misleading. Apple sold 450,000 in the first week, 1 million in the first month, and 19 million in the first year. It took Apple six months to catch up with how fast consumers were buying them, and by 2011 the iPad had overtaken the DVD player to become the hottest-selling consumer electronics device of all time.

8

"Mr. Quinn, Please, Don't Make Me Sanction You."

For many, the climax of the Apple/Google fight took place during the summer of 2012. After nearly three years of legal maneuvering, Apple got to face one of the antagonists in a court of law. It wasn't Google, but just as good a target—Samsung Electronics of South Korea. An actual lawsuit against Google would have been hard to win. Google wasn't actually making and selling Android phones, and it was giving Android away for free. But by then Samsung was the largest maker of Android phones and tablets. It was the iPhone's and the iPad's biggest challengers for market share. Apple had sued three Android phone makers in courts in every industrialized country in the world since 2010. But none of the cases had gotten as far as the Samsung suit, which was to be tried in front of a jury in San Jose Federal Court.

Jobs was no longer alive to witness the proceedings. He died in October 2011. But Apple's position was just as forceful. In his opening statement at the trial Harold McElhinny, one of Apple's attorneys, sounded almost parental as he laid out Samsung's sins. Apple had spent hundreds of millions to develop the iPhone and the iPad. Its employees had put their hearts and souls into building those devices. And if the iPhone, especially, had not succeeded, Apple's future as a company would have been in doubt, he said. Despite this, "Samsung did not simply copy the outward appearance of Apple's phone and tablet. Samsung copied every detail . . . This was not accidental. Samsung's copying was intentional,"

McElhinny said. "Samsung's sales have taken sales away from Apple, and they have generated more than two billion dollars' worth of profit for Samsung—profit, as the evidence will show, that they made using our [Apple's] intellectual property."

Business trials can be painfully dull. This one was anything but. Some of the specific legal issues were arcane. But everyone in the world understands you aren't supposed to copy someone else's work without permission. And because both companies had the resources to hire the best trial lawyers in the country for the case, both sides were primed to forcefully debate every issue no matter how big or small. Both sides had close to a dozen lawyers just in the courtroom, and hundreds more working on the case. Depositions and exhibits for each witness typically filled half a dozen file boxes. At about five feet tall by five feet wide when stacked, they looked like some jerry-rigged partition for a student apartment as a legal associate wheeled them into court on a hand truck each morning at seven.

Debate got so heated at the beginning of the trial that Judge Lucy Koh threatened to sanction John Quinn, whose firm, Quinn Emanuel Urquhart & Sullivan, represented Samsung. Quinn wanted to show the jury evidence that Apple had just as "slavishly copied" Sony in designing the iPhone as Samsung had "slavishly copied" the iPhone. The point Quinn wanted to make, as laid out in Samsung's pretrial brief, was that "Samsung has used the very same public domain design concepts that Apple borrowed from other competitors, including Sony, to develop the iPhone." Judge Koh had excluded the evidence because it had been introduced too late in the discovery process. Quinn refused to back down.

QUINN: May I address the issue of Slides Eleven to Nineteen, which I was prepared to argue—

KOH: No. We have had three reconsiderations on that, okay? You've made your record. I've ruled. We need to go forward.

QUINN: Your Honor, I beg the court.

KOH: Samsung has had ten motions for reconsideration. I'm doing, as quickly as I can, rulings to give your team as much advanced notice for your preparation of witnesses and exhibits.

QUINN: Your Honor, I've been practicing thirty-six years. I've never begged the court like I'm begging the court now to hear argument on this issue. This relates to a central issue that has been in the case from the very beginning. They [Apple] say in their papers they filed last night that we didn't disclose it in the contention interrogatories. Your Honor, there is no interrogatory that required us to disclose that, and we did. All of that was served—all those images in those slides were served in February—

KOH: I've given you—

QUINN:—in the preliminary injunction—

KOH:—an additional opportunity to brief this issue yesterday, okay? I reviewed what you filed yesterday. I heard argument on this yesterday.

QUINN: All right. Your Honor, what's the point—

KOH: I've given you three motions for reconsideration.

QUINN:—of having the trial? What's the point? They want to create the completely false impression, Your Honor, that we came up with this design after January of 2007 [when the iPhone was unveiled], and, Your Honor, what this suggests, what they're seeking is to exclude indisputable evidence that we had that design patent in 2006 [before the iPhone was unveiled]. And we came out with that product in February of 2007.

KOH: Mr. Quinn, please. Please. We've done three reconsiderations on this and we need to move forward. We have a jury waiting. You've made your record. You've made your record for appeal. Okay?

QUINN: All right. Can I ask the court for some explanation, Your Honor? There is no interrogatory that required

it. We did disclose it in the preliminary injunction papers. We gave them [Apple] the documents—

KOH: Mr. Quinn, please, don't make me sanction you.
Please. Please.

QUINN: So I won't get—

KOH: You've had three reconsiderations motions. You've
had at least two, if not three, if not four opportunities
to brief this. Okay? Please, take a seat.

The standoff didn't end there. Later in the day Samsung
decided that even if the jury wasn't allowed to see the evidence,
the rest of the world could. It issued a press release with all the
excluded documents. Apple's McElhinny accused Samsung of
trying to "pollute the jury," adding, "I'm not sure exactly what the
right remedy or penalty is. But this is contempt of court. I've just
never seen anything as intentional as this in my entire career."
Koh demanded Quinn file an affidavit of explanation. She polled
each juror individually to make sure they had not seen any stories
about the case. Ultimately the jockeying for position got so fierce,
supported by dozens of legal motions filed every night in advance
of the next day's arguments, that Koh insisted that all motions be
argued in front of the jury and count against each side's argument
time.

Apple even allowed three of its top executives to testify. Christopher Stringer, one of Apple's top industrial designers, Phil
Schiller, who was in charge of Apple's worldwide marketing, and
Scott Forstall, who was in charge of software in iPhones and iPads,
all spent a day on the witness stand. Stringer, looking every bit the
artist with shoulder-length hair and wearing a white linen suit,
talked about the whimsical process he and the fifteen-member
design team used to create beautiful products: "There is a table in
the kitchen. It's where we're comfortable. It's where we are most
familial. We throw ideas around and we—it's a brutally honest
circle of debate. We're just very comfortable there. That's where
the ideas happen."

Phil Schiller talked about the organization, coordination, and discipline required to launch a product such as the iPhone or the iPad. He said the iPad cost more to market in the United States during its first year than the iPhone. In 2008, Apple spent $97.5 million on iPhone ads in the United States, compared with the $149.5 million it spent on the iPad in 2010.

Scott Forstall talked about what it had taken to recruit his team and the incredible stress he had put them under to deliver products on time. He also explained how some of Apple's signature software flourishes were conceived, such as the "slide to unlock" feature when iPhone and iPad are turned on, the tap-to-zoom feature, which he said he invented himself, and the rubberband bounce that occurs whenever the end of a list or a page has been reached. He wore a blue suit to court, an outfit few had ever seen him in. When asked about it by an aide as he walked out of court for lunch, he said, "I've worn it twice. Once to the White House. Now here."

All of them made the same point: they were shocked, offended, and angry when they first saw Samsung's Android phones and tablets. Schiller said he was worried that consumers would confuse their devices and said he eventually came to believe that was indeed happening. Stringer was particularly emotional. "We'd been ripped off. It was plain to see," Stringer said when asked how he reacted to seeing Samsung's Android phones for the first time. "It's a huge leap of imagination to come up with something entirely new [such as the iPhone]. It's a process by which you have to dismiss everything you know . . . because if you pay attention to the competition, you end up following. And that's not what we do. We wanted to create originality. It's a very difficult process. It takes a huge amount of time and resources and conviction to do so. So we were offended [by what Samsung had done]."

Quinn and Samsung's other lawyers tried to establish that Apple's case was frivolous. They said that the inventions Apple claimed Samsung copied either had invalid patents or weren't patentable at all because they were obvious. You can't patent shapes and designs that are required for something to function. You can't, for example, patent that a phone is a rectangle, with a speaker at the top and a microphone at the bottom. They pointed out that while Samsung's phones were similar to the iPhone in that they all had touchscreens and were about the same shape, the Samsung phones also demonstrated that Apple had not invented the touchscreen.

The lawyers showed the obvious differences in the devices that were easy for anyone to see—such as where the buttons were placed, and what users saw when they turned the phone on. During his cross-examination of the three Apple witnesses, Samsung attorney Charles Verhoeven took pains to get each of them—particularly Stringer—to acknowledge that Samsung phones have a different home screen that shows up when the phone is turned on, and that Samsung phones had four virtual buttons to navigate the software on the phone whereas the iPhone has one physical button.

VERHOEVEN: Do you remember, yes or no, when you looked at the Samsung phones to form the opinion and the testimony that you gave before the jury, whether they had four soft buttons at the bottom?

STRINGER: I have seen many Samsung phones. I do not remember the exact details of software buttons.

VERHOEVEN: So you don't remember whether they had buttons on the bottom?

STRINGER: Like I said, I've seen many Samsung phones. I do not know that they're all the same in terms of their button arrangements at the bottom.

VERHOEVEN: Have you ever seen any Samsung phones that have four soft buttons at the bottom?

STRINGER: I would like you to show me the phone. This could be a trick question. I don't know.

VERHOEVEN: I'm just asking you, have you ever seen a Samsung phone that had four soft buttons at the bottom?

STRINGER: If you showed me the phone, I could deter-
mine that there are four soft buttons.

VERHOEVEN: That's not my question, sir. My question is,
have you seen a Samsung phone that had four soft
buttons at the bottom?

STRINGER: I cannot recall if it's three or four. I cannot
recall.

VERHOEVEN: Have you seen any phone, any smartphone,
that had four soft buttons at the bottom?

STRINGER: Quite possibly.

VERHOEVEN: Did you think they were beautiful?

STRINGER: Clearly they did not stick in my mind.

VERHOEVEN: Now, you testified about buttons and how
sometimes you might do fifty different models of a
button (as part of the design process). Do you remember that?

STRINGER: That's correct.

VERHOEVEN: How many models did you do of the home
button?

STRINGER: I could not give you an exact number, but I'm
sure there were many.

VERHOEVEN: Over ten?

STRINGER: Very likely.

VERHOEVEN: Over a hundred?

STRINGER: Maybe not.

VERHOEVEN: What's your best estimate?

STRINGER: I will not estimate because I do not know.

VERHOEVEN: Did you work on the different models of
the home button?

STRINGER: Yes.

VERHOEVEN: And why were there so many models of the
home button done?

STRINGER: To get it exactly right.

VERHOEVEN: Because small details matter, right?

STRINGER: Absolutely.

The case was riveting not just because the plaintiff was Apple suing to protect the iPhone and the iPad but also because taking anything to trial was an incredibly un-Apple thing to do. Corporations, in general, avoid trials. They are public venues where all testimony is given on the record, under oath, and subject to cross-examination. Only about 3 percent of all patent-infringement cases go to trial. And Apple is one of the most secretive, controlling companies in the world. Juries are unpredictable in any legal situation, and they tend to be particularly unpredictable about business and technology issues. The press coverage generated by courtroom disputes is typically not good for either company's employee morale or focus. And taking a corporate dispute to trial costs tens of millions of dollars in legal fees.

Samsung looked as if it had a powerful defense, but the jury didn't agree. Three weeks after the trial started, the jury of seven men and two women got to deliberate. Koh's jury instructions took two hours, and the jury form was 109 pages long. But twenty-two hours later—a remarkably short time for such a complex case—it held Samsung liable for virtually all the accusations Apple had leveled. It rejected Samsung's countersuit against Apple. And it ordered Samsung to pay Apple more than $1 billion.

. . .

We are all taught in school that patents are one of the foundations of America's innovation economy—that they are hard to get, ironclad, and straightforward to adjudicate. The stories about how a couple of smart kids with brains, drive, and guts build a company that changes the world for the better are endlessly compelling. The stories of people who steal from them are as painful to hear as those of bullies on the playground. Apple was once one of these young, start-up companies, and throughout Jobs's attack on Android he shrewdly wrapped himself and Apple in a cloak of moral outrage. After his death, that outrage became the foundation of everything Apple did and said leading up to, during, and after the Samsung trial. CEO Tim Cook laid it out in the following memo to employees in the hours after the Samsung verdict:

> Today was an important day for Apple and for innovators everywhere. We chose legal action very reluctantly and only after repeatedly asking Samsung to stop copying our work. For us this lawsuit has always been about something much more important than patents or money. It's about values. We value originality and innovation and pour our lives into making the best products on earth. And we do this to delight our customers, not for competitors to flagrantly copy. We owe a debt of gratitude to the jury who invested their time in listening to our story. We were thrilled to finally have the opportunity to tell it. The mountain of evidence presented during the trial showed that Samsung's copying went far deeper than we knew. The jury has now spoken. We applaud them for finding Samsung's behavior willful and for sending a loud and clear message that stealing isn't right. I am very proud of the work that each of you do. Today, values have won and I hope the whole world listens.

It was brilliant rhetoric. Jobs had been dead nine months, but it felt as if he had written the note himself. The public bought it. The hours and days following the verdict became a public relations bonanza for Apple. Media worldwide wrote breathlessly about the case, wondering how Samsung and Google could possibly recover from it. Samsung's stock fell more than 6 percent in the weeks after the verdict. Apple's already buoyant stock price rose 6 percent. By the middle of September—days before it unveiled the iPhone 5—Apple's stock price had hit an all-time high that made the company worth $656 billion—the biggest market capitalization ever recorded by a U.S. corporation.

In truth there was precious little principle driving Apple's lawsuit. It wanted to win, and everything it did was driven by the tactics and strategy necessary to achieve that goal, according to those who worked on the case. But for all of Apple's rhetoric that's hardly surprising. Most patent lawsuits work this way. Going after Samsung in court was just another way for Jobs and his successors to attack Android. Samsung's Android phones and tablets were closing the market-share gap between them and the iPhone and the iPad. The likelihood that Apple and Google were in a winner-take-all platform war was high. Apple thought a nasty, protracted lawsuit might slow Samsung's and Android's progress.

In fact, the legal assault on Samsung and Android was a marvel of Jobs's mercenary thinking, according to one of the attorneys involved in the case. It wasn't just that Apple had sued a member of the Android community in virtually every industrialized country in the world. Apple effectively created one of the largest patent law firms in the world to do it. It kept its in-house legal staff small. But by the time of the Samsung trial, its four outside law firms had roughly three hundred attorneys worldwide working on the case nearly full-time. The attorney estimated the fees to come to about $200 million a year. As of 2012 Apple had about fifty lawsuits going against Samsung alone in ten different countries.

And while Apple stoked the perception that it was taking a big risk standing up to Samsung in public, executives knew Apple wasn't taking a big risk at all. For a company with more than $100 billion in the bank, the legal fees were a rounding error. It had home-field advantage. San Jose Federal Court is ten miles away from Apple headquarters and five thousand miles from Samsung's. For the three weeks of testimony in August 2012 that the trial took up, media worldwide would be filled with Apple executives' testimony accusing Samsung of copying their work and hurting their company. That, no doubt, would help sell more iPads and iPhones. Apple believed that even if it lost, it would win. Legally, it would be on no different ground than before the trial, but it would have sent a message to competitors that Apple would stop at nothing— including a dreaded jury trial—to bludgeon those who would challenge it in the marketplace.

It's cynical, perhaps, to look at Silicon Valley and the world-changing innovation that bursts out of companies there this way. But in practice, you can't be a successful entrepreneur without lawyers to help protect your ideas. And your attorneys not only need to play defense by drafting hard-to-challenge patent applications but also to game the patent system aggressively to succeed—to play offense, if you will. Despite conventional wisdom about patents, almost any invention can get one with enough lawyering. Any patent can be challenged in court, and patents often are. With the exception of drug patents—when the patent is for a new and distinct molecule—patent fights typically drag on for years. When they are finally resolved, the winner is often not the true inventor, but the litigant with the biggest bankroll for legal fees.

This is especially true in the software industry today, where, unlike in the drug industry, no one single patent can offer effective protection. Now, when patent attorneys talk to companies about their intellectual property, they divide the pile in two. There's the pile with the true inventions that the company is proud of. Then there is the bigger pile—prior inventions supplemented with minor or obvious ideas recast to look important by lawyers—that the company tries to patent.

These discussions are not just about how to keep predators away, but how to prey on competitors. Entrepreneurs, executives, and lawyers look at patents the same way the United States and former Soviet Union waged the Cold War: There are allies and enemies. Both sides are in an arms race. They want to stop building weapons, but they don't trust one another enough to do that. Both worry that if one side gets an edge, that side will attack. So, oddly, the sides seek safety in parity, despite its enormous cost.

Few understood this dynamic better than Jobs. He'd tried to protect the ideas behind the Macintosh from being copied in the early 1980s. He got Gates to agree not to make similar software until a year after the Macintosh shipped in January 1983. The biggest immediate problem with this deal was that the Mac didn't ship until a year later, and the deal made no provision for that kind of delay. Despite Jobs's fury, Gates had every right to tell the world about the system that became Windows at the end of 1983. The longer-term problem was that later, when Apple sued, claiming Microsoft had violated copyright law by ripping off the look and feel of the Macintosh, the courts did not agree. Despite more than a decade of legal fights, the courts said copyright law offered little protection for software in which the code itself wasn't plagiarized. Jobs had no other recourse then, however. In the early days of the software industry, patent protection was not available for software code.

Echoing what a number of Apple executives have said to me, one of them, who would not give his name, said, "Steve was very colored by the feeling that his company had been the first to innovate in the space [making PCs more user-friendly] . . . and that when Apple tried to stop [Microsoft from ripping it off], it had not been successful. And so his view about patents was 'We don't have patents to make money on them. We don't have patents to trade them. We have patents to protect the innovation and the investment in innovation of the company.' And for him that really got reduced to a very simple proposition, which is that, if you have patents, you can tell someone to stop using your technology and sue them if they don't stop."

• • •

Nothing illustrates Jobs's obsession with patents as weapons better than his comments about them during the first iPhone launch in 2007 and the private meetings he had surrounding them in 2006. In the fall of 2006, as Apple's engineers were scrambling to ready the iPhone for its January unveiling, the topic of what technologies Apple should patent in the iPhone came up at one of Jobs's weekly senior-management meetings. It was a short discussion. Before anyone could begin to ponder the question, Jobs answered it completely and definitively: "We are going to patent it all."

The ripple effects inside Apple were immediate. Soon, Apple's

engineers were asked to participate in monthly "invention disclo-
sure sessions." One day, a group of software engineers met with
three patent lawyers, according to *The New York Times*. The first
engineer discussed a piece of software that studied users' prefer-
ences as they browsed the web. "That's a patent," a lawyer said,
scribbling notes. Another engineer described a slight modifica-
tion to a popular application. "That's a patent," the lawyer said.
Another engineer mentioned that his team had streamlined some
software. "That's another one," the lawyer said.

The aggressive filing procedures were designed not just with
maximum protection in mind, but maximum stealth. Patent filings are public, and Apple's competitors are always on the look-
out for them as a way of divining what the company is going to
do next. So Jobs would file them in bunches. That way the public
saw a slew of ideas all seeming to contradict one another, said
Andy Grignon, the early iPhone engineer. Grignon said his patent on one of the early iPhone dialers—it turned the iPod click
wheel into a rotary phone dialer—was conceived in early 2005, but
it wasn't filed until late 2006. That was not only more than a year
after conception but nearly a year after Apple had decided not to
use the invention in the iPhone at all. "We basically tried to patent
everything," an Apple attorney said. "And we tried to patent it as
many different ways as we could, even the stuff that we weren't
one hundred percent sure would go in a product," because it would
prevent another company from trying to patent an idea that
Apple had thought of first.

Jobs was clever when he talked about these issues. Seven and
a half minutes into the first iPhone presentation in January 2007,
he introduced the iPhone's touchscreen like this: "We have invented a new technology called multitouch, which is phenomenal.
It works like magic. You don't need a stylus. It's far more accurate
than any touch display that's ever been shipped. It ignores unin-
tended touches. It's supersmart. You can do multifinger gestures on
it. And, boy, have we patented it."

It was a great laugh line; but Jobs had much more tactical reasons in mind. Jobs knew that defending patents is as much about bluster as about the law. Apple was unveiling a product in an industry—cell phones—that was jammed with big, well-financed companies sitting atop enormous patent portfolios of their own. Nokia was the largest cell phone maker in the world. RIM was the leading smartphone maker for businesses. And Motorola had invented the modern cell phone in 1973. If the iPhone was successful, they and others in the cell phone business would likely want to sue Apple for patent violations as a way of slowing the iPhone's rise. Jobs wanted to make sure they thought twice about that, according to Nancy Heinen, who was Apple's chief counsel until 2006.

Jobs hadn't invented multitouch, and everyone inside Apple knew it, but he'd certainly improved it by sticking it in an iPhone and adding other innovations, and he wanted those innovations protected. So he was following the centuries-old game of chicken: make your enemies worry that you are crazy enough not to swerve in hopes that they don't even bother to challenge you.

"Remember, [Jobs] was the best marketer on the planet," Heinen said. He didn't have to have invented multitouch as much as convince the cell phone industry that he had the money and the will to defend that assertion in court for a long time. "So he was sending a message . . . I've a got a sledgehammer, and I am going to use it anytime you come too close," she said. "It's a business strategy. There were true innovations in the iPhone, but we were not first by a long shot into this area. So if you're not the first in, you have to be robust in covering every possible invention or feature or little thing because it's a crowded environment. You don't know what is going to survive [patent-office and legal challenges], and you don't know what other things are going to be coming out from competitors in the space."

. . .

The Apple-Samsung verdict produced a stream of hand wringing from lawyers, entrepreneurs, and executives, who accused Apple of recklessly twisting the legal process to their advantage. America's innovation economy could not survive long term in the face of such bullying, they said. The problem was that advances in technology were happening so fast, especially in software, that they had outstripped the U.S. patent office's ability to read, analyze, and hand down credible patents.

There is some truth to this. The number of patent applications has been steadily on the rise. In 2000 the U.S. Patent and Trademark Office (USPTO) received 315,000 applications; in 2010, 520,000; and in 2012 it processed 577,000 applications. And while the backlog of unprocessed patent applications fell in 2013, it was after at least a decade of steady increases. The agency hadn't hired enough examiners to keep pace with the increased workload. By the time of the Samsung verdict, the typical wait time for a patent decision had grown from 25 months in 2000 to 32.4 months in 2012, and the patent backlog had ballooned from 158,000 in 2000 to more than 600,000 in 2012.

Also, the rules that enable software to get a patent are far squishier than the rules governing what merits a patent on a drug. With a drug you have to actually create a new molecule. With software you can get a patent simply for coming up with a new way of doing something even if there are many different ways to write the software to accomplish that. One of the most famous and controversial examples of this is the "Buy now with 1-Click" button on Amazon.com. Amazon has a patent on that, meaning any other website that wants to let customers buy with one click has to pay Amazon a license fee.

A patent for 1-Click, known as the "method and system for placing a purchase order via a communications network," was issued to Amazon in 1999. The company now has licensees worldwide, including Apple, which licensed the 1-Click method in 2000 for use in its online store and then later for iTunes. The patent has even withstood court challenges. In 2006 it was challenged by an Auckland, New Zealand, patent enthusiast and actor, who produced prior art filed by a company called DigiCash a year before Amazon's patent. The actor, Peter Calveley, told reporters

at the time that he challenged the patent "because he was bored."
The USPTO reexamined Amazon's claim, Amazon amended it,
and the USPTO regranted the patent in 2010.

There is something slightly misleading about all the howling,
however. The rhetorical premise behind it is that we are living in
unprecedented times. That's false. If you spend enough time talking to patent historians and lawyers, you discover long, drawn-out
patent fights over new and important technologies have been remarkably common since the USPTO was established in 1871.

We celebrate entrepreneurs in history textbooks, and that is a
good thing. But the distillation necessary to make these tomes
palatable—and to establish entrepreneurs as heroes—often leaves
out the scheming, conniving, and hard work of getting this recognition. Virtually all of these entrepreneurs ended up in history
books not just because they invented something but because
they were able to defend it in court better than competitors.

Alexander Graham Bell and Elisha Gray fought for a decade
over who had the right to call himself the inventor of the telephone. The title is still controversial among telephone-history
enthusiasts. Bell and Gray submitted their patents to the USPTO
on the same day—but Bell's was the fifth patent application of
the day and Gray's was the thirty-ninth. The USPTO ignored the
fact that Gray's patent was a kind that required Bell's application
be put on hold until the two patents could be compared. Despite
the nearly six hundred lawsuits filed because of the oversight,
courts consistently sided with Bell.

The Wright brothers spent years defending their patent on
the method for controlling flight. The most famous case, brought
against them by aviation pioneer Glenn H. Curtiss, lasted four
years. Patent suits against the Wrights would have gone on longer
but for the start of World War I. The U.S. government was in
desperate need of planes to fight its battles and ultimately forced
the industry to pool its patents and create cross-licensing agreements so they would stop fighting one another and assist with
fighting the war instead.

In the 1950s the inventor of the laser, Gordon Gould, was unfamiliar with the process of submitting a patent. Rather than immediately submitting an application, Gould had his book of ideas notarized. By the time he applied, his ideas had already been patented by another physicist, Charles Townes. Gould spent the next thirty years attempting to rend the patents away from Townes and get the legal rights to laser technology. This was so expensive that he ultimately spent 80 percent of his royalties to cover his court costs. "The slowly ticking legal clock can exhaust an inventor's financial and emotional resources; large, rich corporations and their lawyers have thwarted many an independent inventor's claims until he has lost the will and ability to fight," said Nick Taylor in his book *Laser: The Inventor, the Nobel Laureate, and the Thirty-Year Patent War.*

One of the most famous of all patent wars was one of the first, during the middle of the nineteenth century. Isaac Singer, the man most of us associate with inventing the sewing machine, was involved in some kind of patent litigation for twenty years. He seemingly lost as many of these lawsuits as he won. Yet because Singer had enough money to fight for the duration and was better at marketing and selling his company to the public than his competitors, he, not the many other inventors of sewing machines, is remembered.

Singer wasn't even the first to patent a sewing machine. In fact, he was one of the last. The first patent went to inventor Elias Howe, Jr., in 1840. His machine was crude. It combined only three of the ten parts that are typically associated with sewing machines. It sewed vertically while the needle moved horizontally—not exactly practical for sewing in a straight line when you have to hold the fabric up in the air and feed it through the machine. Modern machines sew horizontally while the needle moves vertically, allowing the sewer to use a table to support the fabric.

From 1840 to 1850 inventors received at least seven more sewing machine patents, but there were few commercial successes. Only then—after watching others fail—did Singer bring his machine to market in 1850. His machine's advantage was that it had a presser foot, which moved the fabric mechanically through the machine and could sew up to nine hundred stitches per minute. The typical seamstress at the time sewed about forty.

Singer and Howe fought viciously for the next decade. Singer's success enraged Howe, who felt that Singer had merely improved on his ideas and not invented anything. This accusation didn't bother Singer much. Singer was famous for saying that he was "interested in the dimes not the invention," according to Adam Mossoff, George Mason University professor of law and intellectual property, in his paper "The Rise and Fall of the First American Patent Thicket: The Sewing Machine War of the 1850s." When Howe came to Singer's shop in New York City to demand royalties, Singer turned him down and threatened to kick him down the stairs. "Singer was an irascible fellow who lived a very colorful life; he was a bigamist who married under various names at least five women over his lifetime, fathered at least eighteen children out of wedlock, and had a violent temper that often terrorized his family members, business partners, and professional associates," Mossoff wrote.

By the mid-1850s I. M. Singer & Co. was embroiled in twenty different lawsuits in the United States—defending itself in some and bringing cases against its major competitors in others. Howe actually won some of the early lawsuits, but that only emboldened Singer to fight harder. The battles stopped only after it became clear to the various sewing machine makers that they would all make exponentially more money by ending their war than by continuing it. The sewing machine had revolutionized one of the biggest markets in the world—clothing. It allowed clothes to be mass-produced and sold for a fraction of their former cost. That caused a great rise in demand for garments, which in turn caused a great rise in demand for more sewing machines.

The solution was one that many today are suggesting is Apple's way out of the current patent thicket. The suing companies, in-

cluding Singer, Howe, and two other companies, set their differences aside and created America's first patent pool. Called the
Sewing Machine Combination, the group agreed that all participants would be entitled to equal access to the technology necessary to make a basic sewing machine and then created terms for
cross-licensing deals that allowed each company to specialize and
continue competing with one another.

. . .

The similarities between Singer's and Howe's patent fight and the
smartphone wars of today are striking. It's tempting to distinguish
today's fights by arguing that software is so much harder to understand. But USPTO judges and juries have always struggled
with understanding technologies. In 1912, Judge Learned Hand
was overseeing a patent case in the biomedical industry challeng-
ing whether adrenaline could be patented. He ruled that it could
be, but he also wondered why he was being asked to decide at all.
"I cannot stop without calling attention to the extraordinary condition of the law which makes it possible for a man without any
knowledge of even the rudiments of chemistry to pass upon such
questions as these. The inordinate expense of time is the least of
the resulting evils, for only a trained chemist is really capable of
passing upon such facts."

What *is* different with software patents today is that despite
thirty years of trying, the legal precedents governing what makes
a good or a bad patent remain in dispute. In the early days of the
computer industry the answer to this question was easy: software
wasn't patentable. It wasn't viewed as a product separate from
the computer itself. Courts didn't think software did much anyway beyond telling a machine to do mathematical calculations
faster. Math, being a part of nature, was unpatentable.

But by 1981, with the PC gaining traction in businesses and
an entire industry of software entrepreneurs emerging, the U.S.
Supreme Court changed that in *Diamond v. Diehr.* It said that a

computer program used to calculate how long a machine would heat and cure rubber *was* patentable. The software was more than just a series of mathematical equations, the court ruled. It was a unique process for determining the best way to mold rubber. The patent on molding rubber without software had long expired. But the addition of software had created a new, unique, and patentable way of doing it.

This decision became critical to Silicon Valley entrepreneurs in the 1990s. Up until then the legal convention had been to protect software under copyright law, given courts' previous resistance to permitting software patents. Writing software is creative just as writing books or music is, so it should be protected the same way, attorneys thought. With the English language, letters are used to form words and express ideas. With the language of music, notes are used to tell musicians what sounds to play with their instruments. With computer language, software code is written to tell machines what to do.

But in 1987 Quattro, a spreadsheet software program from Borland, pushed the limits of copyright law in software and successfully rendered it useless. Back then there were many spreadsheet programs for the PC, with Lotus 1-2-3 being the most dominant and successful. Quattro, in an effort to make its product easier to use, copied the words and menu hierarchy of Lotus. It didn't want customers to be confused switching back and forth between Lotus and Quattro. It didn't use any of Lotus's underlying code, it just provided users with a "Lotus Emulation Interface," which allowed them to switch between the Quattro look and the Lotus look.

Lotus sued, saying its menu system was protected under copyright law. But, to the surprise of all Silicon Valley, it lost. "In many ways, the Lotus menu command hierarchy is like the buttons used to control, say, a video cassette recorder ('VCR')," said Judge Norman Stahl of the First Federal Circuit Court of Appeals in New Hampshire in 1995. "A VCR is a machine that enables one to watch and record video tapes. Users operate VCRs by pressing a series of buttons that are typically labeled 'Record, Play, Reverse, Fast Forward, Pause, Stop/Eject.' That the buttons are arranged and labeled does not make them a 'literary work,' nor does it make them an 'expression' of the abstract 'method of operating' a VCR via a set of labeled buttons. Instead, the buttons are themselves the 'method of operating' the VCR."

The repercussions were huge. Apple's lawsuits against Microsoft, which continued into the 1990s—long after Jobs had left the company—would run afoul of this ruling, for example. Left with no other tool to protect entrepreneurs' creations, attorneys turned to the *Diamond v. Diehr* case and started using patents for protection instead.

Using patents to protect software has proven only slightly more effective than using copyright, however. One big problem is simply technological: The patent office database is searchable, but the search is not sophisticated like Google's, for example. Google's search engine not only finds items you are looking for, but similar items it *thinks* you are looking for based on your search history. That means that when the patent office tries to find previously issued patents on an idea, it often misses relevant filings.

Two years before Apple even started working on the iPhone—in 2003—a company called Neonode received a patent for activating their handheld device by swiping a finger across the screen. Apple later received a patent for exactly the same thing, known to many as the "slide to unlock" feature on the iPhone and the iPad. The patent office didn't know it had already issued this patent because Apple and Neonode described the same behavior slightly differently. Neonode's patent called the process "gliding the object along the touch sensitive area from left to right" instead of "slide to unlock." Though the Apple patent has been challenged in Europe, it is still valid in the United States. And Apple maintains that its and Neonode's patents describe different things. "Apple's lawyers claim that continuously moving the finger isn't specified in other prior art," said Boston University economist James Bessen at a Santa Clara conference on patent reform. "We're into a world of magic words, of word games. Courts and patent drafters play word games."

Mark Lemley, director of Stanford University's program in law, science, and technology, whom many consider to be the leading guru of reforming software patent law, says that the problem is more the patent office's fault: the office hasn't stopped thinking about software the way it was originally conceived—as a set of processes run by a computer. No one else thinks of software that way anymore, he said. People categorize software innovation by the solution it provides to some problem. At issue is not whether the code itself or the process it runs is unique but whether the software taken as a whole does something unique.

"We let people get away with claiming the invention in terms of the problem they solved, not the solution they provided. We don't allow that in anything else," he said. "We don't allow people to claim a configuration of atoms to cure cancer. Your solution is a particular chemical."

9

Remember Convergence?
It's Happening

Within a year of the iPad's release it seemed remarkable that Jobs had spent a moment worrying about Android's rise in 2009 and 2010—or at all. Android continued its astonishing growth, but iPhone sales accelerated just as fast. Quarterly sales of the iPhone 4, unveiled in 2010, doubled those of the iPhone 3GS. Sales of the iPhone 4S, unveiled in 2011, doubled those of the iPhone 4. By the fall of 2011, Apple was selling nearly 40 million iPhones a quarter. Google was doing well. It said Android was profitable. But it was still hard to see Android's financial impact on the company. Meanwhile at Apple, the iPhone and the app store were propelling the company to record profits. In 2011 Apple made $33 billion, as much as Google and Microsoft combined. In 2010 it had passed Microsoft to become the biggest technology company in stock market valuation. In 2011 it had passed Exxon to become the biggest company, period, in stock market valuation. By the end of 2011 it was sitting on so much cash—$100 billion—that if it had wanted to use that money to become a bank, it would have ranked among the top ten in the world.

Most notably, by the middle of 2011, the iPad was proving to be a more revolutionary product than even the iPhone—and certainly the iPod. The iPod and iTunes changed the way people bought and listened to music. The iPhone changed what people could expect from their cell phones. But the iPad was turning *five* industries upside down. It was changing the way consumers bought and read books, newspapers, and magazines. *And* it was changing the way they watched movies and television. Revenues from these businesses totaled about $250 billion, or about 2 percent of the GDP.

The iPad wouldn't have been possible without the iPhone. It would have been too expensive to build and sell for $600 in 2007. The required low-power ARM chips weren't fast enough to run something with a screen that big. And without all the content in the app store, consumers would not have known what to do with it. At least that's what Apple thought. But by 2011, with the app store in place and the learning curve for using Apple's touchscreen eliminated, the iPad was spawning seemingly endless new ways to consume and interact with content.

On top of all that, the iPad was also upending the personal computer business. It was eating into PC sales the same way that in the 1980s PCs ate into sales of minicomputers and mainframes from such companies as Digital Equipment and IBM. Some iPad buyers did indeed make the iPad their third device, as Jobs had predicted. But many others decided they now needed only two, and they started ditching their Microsoft-run Dell, HP, Toshiba, Acer, and Lenovo laptops at an accelerating clip. The shift hit Dell so hard that by the beginning of 2013 it was trying to take itself private to retrench.

Jobs was particularly satisfied with this development, a confidant said—even though in the context of the other upheavals the iPad was unleashing it was almost a footnote. Thirty-five years after starting Apple with Steve Wozniak, Jobs was finally doing what he had set out to do all along: he was transforming what consumers and businesses expected from their computers. The Macintosh in 1984—the first mainstream machine to use a mouse—was supposed to have been the machine that did this. It was supposed to have taken a complicated device—the PC—and made it a consumer product that anyone could use. That failed. As everyone knows, Macs didn't go away, but Microsoft Windows and Office get the credit for making the PC mainstream.

Yet by 2011 the world had come full circle. If you counted desktop *and* mobile operating systems together, Apple's computing platform was now about as big as Microsoft Windows and Windows Mobile. And it was fitting that Dell had been hit among the hardest. When Jobs returned to Apple in 1997, Michael Dell had declared he had so little faith in an Apple recovery that if he were Jobs, he'd "shut Apple down and give the money back to the shareholders." "Steve hated the fact that the Macintosh wasn't mainstream right away—that everyone wasn't just fucking sweating to get one," the Jobs confidant said. "So we talked a lot about how we could make sure the iPad caught on right away."

Andy Rubin and the Android team at Google scrambled to keep up with the relentless pace of Apple's innovations. But in 2011 they were being outflanked on almost every front. Yes, there were more Android devices in use than iPhones or iPads combined. But platform size was turning out to be just one, not the only, measurement of dominance in the Apple/Google fight. With the iPhone *and* the iPad, Apple still had the coolest, most cutting-edge devices. It had the best content for those devices. It had the easiest-to-use software. And it had the best platform for making content owners and software developers money. What Jobs understood—and what Google executives were furiously trying to get their heads around—was that this was more than just a fight over which company would dominate the future of technology. It was a battle over which would control the future of media too. The iPod was a great-looking device, but what made it popular was all the music consumers could easily buy for it. iPhone sales didn't really take off until Jobs introduced the app store. And the iPad became mainstream only when Jobs convinced big media companies to let consumers shop for an endless supply of books, newspapers, magazines, movies, and TV shows.

Indeed, the more successful Apple became, the more Google and Android hewed toward Apple's "we control everything" approach. To make Android software look cooler and be easier to use, Rubin hired the designer Matias Duarte from Palm in the middle of 2010. And to make Android phones and tablets sell better he started dictating how certain Android phones were designed. While these so-called Nexus devices are built by manufacturers such as Samsung or LG or HTC, they are largely designed and sometimes even marketed by Google.

But this was not an easy adjustment for Google's and Android's very engineering-driven culture. It wasn't until Google released the Nexus S at the end of 2010 that it had a top-selling phone made this way. And it wasn't until it released the Nexus 7 in 2012 that it had a top-selling tablet. Google didn't have a meaningful competitor to the iTunes store until it released Google Play in 2012, which combined its Android app store with its own efforts at distributing movies, books, games, and TV shows.

You'd think that over the years Google would have developed *some* affinity for the sales and marketing skills necessary to make a dent in the media business. Virtually all its revenue came from advertising. It owned YouTube—arguably the biggest distributor of video in the world. But Google had succeeded because it *rejected* these social and business mores. It had used technology to take most of the sales and marketing *out* of advertising and distribution and turn them into giant number-crunching exercises.

Google is trying to develop these sales and marketing skills today, but throughout 2012 and 2013 it continued to demonstrate that it has a long way to go. In 2012, when Google showed off an orblike device called the Nexus Q—which wirelessly streamed music, TV shows, and movies to any device in the house—the public response was so negative that Google decided to scrap the project entirely and not even offer it for sale. The Nexus Q was supposed to challenge the dominant streaming-media devices made by Apple and Roku. But Google said the Nexus Q would cost three times that of its competitors' boxes and would work only with consumers' existing entertainment libraries or with Google-supplied content from its store. Consumers couldn't, for example, watch Netflix or Hulu Plus on it. In mid-2013 Google tacked the opposite way with Chromecast, a $35 TV dongle that turns any smartphone into a remote.

In 2013, it also offered the Chromebook Pixel, a laptop with a touchscreen that was one of the sharpest ever made. But it seemed like more of an experiment than a real product that anyone would buy. Conceptually it worked like a smartphone or tablet— that is, with most of consumers' information stored not on the machine but in the cloud. It came with a tiny 64 GB hard drive, no DVD drive, and not an operating system from Microsoft or Apple but Google's own browser-based setup called Chrome. It wouldn't run Microsoft Office.

Consumers might have made that adjustment if the Pixel were lighter than a typical laptop, had a cooler, more functional design, or better battery life. Google's Office substitutes have become very competitive. But the Pixel wasn't lighter, better looking, or less power hungry. And it cost $1,300, twice the price of an iPad with a similar screen.

. . .

In retrospect it's odd that it took the iPad and not the iPhone to help the media business see a future they wanted to be part of, not fight. One of its holy grails has always been to reach customers wherever they might be. Nothing was better at that than a smartphone connected to the Internet. No other device could consistently reach customers *everywhere*—not only when they planned on reading a book or watching a movie, but also during their many in-between moments—while they were standing in line, using the restroom, or having a moment of boredom in a meeting or a show. But back then content executives thought the screen was too small—they couldn't imagine their customers watching a movie or reading a book on it. And advertisers couldn't imagine flashy, high-budget campaigns on it.

The iPad, on the other hand, with a screen nearly the size of some magazines, offered all manner of possibilities. Could publishers offer digital subscriptions that consumers would actually pay for and wean them off the expectation that their content would always be free? Could publishers sell advertising at the same price as in their printed publications? Could Hollywood change the way it charged cable and satellite distributors for its content by making it more mobile and offering new interactive features?

The answer to most of these questions turned out to be yes. By the time Jobs died, in October 2011, users could read or watch virtually anything on an iPad. Fueled with books, magazines, newspapers, movies, and TV shows from iTunes and the app store, live TV from cable, plus content from other online services such as Amazon, Netflix, Hulu, and HBO, the iPad had become the most important new media-consumption device since television. Subscriptions to hundreds of magazines were available through iTunes. More than 1 million e-books were available for instant download through Amazon's Kindle app or the iTunes bookstore. Almost any movie or TV show you could think of could be found on one of the streaming services.

Media executives' negotiations with Apple and one another were bumpy at first. Newspaper and magazine publishers were worried that selling their content through iTunes would give Apple ownership of their subscriber lists, perhaps their most critical asset. Television studios such as Viacom and News Corp. worried that the cable companies would use the iPad to massively expand their audience and ad revenues but not pay them a cent.

Indeed, for about eighteen months it looked as if few of the issues would be resolved. In 2010 and 2011 separate teams of executives from Condé Nast and Time Inc. made almost monthly pilgrimages to Apple's headquarters in California to explain why they would never negotiate the rights to their subscriber lists. But after roughly a dozen meetings, it still seemed as if Apple didn't understand. Apple's only big concession was agreeing to put up an "opt-in" notice each time someone subscribed through iTunes. Apple would ask subscribers, in effect, "Would it be okay if we shared the name, address, and contact information you've just given us with the publisher?" Condé Nast and Time Inc. executives were convinced this was just a mealymouthed way of turning them down. Their research showed that subscribers almost always responded no when presented with questions like this.

Instead, it turned out, most subscribers said yes. Within six months most of the big magazine and newspaper publishers were selling subscriptions to their content through the app store. They had to give Apple 30 percent of whatever new subscriptions they generated, but given what it cost to acquire new subscribers via analog methods, that seemed like a bargain. It typically costs $10 to $15 to acquire each magazine subscriber. In addition there is roughly $1 of manufacturing and distribution costs built into each magazine copy, compared to about ten cents for each digital copy. "The early response [when subscribers were first asked to share their information] was better than fifty percent, and now [in 2013] it's running at better than ninety percent," said Scott Dadich, editor in chief at *Wired*. As the magazine's design director at the time he was part of the negotiating team for Condé Nast.

The row in the television industry was even more heated. In early 2011 Time Warner Cable, Cablevision, and Comcast all came out with slick iPad apps that enabled the device to be used as a portable TV in different rooms of a customer's house. Content companies such as Viacom and News Corp. said that watching their shows on anything but a television degraded their value and violated their copyrights. For a few months starting in April 2011, Time Warner Cable pulled News Corp. and Viacom programming such as the *Daily Show* from their iPad apps. And in June, Viacom sued Cablevision for *not* pulling its programming from their iPad apps. On the one hand Viacom's position seemed preposterous. How was it possible that a small TV screen was okay but an iPad was not? That no doubt explains why the suit was settled quietly three months later. But it also illustrates how important and disruptive the iPad had become.

Once media companies were freed of their initial worries about the iPad, most of them embraced it. Indeed, it sparked a wave of new, innovative, and popular approaches to consuming news and entertainment that few had seen out of the media industry in decades. Book publishers rushed to make all their titles available in downloadable formats. Newspapers and magazines scrambled to develop well-designed iPad editions. Cable companies such as Comcast and Time Warner Cable developed the watch-TV-anywhere software mentioned above. By the middle of 2011 one of the hottest new iPad apps was HBO GO, from the HBO division of stodgy Time Warner.

With an HBO cable subscription, HBO GO allowed consumers free access to every episode of every show HBO had ever produced. If you had ever missed an episode of *The Sopranos, Curb Your Enthusiasm,* or *Entourage,* you could find it there, not to mention the roughly two hundred movies that were available to every HBO subscriber on his or her television. Previously a show's fans had had to spend hundreds of dollars buying DVDs if they wanted to catch up on missed episodes or watch a series they'd missed completely. Released in early 2011, HBO GO had 4 million users four months later. Total users have settled at about 7 million, or 20 percent, of HBO's total 35 million subscribers. The question HBO president Eric Kessler gets the most often now is when consumers will be able to get HBO *without* getting cable.

The iPad also sparked a flurry of start-up companies that saw it not just as another means to read or watch but as a device that could change that experience altogether. The software entrepreneur Mike McCue and the Apple veteran Evan Doll started Flipboard in 2010 by asking a simple question: What if web pages looked like well-designed magazine pages instead of the jumble of headlines on a monitor we'd begun to grow used to? What if they were updated in real time and customized with personal Facebook and Twitter feeds? "The web isn't broken. It just needs a face-lift," McCue likes to say.

It was a captivating conceit: the World Wide Web had revolutionized the world, but in the nearly twenty years since Netscape started it all with the first Internet browser, it had never undergone a redesign. Since the iPad now forced users to change the way they interacted with their screens—with their fingers instead of a mouse—why not also change the design assumptions underlying the content being interacted with? And moreover, said McCue, why not address the concerns of advertisers in the redesign process? Advertisers considered buying ads on news websites to be a necessary evil rather than something they sought out. Why not create a platform that actually proved attractive to and effective for advertisers?

McCue was an old hand at the start-up game. He'd been the vice president of technology at Netscape in the mid-1990s before leaving to cofound Tellme Networks, a company that built automated call-answering software for corporations. Microsoft bought it in 2007 for $800 million. So when McCue and Doll started Flipboard, they had the credibility and contacts needed to get attention for their idea. Jobs himself took the time to look at the app before Flipboard launched, and by the end of 2011 it had become App of the Year and one of the best-known start-ups in Silicon Valley. Money and attention from top venture capitalists such as John Doerr flowed in. So did résumés, and not just from people at top engineering companies such as Google, Apple, and Facebook, but from people at top media companies such as Time Inc. McCue hired Josh Quittner from there to manage all of Flipboard's media partnerships. Besides being a top tech writer at *Time*, he'd edited *Business 2.0* and helped lead Time Inc.'s iPad app development.

The iPad also spawned Atavist, a rethink of what a magazine would look like in the digital age. When they started it 2010, the journalists Evan Ratliff and Nick Thompson, along with the programmer Jefferson Rabb, wondered whether a newly conceived publication would be just text, photographs, and graphics or include video and audio too. Could readers be allowed to choose how much or how little beyond the words they would experience? Previous attempts at "enhancing" the written word had often seemed little more than distractions. Was there a way to employ these new ways of experiencing stories to ensure they were true and enriching additives?

The founders called their venture Atavist because they were trying to breathe new life into old-fashioned storytelling and long-form journalism. It had become fashionable to conclude that soon there wouldn't be *any* long-form journalism, but Atavist set out to prove otherwise by reconceptualizing what form that journalism took and how it was created. But it wasn't just that these authors wanted to experiment with this concept, it was because Atavist offered to pay them differently. Traditionally a writer is paid by the word. It can be tough to make a decent living this way. A good four-thousand-word piece, including editing time, can easily take three months yet generate only $8,000. But Atavist devised a different business model. They sold downloads as part of Amazon's new Kindle Singles category and evenly split with their writers whatever was left after Amazon's take. One of Atavist's stories, by David Wolman, was nominated for a National Magazine Award in 2012. Byliner, a startup cofounded by two former *Outside* magazine editors, teamed up with *The New York Times* on its "Snow Fall" project by John Branch. It won the 2013 Pulitzer Prize for Feature Writing. Both writers made a lot more money than they could have publishing their stories traditionally.

What really got Atavist attention from investors and then mainstream media, however, was the sophistication of its software. Rabb had designed it to work with all the e-book and e-mag formats in existence. So as Amazon and Apple tried to lock authors into their proprietary formats—Amazon with its Kindle e-books, Apple with iBooks—Atavist became an attractive intermediary. Eric Schmidt of Google and the venture capitalists Marc Andreessen, Peter Thiel, and Sean Parker were part of an outside-investor group in mid-2012. By the end of 2012 the media moguls Barry Diller and Scott Rudin had teamed up to create their own e-books start-up called Brightline. Atavist, with its software, was to be their exclusive online publisher.

The iPad's impacts weren't just limited to media. It seemed to change . . . everything. Pilots stopped carrying bulky bags of navigation charts, runway data, and weather reports. It all fit on an iPad—and was more up-to-date. Because children could figure out how to use an iPad long before using a personal computer, teachers started integrating them into the curriculum as early as kindergarten. Doctors began using iPads on rounds because they were easier to use one-handed by a patient's bed than a PC and had battery life that lasted all day. The iPad had similar appeal on Hollywood sets, amid the controlled chaos of filming. It eliminated the time-consuming distribution of paper script changes. Corporations loved the iPad, and by the end of 2011 Apple reported more than 90 percent of Fortune 500 companies were using them in some way. It turned professional baseball players into data junkies, allowing hitters to use algorithms to better guess what pitch was coming and fielders to better guess where each batter was likely to hit the ball. The iPad even spawned a new kind of virtual painting—on an iPad canvas instead of a real one.

■ ■ ■

The convergence of so much media into one device, the iPad, happened so fast that even if media executives had wanted to resist, it would have been futile. One of the truisms of American media is that it follows its customers' eyeballs, and by 2012 an enormous number of them were staring at iPads. By 2012, 16 percent of Americans had one. For thirty years the media had been dreaming and scheming about how to take advantage of the inevitable collision of digitized content with the integrated circuit—the silicon chip that powers everything from servers to the smallest iPod. But their bets about how it was going to happen had failed so often and so catastrophically that most had given up on the idea. Now they were scrambling to digitize anything they could to keep up with all the content consumers were suddenly willing to pay for.

The list of tycoons who had been flummoxed by media convergence included not second-tier dreamers but some of the smartest, richest, and most successful entrepreneurs and executives in the world. Bill Gates spent more than $6 billion of Microsoft's money on stakes in the big cable and telecom companies in the late 1990s and spent another $425 million to buy WebTV. He hoped to leverage Microsoft's dominant position in personal computers into a controlling position over what we watched on our televisions.

Earlier in the decade, TCI cofounder John Malone had tried to drive convergence by building the largest U.S. cable system, buying interests in more than two dozen cable programming operations—such as CNN, TNT, the Discovery Channel—and then attempting to merge all that in 1993 with Bell Atlantic, one of the big telephone companies. Had the deal not fallen apart five months later it would have given Malone control of a third of the televisions in the United States. Even back then, before anyone was talking about broadband or wireless anything, Malone was talking about a future in which every television had access to five hundred channels—compared to about two dozen then—and a host of interactive services that they might access through an advanced set-top box. It's what we think of as the Internet today, but few were talking about the Internet at the time. Malone's bold prediction spurred dozens of big companies to speed up their embrace of interactive television. One of the most famous was the Orlando Project in 1994, Time Warner's failed effort in Florida to hook up four thousand homes with cable TV that allowed them to download movies on demand. The dream of convergence was the driving force behind pre–Internet browser dial-up services such as Prodigy and Compuserve, not to mention America Online, as far back as the 1980s.

Those in the media industry—Malone, in particular—believed that controlling the television in the living room would be critical to convergence. They believed that the software and hardware they'd built to run televisions would just as easily run our PCs. Silicon Valley—largely meaning Microsoft and Bill Gates—believed that the same technology that ran our PCs—Windows—would run our televisions.

Former vice president Al Gore may have called Malone the Darth Vader of the information superhighway because of how aggressively he used TCI's size and monopoly control. But the fear Malone engendered paled in comparison to the worries Gates and Microsoft sparked. It wasn't just a bunch of technology start-ups like Netscape that were scared of Gates. He also scared executives at phone and cable companies, and every newspaper, magazine, television, and movie executive too. He already controlled the end points of the network with Windows. If he controlled enough telephone company and cable television lines, they worried he could use those two pillars to get control of the content running through those lines. This is why there was ultimately so much public support for the government when it launched its famous antitrust trial against Microsoft in the late 1990s.

The business calculus for all this dealmaking surrounding digital-content delivery wasn't complicated. If you could stop consumers from stealing content, reducing the friction associated with buying newspapers, magazines, books, TV shows, and movies would boost profits. What executives didn't realize was how long it would take before the technology would allow anyone to do that. It didn't matter whether their background was in technology or media. They all moved too soon.

When Gates was eyeing content as the next frontier to dominate with Microsoft Windows, most homes didn't even have broadband connections that would allow television content and Internet content to be merged. Everyone at Microsoft had a superfast connection and could see the change coming. And Gates thought his multibillion-dollar investments in cable companies would help accelerate the process. But the delivery of broadband connections to homes happened so slowly that it's hard to argue Gates had anything to do with it. It could have happened naturally just as easily. Back then most computers in the home connected to the Internet at 56 Kbps—1 percent of what many homes have today. It took another five years for most homes to have broadband, and another five after that before they had speeds that would allow the things Gates et al. had been dreaming of. Indeed, if Microsoft's investments *did* help, speeding up the adoption of broadband helped the competitors Apple and Google much more. Microsoft divested its media holdings in 2009 for an undisclosed sum.

Media companies tried to make a grab for convergence profits in a different way—through dealmaking—and uncorked a series of mergers that will go down as some of the worst-conceived deals in the history of American business. In the space of ten years, Time bought Warner Brothers for $15 billion. It took nearly eight years for Time's shareholders to break even. Just as that was happening, the company shelled out $7 billion to buy Turner Broadcasting, owners of CNN and a giant movie library. Long before that deal could pay off, the conglomerate agreed to sell itself to America Online in 2000, at the peak of the Internet bubble, for $164 billion in AOL stock. By 2009, when the company finally divested itself of AOL, owners of Time Warner shares in 2000 had seen the value of their holdings reduced to eighteen cents on the dollar. By the beginning of the twenty-first century, media/technology convergence had been so discredited that mentioning it at conferences could make executives wince visibly.

All this flailing on both sides of the convergence equation actually made it seem less, not more, likely for it to happen cooperatively. In 2000, when music fans started exchanging songs through illegal sites such as Napster, the industry didn't reach out to Silicon Valley to find a solution. It sent in battalions of lawyers to shut down the sites and sue listeners—many of whom would happily have paid money to get their music that way. Executives such as Edgar Bronfman, who ran Universal, and Michael Eisner, who ran Disney, accused technology executives of, in effect, running a criminal syndicate, not unlike a bunch of Mafia dons who encouraged and supported theft.

Technology executives endlessly pointed out that the movie studios had expressed the same fears about television in the 1960s and the VCR and DVD in the 1980s and 1990s, and that those technologies had actually helped them *increase* their profits. They reminded music executives of how movie moguls worried that consumers would stop going to the movies if they could watch at home but how new technologies just expanded the amount of time and money consumers spent on entertainment. This argument only made music executives angrier. Even Jobs, after constructing the deal that brought music into the iTunes store, where it could legally be purchased, couldn't stop the entertainment industry's grousing about technology and how it was wrecking their professional lives. He and those in Silicon Valley said that he had saved the industry from being decimated by piracy. The industry maintained that since music industry revenues dropped by 50 percent after iTunes and the iPod took off— because consumers bought music by the song instead of the album—the industry would have found a much better solution on its own.

By 2010, however, the entire media business was in such disarray that new technologies, approaches—*anything*—seemed better than the status quo. Executives at newspapers, magazines, publishers, and studios had seen revenues in the music industry cut in half largely because its executives fought rather than embraced technology. They didn't want the same thing happen to their companies—and it looked as if it might if they didn't take some risks. The Internet had already gutted newspaper and magazine circulation and advertising revenues. Amazon's Kindle had created a new, low-priced market for e-books that wasn't going away. Americans were watching less television because they were entertaining themselves with videos on YouTube and other video sites instead. When they *were* watching television, TiVo devices (known as DVRs, for digital video recorders) were enabling— even almost encouraging—viewers to skip commercials. And movies, which had only yesterday been a profit machine for the studios, were now being ordered from Netflix and either shipped on DVD by mail or simply streamed online.

Scott Dadich, *Wired's* editor in chief, said that while he'd been thinking about what *Wired* would look like on a tablet from the moment he saw the iPhone—he had even put together a presentation of what *Wired* would look like on an Apple tablet—"to be totally blunt, the real motivating factor was that [by 2009] we were scared *Wired* was going to go away [because of the recession and shifts in media consumption]. *Portfolio,* [a sister publication, since closed] had come in at one hundred and two pages. *Wired* wasn't much thicker. We had to do something splashy so that *Wired* could differentiate itself."

Apple's ecosystem of iPods, iPhones, and iPads, all connected to the easy-to-use iTunes store, seemed to offer a lifeline. To the media business the word *online* was an epithet—synonymous with falling profits, piracy, and fear of bankruptcy. But everything Apple touched online seemed to turn to gold. Consumers were used to paying for content on Apple devices, not getting it for free as was their wont with content consumed elsewhere on the Internet.

For years, magazine and newspaper publishers had experimented with getting consumers to pay for their online content, and it had been a disaster. One of the accomplishments Jobs rarely gets credit for is building the system behind iTunes that solved this problem. Media companies had failed not because the concept was wrong but because the sign-up and transaction processes had been so cumbersome. With iTunes Jobs made them frictionless. It's not trivial to cost-effectively enable consumers to spend ninety-nine cents for a song or an app, to make it secure, and to make it as easy as touching an icon and entering a password. But today iTunes processes millions of transactions a day from a database of nearly 600 million credit-card numbers.

• • •

In retrospect, it's hard to imagine how anyone could have competed with Jobs in 2011. By successfully sitting astride revolutions he had spawned in Silicon Valley and Hollywood, he and Apple had become the most powerful businessman and company in the world by the time he died in October 2011. They controlled the most popular smartphone and the most popular tablet—devices that together sold 134 million units the year he died. That was 37 percent of the volume in the entire global PC industry. Most important, they—as Gates and Windows had in the 1990s—controlled the software running on those devices and how every application running on top of that platform operated.

And they used that power to reward friends and punish enemies. When Facebook tried to negotiate too hard with Apple over its integration into iPhone iOS 5, Apple simply did a deal with Twitter. Facebook was much more compliant during the next round of negotiations. "They kept talking about how they'd been burned by Google over Maps, and how they were never going to let that happen again," said someone involved in the discussions. Software developers may not like Apple's brass-knuckled approach. They may not like watching Apple take 30 percent of their revenue for listing in the iTunes app store. But they also know that they make less money if they don't. And together they have made *a lot* of money. By the end of 2011, even after Apple took its cut, developers had made more than $4 billion because of the iTunes app store. Apple generated as much revenue just from content/app sales in 2011 as it had made as an entire corporation in 2003—$6 billion.

Perhaps the most conspicuous example of Google's all-out scramble to keep up with this juggernaut was its decision to buy Motorola for $12.5 billion at the end of 2011. The official position about Motorola is that Google bought it for the patent portfolio. That's true. Having enough patents to disrupt competitors in a lawsuit typically keeps them from suing *you* for patent violations. Motorola invented the modern cell phone. As a result it has some of the most valuable and important patents in the world. They touch virtually every wireless device. But few believe Google bought Motorola *just* for the patents. Motorola is one of the largest phone and tablet makers in the world. That buys Google valuable insurance if, for example, Apple's lawsuits get a court to block sales of Android phones somewhere—or even if Google needs to compete with a member of its own Android ecosystem. While Rubin has insisted that it would be suicide for it to use Motorola to compete with other Android phone makers, it *does* give Google more leverage in case that dynamic starts to work in reverse—if one of the Android manufacturers decides to compete with Android.

This so-called "forking" of Android is arguably Google's biggest challenge in its fight with Apple. The beauty of Android is that it is free and open and allows phone makers and carriers a lot of leeway to redesign its look and feel. PC makers never had this flexibility with Windows. Microsoft owned it, and manufacturers had limited flexibility to modify it. But Android's openness is also its biggest potential problem. It allows its manufacturers to abandon the ecosystem. It allows a manufacturer such as Samsung to take Google's software, modify it to its liking, and build its own end-to-end solution the way Apple has, so that content and apps bought for Samsung phones and tablets work only on those devices. As Samsung's Galaxy phones and tablets became the dominant Android phones and tablets in 2013, Samsung seemed to be heading in this direction at an accelerating pace. By then it had its own mobile apps for email and contacts, calendar and notes. And it had felt free to put its competing app store—the Samsung Media Hub—alongside Google's.

Google has always maintained that its control of the Google mobile stack of applications and the Google Play store will keep such defections from happening—as if it held all the cards. Google's position has been "How are you going to sell your phone or tablet if it doesn't come with YouTube or Google search or Google Maps?" That was indeed true for a while. But it isn't anymore. The iPhone 5 sold better than any previous iPhone even though it didn't come with YouTube, and it came with Apple Maps—which proved to be terrible—instead of Google Maps. Google just made those apps available in the Apple app store and consumers downloaded them there.

Count on Samsung pondering the same thing. It has the top-selling smartphone and tablet in the world now. Its executives are wondering the same thing Apple did: Will customers really slow their purchases of our phones and tablets because we don't include Google's software on our phones and don't allow access to Google's app store?

The likely answer is no. Amazon has an app store that is just as good. Microsoft has a search engine that is just as good. There are half a dozen good mapping applications. Google needs Samsung as much as Samsung needs Google now. Without Google apps on Samsung phones—which are now half of all Android sales—half of Google's mobile advertising base disappears.

Andy Rubin is no longer the Google executive to query about Android's future. In early 2013 he handed Android's reigns to Sundar Pichai, who had also been running Google Chrome. Pichai has long been a favorite of Page's and is well regarded as a seasoned manager. That is something Android needs now that it has grown to include hundreds of Googlers worldwide. Such leadership is something Rubin, more of an entrepreneur than an executive, didn't enjoy providing, according to friends. Indeed, when asked about Google's shifting alliance with Samsung in June 2013, Pichai demonstrated his fluency at tackling such complicated questions. He said the best way to think about the Google-Samsung relationship is to think about how Microsoft and Intel worked together to dominate the PC industry: they didn't always say nice things about each other and sometimes they competed, but they mostly worked together because they both knew that was the best way to make the most money. "Samsung is a very close partner and we owe a lot of the success of Android to what they have done. But it's also fair to say that Samsung has been hugely successful in mobile because of Android. We see a path where we can be successful and so can Samsung. We don't see it as a zero-sum game."

The response was friendly but not conciliatory. It also happens to be truthful. Samsung is competing with Google. Yet, as Pichai announced the month before, the two companies are also finding new ways to partner. Samsung's flagship smartphone, the

Galaxy S4, can now be purchased two ways—with or without Samsung's Android software enhancements. This is a big deal. Many consumers love the S4 but hate Samsung's enhancements. Now consumers can buy an S4 with an unmodified version of Android, with essentially the same software that comes with the Nexus phones and tablets Google oversees. That's not the kind of deal that happens when two companies are nearing war.

10

Changing the World
One Screen at a Time

The upheaval in media and technology that the iPhone started, the Android movement accelerated, and the iPad broadened into a full-on revolution has unleashed a maelstrom in the years since Jobs died that few in Silicon Valley, New York, or Hollywood have seen before in their careers. It's not just that two of the biggest, most influential corporations in their worlds—Apple and Google—are fighting each other to the death. It's that the mobile revolution they set off has suddenly put roughly $250 billion in revenue from half a dozen industries up for grabs.

For those on the wrong end of these changes, the past five years have been unpleasant. Newspaper publishers have seen print advertising revenue and circulation fall to twenty-year lows. The number of journalists employed at newspapers has been cut almost in half in the past five years. Book publishers are worried that they are about to get hit in a similar way. Amazon is not only driving prices down beyond publishers' ability to make a profit but also trying to lure away their most profitable authors. Movie studio executives are already reeling from watching their DVD business evaporate. Now their ability to build audiences for bad movies is being destroyed by moviegoers' loud and instant reactions to films on Facebook and Twitter. The television industry is worried because tech companies such as Netflix and Google's YouTube are competing for their audience with their own content, putting pressure on monthly subscription rates.

But the mobile revolution has also created scores of *new* moneymaking opportunities—particularly in television—and it is enabling business partnerships never before thought possible. Tech companies are making impressive strides partnering with top entertainment-industry directors and producers, whereas the companies had previously shown little interest or affinity. New York and Hollywood big shots are now building slick mobile apps and partnering with software developers, whom they once called criminals for encouraging the theft of their content. Indeed, New York and Los Angeles now boast thriving tech start-up communities. Los Angeles is fast approaching a thousand tech start-ups, while New York now has roughly seven thousand. Top agents and producers, who previously had little reason to visit Northern California, are now making the trek almost every week.

"We've launched five different start-ups [for our clients and others] now," said Michael Yanover, the head of business development at Creative Artists Agency (CAA) in Hollywood. "Every time we launch a start-up, it has to get funded. So we are constantly circling VCs for funding, information, and access. We meet with all of the interesting start-ups and the bigger, established companies. We work a lot with Amazon, for instance, and also with YouTube. We look at anything that is emerging. If it's Pinterest. If it's IntoNow. If it's Shazam. We would like to be part of all of that."

Yanover, who looks fortyish but would not tell me his age, has been thinking about the Silicon Valley–Hollywood axis for fifteen years. He was running his own start-up in Los Angeles when Macromedia in San Francisco recruited him to help it build out the first explosion of web content during the Internet bubble.

We did some very pioneering work with Matt Stone and Trey Parker, the guys behind *South Park*, and Tim Burton and James L. Brooks, to create content on our site in return for equity. It wasn't TV, but it serialized episodically like TV. We bought Atom Films, and I ended up running all the content that was nongaming, which was anything film, animation, music, videos, and even greeting cards.

One of the things I was doing at Macromedia was working on embedded Flash. And Flash, at that point, was driving all rich media [video] on the Internet. What we thought was the natural evolution of Flash [now owned by Adobe] was to embed it into mobile devices, embed it onto set-top boxes, embed it into game consoles, et cetera. So we developed an initiative, which we code-named Columbus, because it was the new world, right? Columbus was all about embedding Flash everywhere, including the mobile phone.

The experience of mobile apps was very primitive in 2002. But to me it was always clear that everything was going to be on your mobile phone. In emerging markets they were already skipping over the PC and going right to the mobile phone. And they were skipping over landlines and going right to wireless. So those two factors in and of themselves told you that, oh my God, the mobile phone is going to be the device where content gets displayed and broadcast.

But most of Yanover's work building web content needed to be shelved for a while because the technology just wasn't ready. Most homes didn't even have broadband back then, let alone wireless connections and devices that were fast enough to show video. He joined CAA in 2003 and represented as many mobile ventures as he could find. "And then Steve Jobs came along with the iPhone," he says,

and suddenly the world opened up and totally emancipated all of these developers and all of these creative people from the stranglehold of the carriers and from the lack of flexibility and the screwed-up platform that existed in the traditional feature phone. And so when the iPhone showed up, it was like Moses leading people out of the

desert into the Holy Land. It was an amazing moment.
And it freed everybody. Of course it made Apple much
stronger. But it was a freeing moment. Today it's much
easier. You have iOS and you have Android and it's very
simple, that's it.

. . .

Experimental—that's what tech companies like to call their
growing interest in media. If so, it's a big experiment. Netflix just
spent two years and $100 million producing its hit *House of
Cards* with Kevin Spacey. It just revived *Arrested Development*,
the Mitchell Hurwitz comedy that ended its three-year run on
Fox seven years ago. It plans to make twenty other shows the
same way. Google is spending hundreds of millions to jump-start
production of dozens of channels for YouTube, effectively turning
it into the Internet's first cable television network. And Facebook,
with a membership that now represents half the Internet—half—
is becoming an important part of the movie money-raising and
distribution process. You can't finance and distribute a Hollywood blockbuster through Facebook, but you can do an independent film with a budget of a few million dollars. Amazon, Hulu,
and Microsoft are now also in the early stages of professional
content financing and distribution.

Most think it is only a matter of time before Apple does something big in TV—either with another revolutionary device or by
using its enormous cash hoard to turn iTunes into the most current and deepest source of content anywhere. Before he died,
Jobs told biographer Isaacson that he'd finally figured out a way
for Apple to do it. There has been no big, splashy announcement
yet, but already Apple TV with Airplay has been incrementally
turning Apple's iPhone and iPad into personalized TV remote
controls. You can start watching a movie on your iPhone or iPad
while cleaning the kitchen and continue it on your TV after you've
finished your chores. Or if you like the two-screen experience,
you can switch the movie to the TV while using the iPhone or

iPad to tweet or Facebook with friends about it—or use the iPhone or iPad to do something else entirely.

Meanwhile, old-line Hollywood agencies such as CAA and William Morris Endeavor (WME) now not only shop their clients to big studios but to app developers too. In 2011, with money from chip maker Qualcomm, CAA created Moonshark, a company that would produce mobile apps the same way the agency packages writers, actors, and producers for feature films or TV shows. Yanover said that all the mobile entertainment apps that exist now are great but could be so much bigger if they could tap into the storytelling and production machinery of Hollywood. Writers could give game characters names and origin stories, for example. "*Angry Birds* was fantastic, but really it's the tip of the iceberg. It's the beginning of what is going to really happen," Yanover said. Last year, in an effort to capitalize on the new money-making opportunities of convergence, big tech investor Silver Lake Capital bought a third of WME for an undisclosed sum. TPG, meanwhile, bought a chunk of CAA. "It used to be the only things the agent did—back when I started—was TV, movies, books, and theater," said Ari Emanuel, the CEO of WME, during an onstage interview last year. "Now there are a wide variety of distribution points and places where artists can start creating content. Clients are now creating games, turning it into a book and then a movie. The agency now has a new media department. Apps are getting developed. It's very dynamic."

Here's an example. Lady Gaga's next album, *ArtPop*, won't be issued initially as a CD or digital download but as a mobile app. Her manager, Troy Carter, has a lot more in common with Facebook founder Mark Zuckerberg than with the traditional rock-star managers of old. He's one of the first to use social media as the primary marketing vehicle for his client. In addition, he is fast becoming known as one of the savviest high-tech angel investors around, with early stakes in apps such as music service Spotify, taxi service Uber, and news service Summly (just bought by Yahoo!). "The music industry is healthier than ever right now, and it's a fantastic time to be in it," he told London's *Guardian* news-paper at the end of 2012. When was the last time anyone said *that* about the music industry?

Emanuel says that from his and his clients' perspectives not only have all the changes been good, they've created an embarrass-ment of riches: just as broadcast and cable companies are bidding for his clients' work, so too are half a dozen tech companies—ones with enough spare cash to outbid any cable or broadcast company. Indeed, if you add up the cash on the balance sheets of Apple, Google, Amazon, Microsoft, Facebook, and Netflix, it approaches $300 billion—enough to buy all the big cable companies and broadcast networks combined. Emanuel has been critical of Sili-con Valley's lack of respect for copyrights. But he says Google especially is getting better about this. And it is hard to ignore how much the tech companies are bidding up the prices of his clients' services. Emanuel said that there were 39 scripted TV shows in 2009. In 2011 there were 139. Yet the quality of pro-gramming, and the bidding for talent and distribution, has increased along with the supply. The quality of television pro-gramming today is accepted as better than it has ever been be-fore. Emanuel has a reputation as one of the toughest negotiators in Hollywood, accused of never having a nice word for anyone. But of the rush of Silicon Valley money into Hollywood, he says, "It's fantastic. I love them."

. . .

For Emanuel to call the blurring of the lines among Hollywood, New York, and Silicon Valley "dynamic" may actually be an un-derstatement. Five years ago the words *television* and *TV show* had unambiguous meanings. Now they have become almost too confusing to use in conversation. Are you watching TV if you are watching *House of Cards* by Netflix exclusively on a smartphone or a tablet? It feels as if you are, but you are watching something backed and distributed by a technology company based in Los Gatos, not Hollywood. And you are watching something that is being distributed outside the cable and broadcast-television infrastructure. The only way to get *House of Cards* is with an Internet connection and a Netflix subscription.

What about the difference between web content and professionally produced content? That distinction used to be clear too. Now, it's no longer rare for hit shows to start on YouTube before getting picked up by big broadcast or cable networks for huge sums. That's what happened with *Burning Love* and *Web Therapy*. And it is no longer rare for the big networks to take advantage of the Internet's reach to play that game in reverse. Last fall, in order to build buzz and audience for a new series called *Go On*, NBC aired part of the pilot on YouTube about six weeks before the series's official debut. Fox did the same thing with *Homeland* and *New Girl*.

The blurring of technology and media is even changing how TV shows are produced, said Michael Lynton, Sony's U.S. boss, during a 2013 interview at an All Things D conference:

> In the past you had a really difficult time creating long-form, open-ended drama. You had to wrap up every episode neatly in a bundle at the end—so that if you had never watched the show, you would know what was going on. That was because that was the way people were used to watching television, and it was because of the syndication side of things [through which series were sold to TV/cable stations complete or in chunks depending on their budgets]. Then when [some shows *did* test those rules] people would say, "I've missed two or three episodes. This is not worth my time and effort."
>
> Then the PVR shows up, and Netflix shows up, and people say, "Oh, I can miss a couple of episodes and catch up."
>
> I personally believe that one of the reasons you are seeing such an explosion in creativity—whether it's *Mad Men* to *Breaking Bad* to *House of Cards* to *Justified* to

Sons of Anarchy—is the fact that you can create thirteen-episode, long-form narratives where characters can be developed over thirteen hours. Better writers come to this because they say, 'Gee, I can't get it done in two hours of a movie.' Better directors come to this. For a long time people have wondered when all this new technology was going to affect the creative side of things. This is the first one I've seen. Generally people think that is a good thing.

All this has been enabled or accelerated by the explosive growth of smartphones and tablets in the past five years. At about 4 billion, the number of televisions in use worldwide is still double the number of smartphones and tablets—about 2 billion. But at current growth rates, there will be more smartphones and tablets than TVs within three to five years. Smartphone sales are growing at better than 25 percent a year, and tablet sales are more than doubling every year. Meanwhile, the sales of TVs worldwide is actually declining. Some of that is because of the global recession. But some of that is because more and more new college graduates aren't bothering to buy one.

Investor Marc Andreessen says that smartphones and tablets have not just exponentially expanded the number of people in the world who can consume media, they have also exponentially increased the number of times and places throughout each day that those people can watch. "You've got your phone and you can watch TV or movies anytime you want. The same with tablets. With a TV you have to be at home—to be sitting still—to watch it."

Andreessen sounds giddy when he talks about all this. He has been thinking about these issues and watching them evolve for more than twenty years, and he has been doing it from one of the best vantage points in the world—with the access to people and information only available to a select few Silicon Valley insiders. At the moment he and his partner, Ben Horowitz, are known as two of the top VCs in technology. But many have forgotten that

Andreessen was also the cocreator of the first Internet browser, Mosaic, which became Netscape Communications in 1994. He helped sell it to America Online for $4 billion in 1999—despite losing the browser wars to Microsoft. Then in 2000 he cofounded one of the first cloud-computing companies, Loudcloud. It nearly failed when the Internet bubble popped. But he and Horowitz changed the name to Opsware, rebuilt it, and sold it to Hewlett-Packard for $1.6 billion in 2007. Most of the best-known VCs took a decade or more to make a splash. Andreessen and Horowitz have become two of the top VCs in four years.

Andreessen says,

In 1993 it was very obvious what the world would be like if everyone had a high-speed Internet connection and a big screen because at the University of Illinois [where he was at college] we had those things. But the only reason we had those things was because the federal government was paying for them, and they were only paying for them at four universities. Our first demo for Netscape showed how you could watch *Melrose Place* [the hot TV show at the time] in the browser.

I actually think mobile is the biggest thing our industry has ever done. Our industry was basically born around 1950 at the end of World War Two [when William Shockley invented the transistor]. And that sixty years was basically a prologue to finally being able to put a computer in everybody's hands. We've never had the ability as an industry to give a computer to five billion people [the number of people with cell phones currently], and that is precisely what is happening right now.

• • •

Nothing illustrates the power of the mobile revolution more than its impact on the U.S. television business. Five years ago the idea that anyone would give up cable TV seemed preposterous.

Consumers were annoyed at rising rates, but there wasn't a lot to watch on the Internet yet. Now, not a month goes by without some entrepreneur or television executive being interviewed about the long-term viability of asking consumers to pay more than $100 a month for cable programming. These aren't theoretical conversations. The threats to the financial stability of cable TV—and by extension broadcast TV—are real and seem to get more powerful every day.

The solutions to cable television's problems are complex, but the origins of the problem are simple: the industry has become a victim of its own success. Network programming began in earnest in the 1950s, but it wasn't until the 1980s and 1990s—when almost everyone could get cable TV—that the television industry really took off. For all the attention broadcast television generated, it was a technology inferior to cable. Consumers were typically limited to fewer than a half dozen channels, and many Americans lived in areas where the reception was so bad they were lucky to get one. The cable industry's bet was that by sending TV signals over a wire it could offer consumers far more channels, flawless reception, and an unlimited array of programming. Cable executives believed that the difference in quality was so stark that consumers would even *pay* for this service. Meanwhile, the media landscape would be transformed. TV purchases would increase. TV watching would increase. And new programs would be spawned.

Most of what the cable companies predicted came true, allowing family-run companies such as Comcast to become one of the largest corporations in the world, and allowing channels such as ESPN, FOX, and HBO to charge billions of dollars a year for their content. Then, beginning about a decade ago, the industry began to hook consumers on "the bundle," a combination of TV service, broadband Internet, and telephone service. That also was visionary. It allowed cable companies to compete with phone companies for new customers. This helped the industry not only win more subscribers but also got them to pay more for their service.

But cable broadband is now so fast that it has allowed competing content providers to grow up on top of it. The cable industry was been built on the assumption that consumers had a theoretical choice whether to pay for TV or get it free over the air. But practically, it wasn't a choice. Watching Internet video on a tablet, smartphone, or even on the television via a game console or other electronics, such as the Apple TV or those made by Roku, *is* a real alternative. It's getting more attractive every day. It's hard to miss the irony. Sure, more and more of the content we consume at home is on a mobile device. But those devices are connected to Wi-Fi networks that are connected typically to cable broadband. Cable is being forced to rethink its business because of Netflix, YouTube, Apple's iTunes, Amazon movies and music, and Facebook. But its bandwidth is what has enabled all of them to exist.

The difference between what is available to watch on the Internet and what is available to watch through cable TV remains vast. But while it is narrowing, the difference in the price of a monthly cable subscription (typically in excess of $100 for a family) versus, say, one from Netflix (less than $10) is not. Baby boomers may talk about the importance of watching TV as a family. Millennials think that's just a rationalization for not having what everyone really wants: TV without programming compromises. So-called cord cutting, when households drop their cable TV subscription and only get broadband, has been overblown. But cable TV subscriptions are no longer growing, and *new* households—those started by adults right out of college—are subscribing to cable in smaller numbers than ever before. This group even has a name in the industry: cable nevers.

• • •

All this is straining the cable companies' relationships with content providers to the breaking point. On one hand, cable companies remain the highest bidders for content, and content creators worry about doing anything to mess that up. About $4.50 out of every cable bill goes just to ESPN for its sports programming.

That's close to $3 billion a year from all cable subscribers. It is what enabled ESPN to agree to pay $15.2 billion to the National Football League through 2021 for *Monday Night Football*. It's not just sports that relies on subscriber fees. Each episode of *Game of Thrones* on HBO reportedly costs $6 million to make.

On the other hand, Internet media networks are proving that the money no longer *has* to come from cable subscribers. Netflix didn't originate *House of Cards*. Independent studio Media Rights Capital took bids from a handful of networks, including HBO, Showtime, and AMC (where you can see *Mad Men*). Netflix outbid them all. Google isn't handing directors such as CSI creator Anthony Zuiker millions to make programming on YouTube because it's being charitable. It thinks that YouTube's audience is so enormous that a good show will pay for itself in advertising revenue. YouTube boss Salar Kamangar said in an interview at an All Things D conference in 2012 that in the traditional YouTube experience, "you have to decide, what do I care about and what do I want to watch every three minutes." The new content will be more interactive and more focused on specific niches. "We think that's going to increase minutes watched, we think that's going to improve the experience," he said.

One of the nastiest fights right now is whether or not a company called Aereo has the right to exist. In 2012 Aereo started offering consumers in the New York City area the ability to get their local broadcast channels live on any device they own for between $8 and $12 a month. Aereo doesn't pay the networks or the cable companies anything for those broadcasts, but it allows subscribers to watch live or automatically record local television on their phone or tablet anywhere there is wired or wireless Internet connection. When Aereo launched, most networks allowed you to watch yesterday's broadcast that way, but not today's. But by the middle of 2013 it looked like that stance was changing fast. ABC said it would begin offering live same-day streaming of programming in some Aereo cities, such as New York, even though not all of its programming was available and users could get it only if they had a cable subscription. By the time you read this, all of the other networks may have followed suit.

What Aereo is doing sounds as if it should be illegal. Cable companies pay broadcast networks hundreds of millions of dollars in fees every year to transmit their broadcast signals over their wires. Aereo is getting away with not paying a cent. But for the moment judges have ruled that because of a loophole in the copyright laws Aereo is completely legal. The cable and television industry sued Aereo as soon as it was launched in 2012, seeking an injunction to shut it down. But they lost. When you subscribe to Aereo, your house is assigned a specific antenna in Aereo's server farm. As long as each house is receiving the broadcast signal on an individual antenna based in the local area, it's legal reception. The law doesn't require the antenna to be based in your house.

This is, of course, terrifying for cable and broadcast companies, and they plan to use every dollar at their disposal to continue their fight. Retransmission fees are a huge source of income for broadcast networks. Meanwhile, Aereo together with a Netflix and Hulu subscription at about $20 a month starts to become a compelling alternative to paying $100 for cable service. One of the things that has kept cable customers from cutting the cord has been the absence of live TV—local sports on local broadcast stations in particular.

It's going to be an enormous battle, because Aereo isn't a half-baked start-up with easy-to-scare venture capitalists. Barry Diller, who built his career in Hollywood at ABC, Paramount, and FOX television, is backing it. He knows and has worked with most of the executives running the networks. But from the early days of his career he has also always been much more interested in disrupting the status quo than in making sure people like him. "I knew there was going to be controversy, but I couldn't find a flaw because I felt that the existing law was so much on the side of what Aereo was doing, and that's what intrigued me," Diller told David Carr at *The New York Times* in March 2013. Those remarks brought the following curt response from Les Moonves, the head of CBS: "It is clear that the whole premise of Aereo is to make money off the back of the hundreds of millions of dollars we invest in programming. We pay the NFL one billion dollars a year. Right now we have a lot of correspondents in Rome. We think it is patently illegal to take our signal and those of the other networks and resell it without paying for it. It is so wrong on so many different levels."

The future of HBO will also be a good proxy for how the mobile revolution is going to evolve. For the last few years the company has successfully been embracing technological change with its hugely popular HBO GO app while professing its loyalty to the cable companies who continue to be the gateway to its high-end programming. That's an understandable position, a kind of straddle. For all its growing popularity as a brand, HBO has never had to sell or manage relationships with its customers. It has had to manage its relationships with the cable companies, and they take care of everything else. This has provided HBO with all the money it needs to buy and produce the top-quality shows it is known for.

HBO's problem is that it is increasingly unclear how long that straddle is going to work. Netflix, with the success of *House of Cards* and its other original programming, has now proven that you no longer need a cable network to offer consumers top-quality programming. HBO knows Netflix's model well. It is similar to the one HBO used to become the dominant cable entertainment channel in the world: Use movies to build a subscriber base, then use the subscriber base to start making your own content. The difference is that you only need an Internet connection and $8 a month to get Netflix programming. You need a top-tier cable TV subscription at more than $100 a month to get HBO.

HBO is keenly aware of this, and in an interview in February 2013 its president, Eric Kessler, said that it had partnered with Tivili, a three-year-old start-up led by two Harvard students, to bring HBO GO to a handful of college campuses. Students won't need their parents' cable-subscription number to sign up. They'll be able to do it for free with their Facebook log-in. Kessler said that

HBO never wants to be associated with an audience of middle-aged adults only—as Oldsmobile became—and said he assumed that many college students today would get most of their HBO programming through HBO GO. But he also said he believed that they would be getting that programming via a cable TV subscription for a long time to come.

But this issue is clearly a moving target inside HBO. Just six weeks later—at the premiere of *Game of Thrones* in San Francisco—fifty miles from Netflix headquarters in Los Gatos—it seemed as if HBO had completely reversed course. Its CEO, Richard Plepler, said that HBO was thinking hard about allowing those without cable subscriptions to get HBO anyway. Customers could pay $50 a month for their broadband Internet and an extra $10 or $15 for HBO to be packaged in with that service, for a total of $60 or $65 per month, Plepler explained. "We would have to make the math work," he added.

The antagonistic standoffs between the entertainment industry and the Silicon Valley of the Napster days back in 2000 are not completely gone either. In early 2012 the entertainment industry thought it could use its lobbying clout in Washington to quietly push two bills through Congress that would have given it new powers to control the content of websites violating their copyrights. But the bills read as if they were as much motivated by a nefarious Hollywood power play as by a desire to stop illegal activity. Big tech companies such as Google blacked out their website names in protest of the SOPA/PIPA bills. Some, such as Wikipedia and Reddit, went dark. And the bills were quickly defeated.

But what happened after the SOPA/PIPA fiasco was as interesting as the event itself. Instead of hardening their positions as they had in the past, executives from Hollywood and Silicon Valley figured out a way to make headway. Hollywood executives, such as Chase Carey, the COO of News Corp., were contrite, acknowledging openly that the industry had been heavy-handed. Meanwhile, companies such as Google agreed to figure out new ways to flag pirated content. Ari Emanuel, who had been publicly critical of the high-tech industry—particularly Google—on this issue in mid-2012, was by the end of the year talking about all the progress that had been made. He said Google had demonstrated to him that it was now moving sites it suspected of piracy down in search results—which, if it takes a site out of the top ten, can be akin to making it disappear. "So Silicon Valley and Hollywood *are* working pretty well on aspects of content and distribution in new media," he said.

"It's still not easy," Michael Yanover said. "But the gap has been bridged much more than it ever was. I think that we've made tremendous progress since I started in this world. There's a mutual respect. Hollywood people have had to embrace the technology because it's either embrace it or get killed. And I think the Silicon Valley people have finally come to respect and understand Hollywood a little bit more. Thanks to Netflix, Hulu, YouTube, and others, they respect content and [do] not treat it quite as fungibly as they have previously. So I think there is much more than ever this coming together that's occurring finally."

Andreessen concurs with this: "Every year for the past twenty years media-company CEOs have told me, 'Someday you guys in Silicon Valley will discover you really need us, and someday you'll start paying us.' And it wasn't true for years numbered one through nineteen. And it literally just became true. And so I think that is a very big change. I think these industries are going to intersect much more in the years ahead than they have so far."

Everyone agrees that the biggest issue in the transition remains finding a way to continue paying top dollar for content. This still makes everyone in Hollywood exceedingly nervous. Hollywood exists not just because it makes movies and television shows people want to watch, but also because executives there have shrewdly figured out how to divide the world into submarkets, allowing them to control the supply of content and sell it again and again for high prices. Without these windows everyone is worried that revenues from content won't be large enough to support the cost of making it. What's different now, however, is that companies in Silicon Valley are also footing the bills—and proving that thanks to their inventions there are indeed new ways of financing, producing, and distributing content. That isn't the sort of challenge Hollywood can ignore or make go away with lawsuits as it has done before.

. . .

In mid-May 2013, at the end of a marathon keynote presentation to open its conference for software developers, Google served up a surprise to its exhausted listeners. At the three-hour mark, Larry Page, the company's publicity-shy CEO, came out to deliver remarks and take questions from the audience.

Page isn't a rock star CEO as Steve Jobs and Bill Gates once were, or as Mark Zuckerberg at Facebook and Larry Ellison at Oracle continue to be. In fact, Page's appearance was notable for the exact opposite reason: few could remember the last time they had seen him center stage. He has been Google's CEO for two years and is one of its cofounders. But during that entire fifteen-year period—Google was founded in 1998—he has taken pains to avoid the limelight. He rarely grants interviews, or makes speeches the way Google's former CEO, Eric Schmidt, does. There are many who believe that Schmidt is *still* Google's CEO because of that. Page had been particularly out of the public eye during the previous year because, as he revealed the day before, he'd been suffering from a condition that has left both his vocal chords partially paralyzed.

His effect was magical. Page is often guarded and stiff in public. But the lack of power in his voice made him seem more human and his remarks more intimate. The six thousand people in the audience and the roughly 1 million watching the live stream worldwide were rapt as Page spun up a vision of the world where technology solved many of its biggest problems—from commuting to education to world hunger. He also did something he rarely does: he talked about himself. He told his listeners how lucky he was to have had a father who was a geek like him. "He actually drove me and my family all the way across the country to go to a robotics conference," Page said. But Larry had been younger than the cutoff age for the conference and was going to be turned away. The elder Page was adamant. "He thought it was so important that his young son go to the conference, it was one of the few times I've seen him really argue with someone." His dad, who died a decade ago, convinced the conference organizers to make an exception.

> You take out your phone, and you hold it out, it's almost as big as the TV or a screen you're looking at. It has the same resolution as well. And so if you're nearsighted, a smart-phone and a big display are kind of the same thing now. Which is amazing. Absolutely amazing . . . We haven't seen this rate of change in computing for a long time—probably not since the birth of the personal computer. But when I think about it, I think we're all here because we share a deep sense of optimism about the potential of technology to improve people's lives, and the world, as part of that.

He went on like this for ten minutes, taking audience questions for another ten. In that short span he was alternately optimistic and visionary, and arrogant and sanctimonious. About Google's fights with Apple and other competitors, he said,

> You know, every story I read about Google, it's kind of us versus some other company, or some stupid thing. And I just don't find that very interesting. We should be building great things that don't exist. Right? Being negative is not how we make progress. And most important things are not zero sum. There's a lot of opportunity out there. And we can use technology to make really new and really im-portant things to make people's lives better.

This was more than a coming-out party for Page. Only execu-tives atop companies that are winning in the marketplace make speeches like this. And Page, it appeared, wanted the world to know that this was indeed how he felt. The cynical might have called it Page's "What's good for the world is good for Google" speech—a reference to GM president Charles Wilson's remark in the 1950s about the automaker. After all, it's hard to imagine Page, or anyone at Google, calling its fight with Apple uninteresting in 2011, when the iPad controlled the entire tablet market, or in 2007, when Google was scrambling to get Android off the ground—or when Apple and Jobs began accusing Google and its Android manufacturers of wrongly copying their work. Page knows that Google's five-year fight with Apple hasn't been a distraction for either company. It's made both companies better. Apple might not have had an app store if Google hadn't planned one first. Android phones and software might still look as if they were designed for engineers, not consumers, if Google hadn't been forced to compete with Apple. The list is enormous.

But the momentum in Google's mobile-platform war with Apple was definitely in Google's favor by the middle of 2013. Google seemed as dominant in that fight as Apple had seemed in 2011 and in the three years after it unveiled the iPhone. Android's share of the mobile phone and tablet markets was continuing to rise, clearing 75 percent in smartphones and 50 percent in tablets. Moreover, the competition had pushed down the prices Apple could charge for some devices and that was eating into Apple's once unassailable profit margins. Apple's stock price, which had doubled to more than $700 a share in the year after Jobs's death in 2011, had deflated almost as fast during the following year. By 2013 Apple was no longer the most valuable company in the stock market. And Google's stock price was at an all-time high.

Apple's losing its ranking as the most valuable company was, of course, just a symbolic change. What wasn't symbolic were the scores of angry investors left in the wake of Apple's plunging stock price. For four years Apple shares had been some of the best-performing of all time, rising nearly tenfold from about $80 in 2008. But investors who bought Apple shares in the fall of

2012—believing, as many did, that its stock was headed to $1,000 a share—watched their investment lose 40 percent of its value while the rest of the stock market was up around 15 percent. Jobs never discussed Apple's stock price with investors. He rarely even met with them. But by early 2013 the shareholders refused to be ignored, forcing CEO Tim Cook to pledge more than $100 billion in dividends and stock buybacks.

Indeed, when Page made his remarks, the innovation gap between Apple and Google for dominance of the mobile Internet looked downright stark. In the fall of 2012, Apple had released the iPhone 5, its bestselling phone to date, and the iPad mini, which was also a success despite its smaller profit margins. But it had been more than three years since the last breakthrough product—the iPad. And the TV/device that Jobs had mentioned in Walter Isaacson's biography, and which Cook has also alluded to, was nowhere to be seen.

Meanwhile, Google had unleashed a slew of new and improved software that was astonishing in its breadth and depth. Google unveiled Google Now, a mobile application that slickly anticipates and displays information users might need on the fly, such as travel and restaurant reservations and their expected commute time. It launched a music streaming service to compete with Spotify, leaving many wondering how Google had beaten Apple—the inventor of iTunes—to that market. It showed off a remarkable automatic photo editing feature for Google Plus. Using the horsepower in Google's millions of servers, the feature goes through your entire photo library, auto-selecting and auto-editing the best pictures. And it demonstrated improvements to Google's voice search that would make it finally useful for every-day tasks—like the voice-activated computers in *Star Trek* and other science fiction movies. When it's rolled out, Google says, you'll be able to ask your laptop, smartphone, or tablet anything—and it will respond accurately. The improvements made Siri, Apple's voice-command technology in the iPhone, seem quaint. In August 2013 it unveiled its first Motorola smartphone.

Even the products Google had no intention of selling immediately were generating enormous buzz. It demonstrated that its driverless-car software actually works. It showed that Google Glass—a computer in a pair of eyeglasses—may indeed fuse man and his machine.

It's tempting to predict that it's only a matter of time before Apple comes back with its own new revolutionary device. Certainly that's how the competition between the two has been up until now. What's unclear is whether Apple can do it without Jobs at the helm. Apple certainly encouraged investors to feel as if this question had been answered when its stock and profits skyrocketed after Jobs's death. But a year later, by the fall of 2012, Jobs's absence was, if anything, becoming more obvious by the day.

Take Apple's advertising, for example. It no longer sparkled. Jobs had personally reviewed Apple's advertising, and its TV spots had always been iconic. But the television ads that aired during the 2012 London Olympics—the Genius Bar employee spots—were so bad, they generated headlines. Indeed, the best phone ads of 2012 and 2013 came from Samsung, Google's biggest Android phone maker. After Apple unveiled the iPhone 5, Samsung pounced with a barrage of TV spots that amusingly depicted iPhone users as misguided elitists waiting in line for a phone that was inferior in every way to the Galaxy S III.

Apple was also taking heat for the way it was making its phones. *The New York Times*, in a handful of long articles about the "iEconomy," presented evidence that Apple was making its iPhones and iPads in Asian sweatshops, forcing CEO Tim Cook to acknowledge Apple could do more to make its contractors provide safer workplaces. A year later he was apologizing to Chinese customers for Apple's unresponsiveness to customer service and technical support issues.

But perhaps the most notable example of Jobs's absence was the public relations disaster surrounding Apple's new mapping application. Apple had made a big deal about how it and Google had parted ways over maps, saying that Google was using its control of the technology as a cudgel in negotiations. But when Apple unveiled its homegrown solution along with the iPhone 5, the application was full of bugs. For nearly a month chat boards and social networks teemed with examples of egregious errors— the Washington Monument in the wrong place, the Brooklyn Bridge melting, and directions that led drivers to the wrong desti- nation—that made the app effectively useless and prompted Cook to apologize to customers and then push out many of those respon- sible, among them the iPhone software boss, Scott Forstall. Most of all, it made many wonder whether Jobs would ever have allowed such a blunder to get through.

The maps fiasco not only made Apple look bad, it made Google look heroic. Google quickly rewrote its own maps application, making many improvements. Then, when Google updated it three months later, headlines worldwide made note of how much better it was than Apple's. Ten million users downloaded the Google maps application in forty-eight hours.

Apple's Tim Cook knows all the challenges he faces and says he has the answers. "We're still the company that is going to do that [change the game]. We have some incredible plans that we have been working on for a while. The culture is all still there, and many of the people are still there. We have several more game changers in us," he said during an onstage interview at the end of May 2013. Apple was widely believed to be working on a complete redo to the look of its iPhone and iPad software. Cook didn't deny this in the interview. And Cook continued to talk generally about Apple's interest in making the television-watching experience better.

But there wasn't much more to Cook's remarks. Instead of using the stage—as Google's Larry Page had—to lay out a broad vision for the future, it seemed that Cook's overall goal was to say as little of substance as possible. He said "I don't want to go into detail about that" often. That's typical for many CEOs in these situations. Cook's problem is that he is not being compared to most CEOs. He is being compared to Google's cofounder Larry Page and, of course, to his predecessor, Steve Jobs.

Jobs was a master at moments like this. In 2010, when he was asked about why the iPad was important, he said, "When we were an agrarian nation, all cars were trucks, because that's what you needed on the farm. But as vehicles started to be used in the urban centers, cars got more popular. Innovations like automatic transmission and power steering and things that you didn't care about in a truck as much started to become paramount in cars . . . PCs are going to be like trucks. They're still going to be around, they're still going to have a lot of value, but they're going to be used by one out of X people." Jobs was equally unspecific about future products, but his vision was so clear and compelling that it seemed not to matter.

Comparing anyone to Steve Jobs is unfair. And during his two years as Apple's CEO, Tim Cook has taken pains to point out that Jobs himself had made it clear to him that he didn't want Cook running Apple the way he thought Jobs would want to but the way Cook thought it should be done. It's nice that Jobs let Cook off the hook like that. What isn't clear is how meaningful a gesture it was. Jobs is gone, and Apple's customers, vendors, investors, employees, and fans *do* want Cook to be just like him—even if they won't admit it. They are unlikely to leave him alone about that shortcoming until Cook shows the world his own revolutionary new thing. During the audience question-and-answer period, Dan Benton, the well-known technology hedge fund investor, laid out these concerns plainly: "Why won't you give us a view of the future," Benton asked, suggesting that Google has become better at painting a picture of things to come. Cook's response: "We believe in the element of surprise." Perhaps by the time you read this, that will once again, from Apple, be considered a good thing.

A Note on My Reporting

This book is the outgrowth of, depending how you count, two, seven, or sixteen years of work. I've been writing about technology and media since 1997, first for *U.S. News & World Report* and *Fortune*, and since 2006 for *Wired*. I've been writing about the mobile revolution since the iPhone was unveiled in 2007. The reporting and writing for this project has been my full-time job since 2011. Along with previous reporting I had done, it is the product of more than a hundred interviews. That was supplemented by my reading thousands of pages of books, newspaper and magazine articles, trial transcripts, and exhibits. It was also supplemented by my attendance at dozens of Apple and Google public presentations, industry conferences, and the *Apple v. Samsung* patent trial in 2012. Where I was unable to attend presentations and conferences personally, I relied on official video feeds cross-checked with unofficial video and other reporting. I have relied on court transcripts for both the *Apple v. Samsung Electronics* trial and the *Oracle America v. Google* trial—both in 2012—even for the days when I attended. Where I relied on books, articles, transcripts, and video for my reporting, I have footnoted it. Where I relied on information from interviews, I have not.

For the history of patent law—about a third of chapter 8—I relied on the skilled research and writing help of Erin Biba, whom I worked with when she was a correspondent at *Wired* and who is now a columnist for *Popular Science*. I received fact-checking help from Bryan Lufkin, Katie M. Palmer, Elise Craig, and Jason Kehe. I found Bryan through my *Wired* contacts. He found Katie, Elise, and Jason. I take full responsibility for all errors and omissions, however.

Writing about any company is hard. It, like all of us, wants the world to see only its triumphs, not its worries, fights, and failures. So it is a journalist's job to get behind that facade and find out what is really going on. Writing about Apple presents an even greater challenge. More than just about any other company, Apple goes out of its way to make it difficult for outsiders to see behind the facade. There are roughly half a dozen journalists with whom it occasionally cooperates around product launches. It also cooperated with my friend Steven Levy for a book about the iPod that was released in 2006. And Jobs himself solicited Walter Isaacson to write his acclaimed biography, which was published at the end of 2011. Every other book in the past twenty years that has involved Apple or Jobs has been done without his and Apple's cooperation. That includes this one. I informed Apple about the project at its inception, and I kept them informed until the manuscript was finished. But they did not make anyone at the company available for an interview. Google did cooperate somewhat—it didn't make Larry Page and Sergey Brin available for an interview, but it has made many other executives available over the years for this project and/or for other stories I have written, including its former CEO Eric Schmidt and former Android boss Andy Rubin.

The most important sources for this book weren't officially sanctioned interviews anyway. They were the myriad engineers and executives who actually worked on these projects but have gone on to do other things. All of them were proud of the work they did and graciously spent hours with me making sure I recounted accurately what happened—many on the record. Although Steve Jobs and Google executives such as Eric Schmidt, Larry Page, Sergey Brin, and Andy Rubin get all the credit for building the iPhone, the iPad, and everything that has grown out of Google's Android project, these people are the unseen heroes of Silicon Valley. They felt, as I did, that they were part of history. They didn't want their work to be forgotten. I felt their stories deserved to be told.

Notes

Introduction

4   *The iPhone has become*: Apple financial statements and presentations.

4   *Apple is now the largest*: Philip Elmer-DeWitt, "Chart of the Day: Apple as the World's No. 1 PC Maker," *CNN Money*, 2/7/2013; Apple financial statements; Andrea Chang, "Global TV Shipments Fall in 2012, Recovery Not Expected Until 2015," *Los Angeles Times*, 4/2/2013; John Sousanis, "World Vehicle Sales Surpass 80 Million in 2012," *WardsAuto*, 2/1/2013.

5   *To Apple's astonishment*: Killian Bell, "Android Powers Almost 60% of All Mobile Devices Sold, iOS Just 19.3%," CultofAndroid.com, 5/10/2013; Jon Fingas, "Apple Counts 400 Million iOS Devices Sold as of June," Engadget.com, 9/12/2012.

5   *During the third quarter of 2012*: Philip Elmer-DeWitt, "Chart of the Day: Apple iPhone vs. Samsung Galaxy Sales," *CNN Money*, 3/16/2013.

6   *Apple has even begun replacing*: Shira Ovide, "Apple Boots Google for Microsoft in Siri" (*Digits* blog), *Wall Street Journal*, 6/10/2013.

8   *Today, 1.8 billion cell phones*: "Worldwide Mobile Phone Sales Fell in 2012: Gartner," Reuters, 2/13/2013; Mary Meeker and Liang Wu, "Internet Trends: D11 Conference," www.kpcb.com/insights/2013-internet-trends, 5/29/2013.

10   *Although most people don't think*: "iTunes Continues to Dominate Music Retailing, but Nearly 60 Percent of iTunes Music Buyers Also Use Pandora," NPD Group press release, 9/18/2012; "As Digital Video Gets Increasing Attention, DVD and Blu-ray Earn the Lion's Share of Revenue," NPD Group press release, 1/30/2013; Colin Dixon, "How Valuable Is Apple to the Movie Business? Not So much!," NScreenMedia, 4/25/2013; Horace Dediu, "Measuring the iTunes Video Store," Horace Dediu, ASYMCO.com, 6/19/2013; Brian X. Chen, "Apple and Netflix Dominate Online Video" (*Bits* blog), *New York Times*, 6/19/2013.

1. The Moon Mission

18   *But Jobs had no choice*: Wikipedia, cross-checked with Apple financial statements;

Buster Heine, "15 Years of Macworld History in Just 10 Minutes," CultofMac.com, 1/29/2013.

19 *It wasn't just his own*: Fred Vogelstein, "The Untold Story: How the iPhone Blew Up the Wireless Industry," *Wired*, 1/9/2008.

23 *Worst of all*: Ibid.

24 *Jobs was personally offended*: Kara Swisher, "Blast from D Past Video: Apple's Steve Jobs at D1 in 2003," AllThingsD.com, 5/3/2010.

24 *It's hard to imagine*: "iPhone," Wikipedia; cross-checked with Apple financial statements.

25 *Publicly, Jobs continued his*: Kara Swisher, "Blast from D Past: Apple's Steve Jobs at D2 in 2004," AllThingsD.com, 5/10/2010.

26 *The tension between the partners*: Frank Rose, "Battle for the Soul of the MP3 Phone," *Wired*, 11/2005.

26 *Jobs successfully pinned the Rokr screwup*: "iPod Sales per Quarter," Wikipedia; cross-checked with Apple financial statements; Peter Burrows, "Working with Steve Jobs," *Bloomberg Businessweek*, 10/12/2011.

27 *Disney, on whose board*: "Disney Teams with Sprint to Offer National Wireless Service for Families," Disney news release, 7/6/2005.

28 *Cingular wasn't just playing defense*: "iPod Sales per Quarter," Wikipedia; cross-checked with Apple financial statements.

32 *No one had ever put*: Christine Erickson, "The Touching History of Touchscreen Tech," Mashable.com, 11/9/2012; Andrew Cunningham, "How Today's Touch-screen Tech Put the World at Our Fingertips," ArsTechnica.com, 4/17/2013; Bent Stumpe and Christine Sutton, "The First Capacitative Touch Screens at CERN," *CERN Courier*, 3/31/2010; "Touchscreen Articles in Phones," PhoneArena.com, 8/26/2008; Bill Buxton, "Multi-Touch Systems That I Have Known and Loved," BillBuxton.com, 1/12/2007.

34 *To ensure the iPhone's*: Vogelstein, "Untold Story."

36 *It all made the iPhone*: Testimony from Scott Forstall, Apple's then senior vice president for iPhone software, at *Apple v. Samsung* trial, 8/3/2012.

37 *Through his friend*: Walter Isaacson, *Steve Jobs* (New York: Simon & Schuster, 2011), 471.

37 *"Steve didn't want"*: Forstall at *Apple v. Samsung*.

40 *To Grignon's amazement*: Steve Jobs's iPhone keynote address, 1/9/2007, available at www.youtube.com/watch?v=t4OEsI0Sc_s.

2. The iPhone Is Good. Android Will Be Better.

43 *But a visual encapsulation*: Drawn from Google's financial statements and my own visits there, cross-checked with Google media-relations executives. Also, Paul Goldberger, "Exclusive Preview: Google's New Built-from-Scratch Google-plex," *Vanity Fair*, VF Daily, 2/22/2013.

44 *"We made an explicit decision"*: Fred Vogelstein, "Google @ $165: Are These

Guys for Real?," *Fortune*, 12/13/2004; interview with Eric Schmidt at Google, Mountainview, CA, 11/2004.

44 *Over the years*: Ari Levy, "Benchmark to join Twitter in S.F.'s Mid-Market," *San Francisco Gate*, 5/25/2012.

49 *The easiest way*: Adam Lashinsky, "Chaos by design," *Fortune*, 10/2/2006.

50 *Larry Page has never been shy*: Google Investor Relations, "2012 Update from the CEO," available at http://investor.google.com/corporate/2012/ceo-letter.html.

50 *This wasn't an exaggeration*: Fred Vogelstein, "Search and Destroy," *Fortune*, 5/2/2005.

51 *"It's hard to relate"*: Testimony of Eric Schmidt in *Oracle v. Google* copyright trial, 4/24/2012.

51 *All these fears and frustrations*: Daniel Roth, "Google's Open Source Android OS Will Free the Wireless Web," *Wired*, 6/23/2008; Vogelstein, "GOOGLE @ $165."

53 *Page listened gamely*: Roth, "Google's Open Source"; Steven Levy, *In the Plex: How Google Thinks, Works, and Shapes Our Lives* (New York: Simon & Schuster, 2011), 214.

56 *Officially, the three*: Fred Vogelstein, "Can Google Grow Up?," *Fortune*, 12/8/2003.

57 *Then there were legal issues*: This comes from reading through trial transcripts and press reports of the *Oracle v. Google* copyright trial in 2012.

59 *This thinking was firmly rooted*: John Battelle, *The Search: How Google and Its Rivals Rewrote the Rules of Business and Transformed Our Culture* (New York: Portfolio, 2005), e-book location 1881–1921.

59 *Google had clearly created*: From Google financial statements, my own interviews, and various news reports.

60 *Executives at companies*: Matt Rosoff, "Other Than Facebook, Microsoft's Investments Haven't Worked Out So Well," *Business Insider*, 5/8/2012.

60 *"Google's vision of Android"*: Ken Auletta, *Googled: The End of the World as We Know It* (New York: Penguin Press, 2009), e-book location 4497.

61 *Rubin believed that*: Trial testimony of Andy Rubin in *Oracle v. Google*, 3/23/2012.

61 *He said the iPhone was*: Steve Jobs's iPhone keynote address, 1/9/2007, available at www.youtube.com/watch?v=t4OEsI0Sc_s.

63 *At Apple in the late 1980s*: John Markoff, "I, Robot: The Man Behind the Google Phone," *New York Times*, 11/4/2007.

3. Twenty-Four Weeks, Three Days, and Three Hours Until Launch

71 *But Forstall had*: Adam Satariano, Peter Burrows, and Brad Stone, "Scott Forstall, the Sorcerer's Apprentice at Apple," *Bloomberg Businessweek*, 11/12/2011; Jessica Lessin, "An Apple Exit over Maps," *Wall Street Journal*, 10/29/2012.

72 *Fadell is not shy*: Leo Kelion, "Tony Fadell: From iPod father to thermostat start-up," *BBC News*, 11/29/2012.

74   *Fadell was truly*: Steven Levy, *The Perfect Thing: How the iPod Shuffles Commerce, Culture, and Coolness* (New York: Simon & Schuster, 2006), 54–74.

76   *Forstall couldn't have been*: Satariano et al., "Scott Forstall."

77   *Despite the feuding*: Christina Kinon, "Say What? Mike stolen during live Q&A on Fox," *New York Daily News*, 6/30/2007; Steven Levy's interview on FOX News is accessible at www.youtube.com/watch?v=uayBcHDxfww.

77   *Levy wrote about*: Steven Levy, "A Hungry Crowd Smells iPhone, and Pounces," *Newsweek*, 12/22/2007.

78   *Looking back, the iPhone launch*: These two paragraphs come from Apple financial statements and various news reports and reviews widely available at the time.

79   *It generates $4.5 billion:* "Apple's CEO Discusses F2Q13 Results—Earnings Call Transcript," SeekingAlpha.com, 4/23/2013.

79   *After the unveiling, when*: John Markoff, "Steve Jobs Walks the Tightrope Again," *New York Times*, 1/12/2007.

80   *Apple helped create and then took*: This comes from the testimony of Phil Schiller, Apple Senior Vice President of Worldwide Marketing, at the *Apple v. Samsung* trial, 8/3/2012.

80   *University Avenue and Kipling Street*: The new Apple store in Palo Alto is at Florence Street and University Avenue.

4. I Thought We Were Friends

83   *the Android team's initial worries*: Information for the following two paragraphs comes from trial testimony and exhibits in the *Oracle v. Google* trial; from Steven Levy, *In the Plex: How Google Thinks, Works, and Shapes Our Lives* (New York: Simon & Schuster, 2011), 213–37; and from my own reporting.

85   *Gundotra's 2007 start date*: Brad Stone, "Larry Page's Google 3.0," *Bloomberg Businessweek*, 1/26/2011; and my own reporting.

85   *But Gundotra thrived*: Levy, *In the Plex*, 219.

91   *For example, the trio*: Ibid., 218.

92   *The secrecy, leaks, and backbiting*: John Markoff, "I, Robot: The Man Behind the Google Phone," *New York Times*, 11/4/2007.

93   *It wasn't just dull*: Ryan Block, "Live coverage of Google's Android Gphone mobile OS announcement," Engadget.com, 11/5/2007; Danny Sullivan, "Gphone? The Google Phone Timeline," SearchEngineLand.com, 4/18/2007; Miguel Helft and John Markoff, "Google Enters the Wireless World," *New York Times*, 11/5/2007.

93   *Google got more attention*: See the first Android introduction and demo by Sergey Brin and Steve Horowitz at www.youtube.com/watch?v=egxNkU5__hU.

96   *Certainly, Google's other initiatives*: Ken Auletta, *Googled: The End of the World as We Know It* (New York: Penguin Press, 2009), e-book location 2842.

97   *Perhaps the most powerful reason*: Levy, *In the Plex*, 213–37; Auletta, *Googled*, e-book location 118–1132; Brad Stone and Miguel Helft, "Apple's Spat with Google Is Getting Personal," *New York Times*, 3/13/2010; and my own reporting.

98 *"One Sunday morning"*: From Vic Gundotra's Google Plus profile, https://plus
.google.com/+VicGundotra/posts/gcSStkKxXTw.

99 *But by spring 2008*: My reporting and Levy, *In the Plex*, 213–37.

102 *One piece of evidence*: For a demonstration of the Star7, visit www.youtube.com
/watch?v=1CsTH9S79qI.

5. The Consequences of Betrayal

106 *Brin and Page refused*: David A. Vise and Mark Malseed, *The Google Story*
(New York: Delacorte, 2005), e-book location 1593–94.

106 *Schmidt was hired*: Affidavit from Lukovsky in *Microsoft v. Kai-Fu Lee*, 2005;
Viacom complaint filed in 2007, https://docs.google.com/viewer?url=http%3A
%2F%2Fonline.wsj.com%2Fpublic%2Fresources%2Fdocuments%2FVia
com031207.pdf; Saul Hansell, "Google and Yahoo Settle Dispute over Search
Patent," *New York Times*, 8/10/2004; see also Google IPO documents (for Yahoo!
settlement).

109 *The final push wasn't*: Steven Levy, *In the Plex: How Google Thinks, Works, and
Shapes Our Lives* (New York: Simon & Schuster, 2011), 213–37.

111 *It had a slide-out keyboard*: Walt Mossberg, "Google Answers the iPhone,"
AllThingsD.Com, 10/15/2008.

111 *Compared to the iPhone's*: My reporting and Levy, *In the Plex*, 227.

114 *"Put yourself in Steve's shoes"*: Isaacson's biography was the first to report that
Jobs had been battling cancer since his first surgery in 2005. Jobs's public position until he died was that his cancer had been cured.

116 *Like Android, Google Voice*: These three paragraphs combine my own reporting with Steven Levy's from *In the Plex*, 213–37.

118 *Almost all the media coverage*: These are publicly available documents that
news organizations secured through a Freedom of Information Act request—
see www.apple.com/hotnews/apple-answers-fcc-questions and www.scribd.com
/doc/18983640/Google-Response-to-FCC.

119 *The Google Voice skirmish*: Fred Vogelstein, "How the Android Ecosystem
Threatens the iPhone," *Wired*, 4/14/2011.

124 *"Our lawsuit is saying"*: Walter Isaacson, *Steve Jobs* (New York: Simon & Schuster, 2011), 512.

127 *But in 2010 he said*: Ibid., 513.

127 *And at the end of 2012, Schmidt*: "Jessica E. Lessin, "Google's Explainer-in-
Chief Can't Explain Apple," *Wall Street Journal*, 12/4/2012.

128 *By 2010, however, big commercial customers*: Wayne Rash, "Microsoft, New
York City Ink Deal for Cloud Application Licenses," eWeek.com, 10/20/2010.

128 *Then, in 2008, it released Chrome*: Steven Levy, "Inside Chrome: The Secret
Project to Crush IE and Remake the Web," *Wired*, 9/2/2008.

6. Android Everywhere

131 *"It [Android] is"*: Brad Stone, "Google's Andy Rubin on Everything Android" (*Bits* blog), *New York Times*, 4/27/2010.

131 *It was as if little else*: This data comes from Google financial statements as well as from annual presentations by Mary Meeker, the former Wall Street technology analyst and current partner of venture capital firm Kleiner Perkins Caufield & Byers.

132 *An electronic poll*: I witnessed this poll at the *Fortune* Brainstorm TECH conference in Aspen, July 2010.

133 *"We have a product that allows"*: This is from a presentation I saw Schmidt give at the DLD annual technology conference in Munich in January 2011.

134 *In the fall of 2010 Vodafone tried*: "Customer Backlash Forces Vodafone to Renege on Software Update" (*Technology* blog), *Guardian*, 8/12/2010.

137 *Intellectually, it's easy to understand*: Stone, "Google's Andy Rubin"; Jesus Diaz, "This Is Apple's Next iPhone," *Gizmodo*, 4/19/2010; Rosa Golijan, "The Tale of Apple's Next iPhone," *Gizmodo*, 6/4/2010; Miguel Helft and Nick Bilton, "For Apple, Lost iPhone Is a Big Deal" (*Bits* blog), *New York Times*, 4/19/2010; David Carr, "Monetizing an iPhone Spectacle," *New York Times*, 4/25/2010; Jeff Bertolucci, "*Gizmodo*-iPhone Saga: Court Documents Reveal Fascinating Details," *PC World*, 5/15/2010.

137 *In June came*: *Fortune* Brainstorm, Aspen, 2010; Matt Buchanan, "Apple, Antennagate, and Why It's Time to Move On," *Gizmodo*, 7/19/10; Nick Bilton, "Fallout from the iPhone 4 Press Conference" (*Bits* blog), *New York Times*, 7/19/2010.

139 *AT&T made this debacle*: Saul Hansell, "AT&T Declares Cold War on Verizon," *New York Times*, 11/3/2009.

139 *By 2010 many consumers*: Fred Vogelstein, "Bad Connection: Inside the iPhone Network Meltdown," *Wired*, 7/19/2010.

139 *Jobs did little to hide*: Jason Snell, "Jobs Speaks: The Complete Transcript," *Macworld*, 10/18/2010.

140 *Because of the iPod*: Apple press release, 4/9/2007.

142 *Jobs said he never saw*: Kara Swisher, "Full D8 Interview Video: Apple CEO Steve Jobs," Steve Jobs interviewed by Kara Swisher and Walt Mossberg (video), AllThingsD.com, 6/7/2010, available at www.allthingsd.com/20100607/full-d8 -video-apple-ceo-steve-jobs.

143 *Apple's three-year head start*: "Apple Says App Store Has Made Developers over $1 Billion," AppleInsider.com, 6/10/2010.

7. The iPad Changes Everything—Again

147 *Starting in 2010 Jobs had*: "Apple's Diabolical Plan to Screw Your iPhone," iFixIt.com, 1/20/2011.

148 *"It turns out"*: Beth Callaghan, "Steve Jobs's Appearances at D, the Full Video Sessions," AllThingsD.com, 10/5/2011.

148 *He laid out his new invention*: See Steve Jobs's iPad keynote address, 1/27/2010, available at www.youtube.com/watch?v=lTNbKCAFHJo.

149 *Alan Kay, who is*: Catharine Smith, "History of Tablet PCs," *Huffington Post*, 6/15/2010; Jenny Davis, "The Tablet's Long History" (*Geekdad* blog), *Wired*, 10/29/11; "Tablet Timeline," *PCMag*, January 2013; Jerry Kaplan, *Startup: A Silicon Valley Adventure* (New York: Penguin, 1996), 1–36.

152 *As the father of the Macintosh*: See Jobs's iPad keynote address.

153 *The immediate reaction*: "The Book of Jobs," *Economist*, 1/28/2010; "Apple's Hard-to-Swallow Tablet," *Wall Street Journal*, 12/30/2009; Claire Cain Miller, "The iPad's Name Makes Some Women Cringe" (*Bits* blog), *New York Times*, 1/27/2010.

153 *The biggest criticism*: Schmidt's comments were made at a press briefing at the World Economic Forum in Davos, 1/28/2010; Brent Schendler, "Bill Gates Joins the iPad's Army of Critics," *CBS MoneyWatch*, 2/10/2010; John McKinley, "Apple's iPad Is This Decade's Newton," *Business Insider*, 1/27/2010; Arnold Kim, "Apple Gives a Nod to Newton with New 'What is iPad?' Ad," *MacRumors*, 5/12/2010.

153 *With so much at stake*: Walter Isaacson, *Steve Jobs* (New York: Simon & Schuster, 2011), 495.

155 *"I spent a year and a half"*: Joe Hewitt, "iPad," JoeHewitt.com, 1/28/2010.

156 *"This guy badgered me"*: Isaacson, *Steve Jobs*, 467.

160 *Cue explained the evolution*: John Paczkowski, "The Apple iBooks Origin Story," AllThingsD.com, 6/14/2013.

160 *Cue said the "page curls"*: Peter Kafka, "Steve Jobs, Winnie the Pooh and the iBook Launch," AllThingsD.com, 6/17/2013.

160 *The problem, Cue said, was*: Paczkowski, "The Apple iBooks Origin Story."

160 *When the first iPads*: Apple quarterly financial statements (10-Q) for April 2010, July 2010, January 2011, and April 2011; Apple annual financial statement (10-K) for October 2010.

8. "Mr. Quinn, Please, Don't Make Me Sanction You."

The first section of this chapter includes testimony and scenes from the *Apple v. Samsung* patent trial in the summer of 2012. I witnessed the first three days of these proceedings and supplemented and cross-checked my reporting with the trial transcripts.

168 *Only about 3 percent*: Paul F. Morgan, "Guest Post: Microsoft v. i4i—Is the Sky Really Falling?," PatentlyO.com, 1/9/2011.

169 *"Today was an important day"*: Mark Gurman, "Tim Cook tells Apple employees that today's victory 'is about values,'" 9to5Mac.com, 8/24/2012.

171 *Few understood this dynamic*: Walter Isaacson, *Steve Jobs* (New York: Simon & Schuster, 2011), 171–75.

172 *Nothing illustrates Jobs's obsession*: Charles Duhigg and Steve Lohr, "The Patent, Used as a Sword," *New York Times*, 10/7/2012; I supplemented this and cross-checked it with my own reporting.

173 *Jobs was clever*: Steve Jobs's iPhone keynote address, 1/9/2007, available at www .youtube.com/watch?v=t4OEsI0Sc_s.

175 *The number of patent applications*: U.S. Patent and Trademark Office annual reports, available at www.uspto.gov/about/stratplan/ar/index.jsp.

175 *A patent for 1-Click*: See Patent US5960411, held by Amazon.com, 9/28/1999; Stephen Hutcheon, "Kiwi Actor v. Amazon.com," *Sydney Morning Herald*, 5/23/2006.

176 *Alexander Graham Bell*: The Telecommunications History Group, "The Telephone Patent Follies," Telecommunications Virtual Museum, available at www .telcomhistory.org/vm/sciencePatentFollies.shtml.

176 *The Wright brothers*: Rose Eveleth, "Five Epic Patent Wars That Don't Involve Apple," *Smithsonian*, 8/27/2012; "The Wright Story," Wright-Brothers.org.

177 *In the 1950s the inventor*: Nick Taylor, *Laser: The Inventor, the Nobel Laureate, and the Thirty-Year Patent War* (New York: Simon & Schuster, 2002), 40; George Stein, "Inventor fights laser patent war," *Lakeland Ledger* (Knight News Service), 11/22/1982; Jeff Hecht, "Winning the Laser Patent War," *Laser Focus World*, 12/1994, 49–51; Kenneth Chang, "Gordon Gould, 85, Figure in Invention of the Laser Dies," *New York Times*, 9/20/2005.

177 *One of the most famous*: Adam Mossoff interview and emails, November and December 2012; Susan Decker, "Apple Phone Patent War Like Sewing Machine Minus Violence," Bloomberg News, 10/8/2012; Mary Bellis, "The Textile Revolution: Sewing Machine Patent Battles & Improvements," About.com; David Zax, "What Smartphone Makers Can Learn from the Sewing Machine Patent War" (*Digits* blog), *Wall Street Journal*, 10/28/2010; Adam Mossoff, "The Sewing Machine War: Howe v. Singer," Volokh.com, 5/1/2009; Alex I. Askaroff, "Elias Howe, Master Engineer," Sewalot.com; Adam Mossoff, "The Rise and Fall of the First American Patent Thicket: The Sewing Machine War of the 1850s," *Arizona Law Review* 53 (2011): 165–211; Richard Cavendish, "The Singer Sewing Machine Is Patented," HistoryToday.com, 2001; Adam Mossoff, "How Many Patents Make a 'Patent War'?," IntellectualVentures.com, 11/15/2012.

179 *What is different with software patents*: LeRoy L. Kondo, "Untangling the Tangled Web: Federal Court Reform Through Specialization for Internet Law and Other High Technology Cases," *UCLA Journal of Law and Technology*, 2002.

179 *But by 1981, with the PC gaining*: Most of this historical case is from BitLaw, which lays out a fantastic timeline and explains how everything connects, at www.bitlaw.com/software-patent/history.html; also, Erin Biba's November 2012 interview with an Electronic Frontier Foundation (EFF) lawyer.

180 *But in 1987 Quattro*: *Lotus Development Corporation v. Borland International, Inc.*, U.S. Court of Appeals, First Circuit, 10/6/1994, https://bulk.resource .org/courts.gov/c/F3/49/49.F3d.807.93-2214.html.

181 *Two years before Apple*: Presentation at Solutions to the Software Patent Problem, a conference at Santa Clara University, 11/16/2012; Jason Mick, "Analysis: Neonode Patented Swipe-to-Unlock 3 Years Before Apple," DailyTech.com,

2/20/2012; Liam Tung, "Apple Secures Patent on iPhone's Slide-to-Unlock Feature," ZDNet.com, 2/6/2013.

182 *Mark Lemley, director*: Presentation at Solutions to the Software Patent Problem; Lemley email, November 12, 2012.

9. Remember Convergence? It's Happening

183 *Within a year*: Apple, Google, and Microsoft financial statements for 2010 and 2011.

184 *Revenues from these businesses*: National Cable and Telecommunications Association data; Television Bureau of Advertising data; and Jack W. Plunkett, *Plunkett's Entertainment & Media Industry Almanac 2012* (Houston, TX: Plunkett Research, 2012).

185 *If you counted desktop* and *mobile operating systems*: "Gartner Says Worldwide Mobile Device Sales to End Users Reached 1.6 Billion Units in 2010," Gartner press release, 2/9/2011; "Gartner Says Worldwide PC, Tablet and Mobile Phone Combined Shipments to Reach 2.4 Billion Units in 2013," Gartner press release, 4/4/2013; Louis Columbus, "2013 Roundup of Smartphone and Tablet Forecasts & Market Estimates," *Forbes*, 1/17/2013.

186 *an orblike device called the Nexus Q*: Fred Vogelstein, "It's Not an Entertainment Gadget, It's Google's Bid to Control the Future," *Wired*, 6/27/2012; Florence Ion, "Google Finally Lists Nexus Q as Not for Sale on Google Play," ArsTechnica.com, 1/17/2013.

187 *In 2013, it also offered*: David Pogue, "What Is the Point of Google's Chromebook Pixel?" (*Pogue's Posts* blog), *New York Times*, 2/28/2013.

188 *More than 1 million e-books*: Rüdiger Wischenbart et al., *The Global eBook Market 2011* (Sebastopol, CA: O'Reilly Media, 2011).

188 *Television studios such as*: Eriq Gardner, "Viacom Sues Cablevision over iPad Streaming," *Hollywood Reporter*, 6/23/2011.

192 *Atavist set out to prove otherwise*: David Carr, "Long-Form Journalism Finds a Home," *New York Times*, 3/27/2011; David Carr, "Maturing as Publisher and Platform," *New York Times*, 5/20/2012; David Carr, "Media Chiefs Form Venture to E-publish," *New York Times*, 9/18/2012.

193 *Pilots stopped carrying bulky bags*: "FAA Approves iPad for Pilots' Flight Planning," *iPadNewsDaily*, 2/14/2011; Nick Bilton, "United Pilots Get iPad Flight Manuals" (*Bits* blog), *New York Times*, 8/23/2011; Christina Bonnington, "Can the iPad Rescue a Struggling American Education System?," *Wired*, 3/6/2013; Katie Hafner, "Redefining Medicine with Apps and iPads," *New York Times*, 10/8/2012.

193 *The iPad had similar appeal on Hollywood sets*: Brian Stelter, "Pitching Movies or Filming Shows, Hollywood Is Hooked on iPads," *New York Times*, 10/24/2010.

193 *Corporations loved the iPad*: Nick Wingfield, "Once Wary, Apple Warms Up to Business Market," *New York Times*, 11/15/2011.

193 *It turned professional baseball players*: "Bowman Says at Bat Application Sales May Triple on iPad," Bloomberg, 3/23/2012.

193 *By 2012, 16 percent of Americans*: Online Publishers Association, "A Portrait of Today's Tablet User: Wave II," study conducted in partnership with Frank N. Magid Associates, June 2012.

194 *The list of tycoons*: Michael Kanellos, "Gates taking a seat in your den," CNET News, 1/5/2005; Matt Rosoff, "Other Than Facebook, Microsoft's Investments Haven't Worked Out So Well," *Business Insider*, 5/8/2012.

194 *Earlier in the decade, TCI cofounder John Malone*: Edmund L. Andrews, "Time Warner's 'Time Machine' for Future Video," *New York Times*, 12/12/1994; Ken Auletta, "The Cowboy," *New Yorker*, 2/7/1994; Mark Robichaux, *Cable Cowboy: John Malone and the Rise of the Modern Cable Business* (Hoboken, NJ: Wiley, 2002), e-book location 1796–2053.

195 *When Gates was eyeing content*: Rosoff, "Other Than Facebook."

196 *Executives such as Edgar Bronfman*: Evelyn Nussenbaum, "Technology and Show Business Kiss and Make Up," *New York Times*, 4/26/2004.

197 *The industry maintained that*: Eric Pfanner, "Music Industry Sales Rise and Digital Revenue Gets the Credit," *New York Times*, 2/26/2013.

199 *They controlled the most popular smartphone*: "Gartner Says Worldwide PC Shipments in the Fourth Quarter 2011 Declined 1.4 Percent," Gartner press release, 1/11/2012; "Smartphones Overtake Client PCs in 2011," Canalys press release, 4/4/2013.

199 *By the end of 2011, even after Apple*: Daniel Eran Dilger, "Apple Has Now Paid $4 Billion to App Store Developers," AppleInsider.com, 1/24/2012.

200 *While Rubin has insisted that*: Nilay Patel, "Google Building 'Firewall' Between Android and Motorola After Acquisition," *The Verge*, 2/27/2012.

200 *As Samsung's Galaxy phones and tablets*: Michael Lev Ram, "Samsung's Road to Global Domination," *Fortune*, 1/22/2013.

201 *He said the best way to think*: Mike Isaac, "Google's Sundar Pichai Is Cool with Samsung's Android Dominance," Sundar Pichai interviewed by Walt Mossberg (video), AllThingsD.com, 5/30/2013, available at www.allthingsd.com/20130530 /googles-sundar-pichai-is-cool-with-samsungs-android-dominance-video.

10. Changing the World One Screen at a Time

203 *For those on the wrong end*: The Pew Research Center's Project for Excellence in Journalism, "The State of the News Media 2013," annual report on American journalism, 3/18/2013, available at www.stateofthemedia.org.

204 *But the mobile revolution*: Nadja Brandt, "Silicon Beach Draws Startups," *Bloomberg Businessweek*, 10/16/2012; Leslie Gersing, "Tech Start-Ups Choosing New York City Over Silicon Valley," CNBC, 2/22/2012.

206 *Netflix just spent two years*: Julianne Pepitone, "Netflix's $100 Million Bet on Must See TV," CNNMoney.com, 2/1/2013.

206 *Most think it is only a matter of time*: Walter Isaacson, *Steve Jobs* (New York: Simon & Schuster, 2011), 554.

207 *"It used to be the only things"*: Ari Emanuel interviewed by Conor Dignam at Abu Dhabi Media Summit, 10/10/2012, available at www.youtube.com/watch ?v=AjMST1m3DVc.

207 *Lady Gaga's next album*: Lisa O'Carroll, "Troy Carter Interview: Lady Gaga's Manager on the Future of Social Media," *Guardian*, 11/4/2012.

208 *Emanuel says that from his and his clients' perspectives*: Emanuel interviewed by Dignam.

209 *The blurring of technology and media*: John Paczkowski, "Sony's Michael Lynton on How the Net and Social Media Are Changing the Movie Business," AllThingsD.com, 2/12/2013; Peter Kafka, "Hollywood Goes Digital—but Not Too Digital: Sony Boss Michael Lynton's Candid Dive into Media Interview," Michael Lynton interviewed by Peter Kafka (video), AllThingsD.com, 2/26/2013, available at www.allthingsd.com/20130226/hollywood-goes-digital-but-not-too -digital-sony-boss-michael-lyntons-candid-dive-into-media-interview.

210 *All this has been enabled or accelerated*: The TV and smartphone numbers are based on an estimate. Based on the most recent data from Display Search for worldwide TV sales, I assumed that the average life of a TV is twenty years and that 200 million are sold a year. I assumed that the average life of a smartphone is two years. Gartner says 2 billion have been sold in the past two years.

213 *All this is straining*: Richard Sandomir, "ESPN Extends Deal with N.F.L. for $15 Billion," *New York Times*, 9/8/2011; Matthew Futterman, Sam Schechner, and Suzanne Vranica, "NFL: The League That Runs TV," *Wall Street Journal*, 12/15/2011.

214 *Netflix didn't originate* House of Cards: Brian Stelter, "A Drama's Streaming Premier," *New York Times*, 1/18/2013; "YouTube Now Serving Videos to 1 Billion People," Associated Press, 3/21/2013

214 *YouTube boss Salar Kamangar*: Peter Kafka, "YouTube Boss Salar Kamangar Takes On TV: The Full Dive into Media Interview," Salar Kamangar interviewed by Peter Kafka (video), AllThingsD.com, 2/27/2013, available at www .allthingsd.com/20120227/youtube-boss-salar-kamangar-takes-on-tv-the-full -dive-into-media-interview.

215 *It's going to be an enormous battle*: David Carr, "Spreading Disruption, Shaking Up Cable TV," *New York Times*, 3/17/2013; Jeff John Roberts, "The Genie Is Out of the Bottle: Aereo's Court Victory and What It Means for the TV Business," *GigaOM*, 4/1/2013; Peter Kafka, "Wall Street to the TV Guys: Please Bail on Broadcast for Cable!," AllThingsD.com, 4/8/2013.

216 *HBO is keenly aware*: "HBO's Eric Kessler at D: Dive into Media," Eric Kessler interviewed by Kara Swisher (video), AllThingsD.com, 2/28/2013, available at www.allthingsd.com/video/hbos-eric-kessler-at-d-dive-into-media; Alistair Barr and Liana Baker, "HBO CEO Mulls Teaming with Broadband Partners for HBOGO," Reuters, 3/21/2013; Peter Kafka, "HBO Explains Why It Isn't Going a la Carte Anytime Soon," AllThingsD.com, 3/22/2013.

219 *In mid-May 2013*: Larry Page's Google I/O 2013 keynote address, 5/15/2013, available at www.youtube.com/watch?v=Zf2Ct8-nd9w; Q&A with Page at Google I/O 2013, 5/15/2013, available at www.youtube.com/watch?v=AfK8h73bb-o.

221 *Android's share of the mobile phone and tablet markets*: "Android Captures Record 80 Percent Share of Global Smartphone Shipments in Q2 2013," Strategy Analytics press release, 8/1/2013; "Small Tablets Drive Big Share Gains for Android," Canalys press release, 8/1/2013.

223 *Apple was also taking heat*: Charles Duhigg and Keith Bradsher, "How the US Lost Out on iPhone Work," *New York Times*, 1/21/2012; Duhigg and Bradsher, "In China, Human Costs Are Built into an iPad," *New York Times*, 1/25/2012; Mark Gurman, "Tim Cook Responds to Claims of Factory Worker Mistreatment: 'We Care About Every Worker in Our Supply Chain,'" 9to5mac.com, 1/26/2012; "Here's Apple CEO Tim Cook's Apology Letter in China" (*Digits* blog), *Wall Street Journal*, 4/1/2013.

223 *But perhaps the most notable example*: Jessica Lessin, "An Apple Exit over Maps," *Wall Street Journal*, 10/29/2012; Liz Gannes, "Google Maps for iPhone Had 10 Million Downloads in 48 Hours," AllThingsD.com, 12/17/2012.

224 *Apple's Tim Cook knows all the challenges*: Ina Fried, "Apple's Tim Cook: The Full D11 Interview," Tim Cook interviewed by Walt Mossberg and Kara Swisher (video), AllThingsD.com, 5/29/2013, available at www.allthingsd.com/20130529/apples-tim-cook-the-full-d11-interview-video.

225 *Jobs was a master*: Peter Kafka, "Apple CEO Steve Jobs at D8: The Full, Uncut Interview," Steve Jobs interviewed by Walt Mossberg and Kara Swisher (video), AllThingsD.com, 6/7/2010, available at www.allthingsd.com/20100607/steve-jobs-at-d8-the-full-uncut-interview.

Acknowledgments

Writing is usually a solitary act. Writing a book—at least one like this—is not a solitary act at all. There have been dozens of people involved in this three-year journey. And so I am pleased to have this space to thank them.

This book never would have happened without a slew of current and former editors, designers, and staff at *Wired* magazine. I wrote the stories that formed the foundation of this project there. I want to thank the magazine's former editor in chief Chris Anderson; its former executive editors Bob Cohn and Thomas Goetz; its current editor in chief, Scott Dadich; its current executive editor, Jason Tanz; its current managing editor, Jake Young; and its features editor, Mark Robinson. Before Jason was executive editor he was my editor, meaning he shepherded all my stories into the magazine.

I want to thank the San Francisco Writer's Grotto for giving me office space and for nourishing my spirit during the day. The Grotto, founded nineteen years ago by Po Bronson, Ethan Watters, Todd Oppenheimer, and others, is a miraculous collection of about five dozen fiction and nonfiction writers. They have come together to share a space and to create a community. Had I not landed there, I would have tried to write the book out of my house or from an office alone somewhere. I would not have succeeded.

Thank you also to Erin Biba, who researched and wrote a

third of the chapter on patents. I met her when she was a correspondent at *Wired*. She has gone on to become a columnist at *Popular Science*. For the first twenty-five years of my career I fact-checked my own stories exclusively. But during my time at *Wired* I discovered that its fact-checking department, run by Joanna Pearlstein, hires some of the smartest and most reliable young writers and reporters in journalism. Thank you to one of those researchers, Bryan Lufkin, who took on the job of helping me fact-check the manuscript and for having the wisdom to bring in his colleagues Katie M. Palmer, Elise Craig, and Jason Kehe when he needed help.

I wouldn't have gotten this project off the ground were it not for the advice about the book-writing process and generous agent recommendations of my friends Joe Nocera and Steven Levy. My friend Jim Impoco read the manuscript and gave me comments. I worked for Jim fifteen years ago. He is one of the best editors walking. Yukari Kane, who is working on her own book about Apple out of the Grotto, provided daily therapy and jelly beans. Our books are different enough so that we were able to support each other without letting competition get in the way.

Thanks also go to my father, John, who provided endless encouragement. I might not have become a journalist were it not for his harping on the importance of the written word at dinner. Also thank you to his wife, Barbara, and my brother, Andrew, and his wife, Monica, for listening to my gripes for three years. I wish my mom were still alive to thank, but many of us in that position feel that way. Thank you to my friend Eric Snoey for all those a.m. coffees, and for making sure I didn't forget about myself.

It's hard to imagine a better agent than Liz Darhansoff, who agreed to take me on when the proposal for this book was barely formed. She was tough with me when she needed to be, she was my therapist when she needed to be, and she had my back at all times.

It's also hard to imagine a better publisher/editor than Sarah Crichton, who has her own imprint at Farrar, Straus and Giroux.

Before I started this project I had heard dozens of publisher/ editor horror stories. They are much like the stories one hears about contractors—about promises made and not fulfilled. That hasn't been my experience at all. Everything Sarah said she would do she did—and more. I feel privileged to have met and worked with her. My thanks also to her assistant, Dan Piepenbring; to production editor Mareike Grover; and to the rest of the editing and marketing staff at FSG. We closed this book quickly, and a lot of people I haven't yet met had to work overtime to get this book ready in time.

Lastly, I want to thank my wife of twenty-three years, Evelyn Nussenbaum. I, like I'm sure many writers, took on this project thinking that somehow I would be the one who got to the end without leaning too hard on his partner. I was wrong. I leaned on Evelyn really hard. She not only handled it. She was a source of endless encouragement. She managed without me on two family vacations and on most Sundays for a year. She managed without me our son's bouts with epilepsy and family issues of her own outside our home. And she gracefully managed the mood-swing rollercoaster that every first-time author—and maybe every author, period—goes through. She was an amazing journalist herself for twenty years, so she understands the writing and reporting process. But that only marginally helps anyone deal with the exhaustion of running a family by yourself. She is an inspiration to me.

Index

A Note About the Author

Fred Vogelstein is a contributing editor at *Wired* magazine, where he writes about the tech and media industries. He has been a staff writer for *Fortune, The Wall Street Journal,* and *U.S. News & World Report.* His work has also appeared in *The New York Times Magazine,* the *Los Angeles Times,* and *The Washington Post.*